W9-AGK-039

What's the Good Word?

Also by William Safire

NONFICTION

On Language (1980)

Safire's Washington (1980)

Before the Fall (1974)

The New Language of Politics: Safire's Political Dictionary (1968, 1979)

Plunging Into Politics (1964)

The Relations Explosion (1963)

FICTION

Full Disclosure (1977)

WILLIAM SAFIRE

What's the Good Word?

Published by TIMES BOOKS, a division of
Quadrangle/The New York Times Book Co., Inc.
Three Park Avenue, New York, N.Y. 10016

Published simultaneously in Canada by
Fitzhenry & Whiteside, Ltd., Toronto

Library of Congress Cataloging in Publication Data

Safire, William, 1929-
What's the good word?

Includes index.
1. English language—Idioms, corrections, errors.
2. English language—Usage. I. Title.
PE1460.S17 1982 428'.00973 81-52568
ISBN 0-8129-1006-0 AACR2

Manufactured in the United States of America

10 9 8 7 6 5 4 3 2 1

To Marshall and Gladys

Introduction

This book is a ripoff.

Why? One reason is that half of the book is a recycling of my Sunday *New York Times Magazine* column, spanning April 1980 to March 1981; it picks up where my last collection of columns, *On Language,* left off. Anybody with a scissors and a subscription to *The Times*—or to any of the hundreds of papers taking its news service—would be able to paste together half of this book for himself.

The other reason is that the better half of this book—the new material—is written by readers who react to the column. Some are irate, some vituperative—most are studious, helpful, scholarly, and funny. These "Lexicographic Irregulars," with their herd of pets, all named Peeve, are not paid for their contributions. I am the one who profits from their labor. Life may be unfair, but it's nice when the unfairness breaks your way.

This book is, therefore, a ripoff; at the same time, it is a steal. Where else, for the piddling (watch out for euphemisms) sum you paid for this book, which you may be putting on your swindle sheet or deducting as a business expense, can you sit in on a Great Conversation? Here are the giants of linguistics sending in their thunderbolts from academe, alongside the bartenders and prison inmates and potheads who know how the language is used firsthand, accompanied by the schoolteachers and grammarians who fear that our last moorings of standards and sanity are in the sanctity of English—all banging their spoons against the high chair of the media, defending the mother tongue from the looseness of the descriptivists or the rigidity of the prescriptivists.

Consider the noun "ripoff," as I have been using it here. It is relatively new slang, coined in the late sixties to mean "a theft, robbery, or con game," with a more recent meaning of "exploitation." As a verb, "to rip off" is more vivid than "to steal" because it conjures up a picture of a thief grabbing a piece of something and running away. As crime in America increases, the vocabulary of the victimized needs expansion, and "ripoff" has filled such a linguistic need; in time, the dictionaries will cease listing it as slang and change it to a colloquialism. There has to be a more resentful way of saying "I was taken advantage of," less severe than "I was robbed"; what better than "I was ripped off"? ("Burglarized" refers only to premises and not people.)

Consider, too, the word "steal" as used above, in "at the same time, it is a steal." The noun meaning is not "theft, robbery, burglary," but an intensified "bargain." That is how language breathes, expressing in a word what used to take a phrase, or was never expressed precisely. I welcome new words, or old words used in new ways, provided the result is more precision, added color, or greater expressiveness.

So my philosophy is anything goes, right? Wrong. Syntaxation with misrepresentation is tyranny. Those uninterested in the misuse of "disinterested," and those zigging "imply" when they should be zagging "infer," are the fuzzy-uppers of our language, and the product of their laziness should not be accepted as our norm.

I was invited to lunch one day with the editor of the Oxford English Dictionary, Robert Burchfield, the New Zealander who is probably the world's most influential wordsman. There at the table were John Simon, the noted paradigm-loser, Edwin Newman, the civil tonguester, and Stuart Flexner, the king of slang. Intra-group communication was lacking; that is to say, nobody was saying much for fear of making a terrible gaffe.

"The reason why I came," I began—and a wave of horror crossed the table. Not one of the Sanhedrin of syntax was so ungracious as to point out my redundancy, but my grammatical stock, never that high, plummeted. "The reason is," I corrected myself, and went on with some innocuous observation about the ripoffs of dictionary publishers; the tension in the room eased.

Icebreaking like that is what I do in my column, stimulating comment and emendation from peering peers (never co-equal) and backseat philologists. If I hadn't overdone the alliteration in the past couple of paragraphs, I would say we have created a semantic symbiosis.

Take the title of this book, for example. What does "good" mean? In the phrase, "the good book," a description of the Bible, the word "good" means "ethical," the same as in "the good fight." In the phrase "the good life," most would say the word "good" means "fun, easy" (I accept "fun" as an adjective), or most often "luxurious." In *"What's the Good Word?"* the word "good" means both "proper, correct" and "upbeat, fun." In searching for the precise word, in reaching for the accepted form, and in knowing the rules well enough to break them consciously and for effect, the writer and reader can luxuriate in the language. Fighting the good fight for the good word leads to the good life of the mind.

A mistake is not an embarrassment; a mistake offers an opportunity to learn. A special glee attaches to the correction of a language pundit, as the letters herein illustrate. But I'm not the only one who's learning.

What's the Good Word?

abortive, *see* ives have it

adjective inflation

When too many words chase after too few ideas, the result is adjective inflation: Words mean less.

One example is the degeneration of "heavy-duty." That compound adjective, once the stern daughter of the voice of auto mechanics, used to denote an item that would take a beating more than any other. Now, when your local grease monkey throws your car on top of his metal cylinder, he takes for granted that you want "heavy-duty shocks"—the kind of shock absorber that used to be reserved for trucks that went bump in the night. If you want *really* heavy-duty shocks, you should ask for the "heaviest-duty" kind.

Have you bought a heavy-duty battery recently? Union Carbide's Eveready sells three types of batteries for flashlights and radios: "General Purpose" is its name for what others might call "Regular," but "regular" is a word frowned on by advertisers except those selling laxatives. Its better battery is labeled "Heavy Duty." But if you want a battery for heavy duty—that is, the longest life—you don't buy "Heavy Duty," you buy the "Alkaline Battery" made by Eveready or its highly charged competitors.

As every acidhead knows, in both General Purpose and Heavy Duty batteries, the can is zinc; in an Alkaline Battery, the can is steel, with both zinc and manganese dioxide generating electricity in an alkaline solution (rather than in the old acidic solution). When Heavy Duty whispers low, "Thou must," the Alkaline replies, "Steel can."

The olive industry is the best-known example of language inflation. Long before "less is more," the olive packers knew that "big is small."

Olive sizes start with the teeny-weeny ones, which are known as "select" or "standard." Next size is "medium," and as you get up to the small ones, the designation is "large." An olive with a diameter of twenty-two to twenty-four millimeters is "extra large," followed upward by "picnics," "mammoth," and "gems." Then come "giant," "jumbo"—now the olives are getting pretty big—"colossal," "supercolossal," and, finally, "special supercolossal."

The State of California, egged on by the United States Department of Agriculture, is trying to get the olive packers to limit their designations to seven, but the bureaucracy is finding it hard to get that first olive packer out of the bottle. The government proposes to banish such movie-mogul designations as "mammoth" and "special supercolossals," but that's not a good idea: As long as the number or specific dimension of the product is printed on the container, there should be no political restraints to the language used. Let ridicule attack language inflation. Hyperbole suits the olives, but censorship is the pits.

Dear Sir:

English is not the only language suffering from adjective inflation; the indication for various Italian trains has always amused me:

Rapido	*Long-distance express luxury coaches*
Direttissimo	*Long-distance train stopping at main stations*
Diretto	*Local train, stopping at main stations*
Accelerato	*Small local train, stopping at all stations*

(Definitions from Berlitz's Italian for Travellers*)*

Mussolini notwithstanding, none of them ever seems to accelerate, go directly (or even most *directly), or be rapid.*

Sincerely,
Judith Holliday
Ithaca, New York

Dear Bill,

The tuna fish industry uses "light" to distinguish some tuna from white, but when you open the can, it turns out to be a light red . . . a rather deep pink. I complained about this to Bumble Bee or some such company and got a two-page letter of such double talk as I'd never read. I still think "light" is deceptive. "Light" is a degree of a color, but they don't say which color.

Sylvia
[Sylvia R. Lyons]
New York, New York

Dear Mr. Safire:

I would like to know about the category known as "Grade A." Did anyone ever see Grade B eggs or Grade C meats in a supermarket? How about "Grade A, fancy"? Has anyone ever seen "Grade A, bourgeois" or "Grade A, drab" eggs?

Best wishes,
Bob Schroeder
Titusville, New Jersey

Mr. Safire—

Out here in Sun Valley, Idaho, "heavy-duty" means something along the lines of sincere, committed, hardworking, nonfrivolous, such as Earl Holding (the owner of Sun Valley) is a heavy-duty Mormon"; "Eric Heiden is a heavy-duty skater"; etc. You are not a heavy-duty writer—too much sense of humor.

Cordially,
George E. Klingelhofer
Sun Valley, Idaho

---

advertising, *see* "bloopies"

---

the affect effect

"People who choose to be in the public eye," I thundered in a political column, "—to affect public policy—should own up to what they own."

Betty Pomerantz, a *Times* copy editor who has saved me from countless embarrassments, and was in no way responsible for the misspelling of "canister" in this space recently, queried my use of "affect."

The confusion between "affect" and "effect" stems from this: When you affect anything, you have an effect on it. As a verb, "affect" means "influence"; as a noun, "effect" means the same thing. The big difference comes when you use "effect" as a verb—its meaning then becomes "accomplish" or "execute." (Watch out for "affect" in another verbal role meaning "to feign"—as in "to affect an accent"—best known in its noun form as an "affectation.")

So which was right? To "affect" public policy means to have an influence upon it, and to "effect" it means to carry out government programs. Which did I mean? I meant both—and although "effect" is not ordinarily applied to people, there's no law against using it that way.

The line came out "who affect and effect public policy"—covering both pundits and politicians. My gratitude, Miss Pomerantz.

Dear Bill,

On "affect": You leave out a usage which was not uncommon until quite recently. You can, for example, say of me, "He affects English bow ties and colored silk handkerchiefs." The implication of the word, when used in this way (as was quite common through the nineteenth century until the first World War), is commonly mildly derisive, implying that what was affected represented a claim to more youth, or higher station, or whatever, than the person in question actually possessed. Unless I am mistaken, you will even find the usage in Kipling. But of course, "affect," when used in this way, is linked to "affected," as in "affected airs and graces."

Yours ever,
Joe
[Joseph Alsop]
Washington, D.C.

Dear Sir:

Your correspondent Miss Pomerantz (who presumably is a cousin of mine) was quite correct when she wrote of the difference in meaning between the words "effect" and "affect." One wonders, however, if either you or she are aware of another meaning of the word. As used by psychiatrists and others in the field of human thought, the word "affect" means feelings / emotions, as in the following sentence: "Her affect, upon hearing the sad news, was of total grief." The word may in this sense also be used as an adjective, as thus: "His affective demeanor was totally out of relationship to the situation." Or to follow your original thought: "Persons in the public eye should control their affect when reaction to public policy does not agree with their own conception of it." Incidentally, in the above sense "affective feelings" is a redundant phrase.

Yours truly,
Ruth Pomaranc
Chicago, Illinois

airish, *see* getting down

à la mode

"We're concentrating entirely on television," said Robert K. Gray, co-chairman with Charles Wick of the Reagan Inaugural Committee. "Every event has a TV mode to make sure it will get across to the country."

"Some management levels were initially terrified," said an unnamed General Foods executive quoted in a *Time* magazine story about boycotts by angry television viewers, "but now it's settled into a wait-and-see-mode."

WHAT'S THE GOOD WORD?

"The all-volunteer force," declared Chief of Naval Operations Thomas Hayward, "is gradually slipping into a failure mode."

"Mode" is all the mode. From the Latin *modus,* meaning "manner" or "method," and later from the French word for "fashion," the word is soaring to a new popularity.

In some uses, the word now means "dimension"—as in the television dimension of the Inauguration Day events. In other cases, the word means "category"—as in a wait-and-see, or failure, mode.

The word began in music (a form of scale) and was taken up by grammar (as a mood—the subjunctive, etc.), statistics, geology, and physics (mode-locking is very big in laser technology). In Kissingerian diplomacy, "modalities" are dismissed as mere techniques and methods to be worked out by assistant secretaries and other clods.

"Mode" could now use a rest. "Slipping into a failure mode" is an admiral's jargon for "failing." Whenever a scientific term is embraced by jargonauts, the parameters are stretched beyond recognition. Let us return "mode" to fashion, and to the large dollop of ice cream that lands squarely on top of the pie.

Dear Mr. Safire:

My letter-writing mode was set off by your remarks on the use of the word "mode." In the OED*-search mode I found that its use for "a way or manner in which something is done . . . a method of procedure" goes back in English usage to 1667 or earlier. As a physicist who has used the word since the cradle—the graduate school cradle—among the grizzled veterans (some as old as thirty) who had developed radar during the war, let me explain how "mode" became a common word among physicists and plead for its usefulness.*

Lord Rayleigh used the word "mode" in 1897 when he discussed wave propagation in pipes. A complex set of problems, lying at the heart of radar technology, is solved elegantly when all possible modes can be described, and the physicists at MIT's Radiation Laboratory had become mode masters. They excited modes, filtered modes, created hybrid modes, converted modes, and suppressed modes. The radar sets they produced had formidable arrays of switches, and it was entirely natural to use "mode" to refer to operation with a given combination of switch settings. Perhaps the usage came from modus operandi, *but I think not. Radars could be operated in "search mode," "tracking mode," "high power mode," "low power mode," "test mode," and the like. Failures occurred, often at the least convenient time, and the usual professional joke called this "operating in the failure mode."*

It follows, therefore, that an admiral's use of "failure mode" should be tested not by the brevity of the equivalent word, but rather by the expression on his face when he said it. Otherwise, when we are in the mode-use mode, we can comfort ourselves with the knowledge that such usage is at least as ancient as its use for pie.

Very truly yours,
Bernard F. Burke
Professor of Physics
Massachusetts Institute of Technology
Cambridge, Massachusetts

Dear Mr. Safire,

You write, "Whenever a scientific term is embraced by jargonauts, the parameters are stretched beyond recognition." "Parameter" is a mathematical term, and the use you make of it here has no relation to the mathematical usage.

*The definitions given in my dictionary (*Webster's *unabridged, 1979) are correct:*

1. *in mathematics, a quantity or constant whose value varies with the circumstances of its application, as the radius line of a group of concentric circles, which varies with the circle under consideration.*
2. *any constant, with variable values, used as a referent for determining other values.*

The engineer's phrase "the parameters of the problem" clearly refers to the second meaning.

Mathematicians often talk of constants (meaning a quantity which does not change) and variables (meaning a quantity which does change). However, whether a quantity is constant or variable may depend on the context. "Parameter" means a quantity which is constant in a narrow context, but variable in a broader context.

The example in my dictionary illustrates this. For each circle, the radius is constant, but for the family of circles, the radius is variable, depending on the circle under consideration.

For another example, consider the problem of finding how far a shell fired from a gun will go before it hits the ground. An approximate answer can be computed if one knows the angle the gun makes with the horizontal, the muzzle velocity, and the height of the point of impact compared to the point the gun was fired from. These are the parameters of the problem of determining the distance the shell goes.

These are parameters also in the first sense, because they are constant for each firing of the gun, but they may vary when the gun is fired more than once.

Of course, "parameters of the problem," like any other phrase, can be jargon, if it is used incorrectly or in a meaningless way. However, your use is an example of the meaning of "parameter" being "stretched beyond reason."

Sincerely yours,
John Mather
Department of Mathematics
Princeton University
Princeton, New Jersey

Dear Sir:

One of the most constantly misused words nowadays is the word parameter. Imagine my astonishment at finding my favorite word maven using it, like any literary hick, as a fancy and scientific-sounding synonym for perimeter. According to the American Heritage Dictionary *"parameter" means "a variable or an arbitrary constant appearing in a mathematical expression, each value of which determines or restricts the specific form of the expression." I'm no mathematician, and, frankly, I don't know what that means. But I do know that it doesn't mean "boundary" or "perimeter" as in your recent sentence: "Whenever a scientific term is embraced by jargonauts, the parameters are stretched beyond recognition." Shame! Jargonaut!*

Yours sincerely,
Winthrop Sargeant
Salisbury, Connecticut

Dear Mr. Safire:

You concluded your remarks pertaining to the word "mode" with "Whenever a scientific term is embraced by jargonauts, the parameters are stretched beyond recognition." How true!

As a physicist I am constantly surprised at the regular misuse of the word "quantum." A quantum (in my limited experience) is a discrete natural unit or packet of energy associated with submicroscopic vibrations in atoms or a very small increment or parcels into which many forms of energy are subdivided. A "quantum jump" is an abrupt transition from one energy state to another in a submicroscopic atom.

How many times do we hear the jargonauts refer to a quantum leap in the cost of living? Don't we wish it? Or a quantum leap in the federal defense spending? Or a quantum leap in the number of traffic fatalities—which, if true, would not be an item of much concern.

Sincerely yours,
Joseph A. Keane, Ph.D.
Director of Continuing Education
St. Thomas Aquinas College
Sparkill, New York

alternate/alternative, *see* nifty

analysts, *see* indecent invasion

the area area

"Welcome to the New York area," says the female flight attendant, once the stewardess. Not welcome to New York, or to La Guardia Airport, or to God's country—always to the New York "area." Wasn't the navigator sure of the landing field? ("Welcome to the Tri-City area" is OK—it covers Saginaw, Flint, and Bay City, Michigan.)

In the same way, "area" is befuzzing other areas of discourse. (To be specific, other nouns.) The word comes from the Latin *arere,* "to be dry"—an arid place, a vacant courtyard. Thomas Gerrity, of the University of Scranton's Department of Education, dryly observes that "subject area" would be better understood as "subject," "wilderness area" would have more of the tang of the forest as simply "wilderness," "Persian Gulf area" would be more crisply written as "Persian Gulf," and even "stomach area" would be better called "stomach" unless the speaker means "near the stomach."

In interior design, "area" has its place: It's hard to call a nook with a table and chairs a "dining room," so we have to grab our grub in "dining areas." But the areazation of apartments was neatly spoofed in a recent Donald Reilly cartoon in *The New Yorker,* as a modern homemaker in a free-flowing kitchen says to her child: "When I saw your bear last, it was near where the talking area flows into the eating area."

Most of the time, area qualifiers are unnecessary. The phrase "the Persian Gulf" denotes not merely a body of water, but is used to describe a region, and includes the countries on that gulf. When used in such an inclusive sense, the addition of "area" is redundant. The word is antiprecision, used by people who like to let their meanings spread out.

"Area" is to "place" what "situation" is to "scene." A crisis is a crisis, not a "crisis situation." My fire engines do not respond to an "emergency situation," and I fall asleep in a "classroom situation." The phrase "in a work-type situation" does not work as well as "at work."

People enmeshed in situations also become involved in "activities." To them, "sports" become "sports activities," and storms become "thunderstorm activity" (in which a howling gale is said to include "gale-force winds").

All these are harrumphing expressions, filled with phony importance, to go along with the "Hak! Kaff! Fap!" of a Major Hoople. Welcome to the situation-activity area.

Dear WS:

Re "The Area Area," thought you would enjoy this from Inside Design *by the late Michael Greer:*

> *Speaking of rugs, there's no more ridiculous term—I suppose the invention of a gushy so-called shelter magazine—in common parlance today than "area" rugs; I defy anyone to show me any rug that doesn't cover an area.*

Yours truly,
Renee F. Lord
New York, New York

Dear Mr. Safire:

The reference to "gale-force winds" in the next-to-last paragraph leaves something to be said. As it appears in the sentence, the term is redundant, but the implication is that the term itself is in a class with the other "harrumphing expressions."

To us, "gale-force winds" seems acceptable, considering the scale that was originated in 1806 by Admiral Sir Francis Beaufort to enable mariners to gauge wind speeds from sea conditions. Beaufort arranged wind speeds in groups from 0, for calm, to 12, for hurricane. (Today the groups have been expanded to include hurricanes of increasing intensity.) When, for instance, the sea is observed to be covered with ripples having the appearance of scales with no foam crests, the term in relation to the wind is "light air," the wind speed is 1-3 knots, and the Beaufort number is 1; when large waves form, with whitecaps everywhere and increasing spray, the term is "strong breeze," the wind speed is 22-27 knots, and the Beaufort number is 6. A "near gale" has wind speeds of 28-33 knots and a Beaufort number of 7. Actually, gales are divided into "gale" and "strong gale," with Beaufort numbers of 8 and 9 and wind speeds ranging from 34 to 47 knots. A "storm" comes in at 48 knots, and a "hurricane" at 64.

Beaufort numbers came to be known as "Force 1," "Force 2," etc. Thus, "Force 8" presents a good picture of sea conditions to the mariner. Conversely, he knows that the wind speed is between 34 and 40 knots when he's out there.

Given the foregoing, it does seem logical to designate winds of 34 to 47 knots as winds of gale force—or "gale-force winds." Do you not agree?

Sincerely yours,
Jack Smith
Associate Editor
Yachting
New York, New York

Asian, *see* heathen Chinese

---

assault rifle, *see* mod modifiers

---

assertive, *see* ives have it

---

asymmetric, *see* neatness counts

---

attributive nouns, *see* for attribution

---

baggage, *see* watch your baggage

---

bargaining chip

One of my goals in life is to discover the metaphoric basis of the phrase "bargaining chip."

" 'Bargaining chip' is a poker expression," writes Peter Fessenden of Brunswick, Maine, "somehow loosely derived from the threat to raise to the roof (or, by a $1,000 chip) if the fellow across the table has the temerity to raise by so much as a penny. It is a throwaway threat, since it is seldom followed through."

A different poker theory is advanced by Ara Daglian of New York: "When playing cutthroat, you can call and raise, but kitchen-style gaming changed that. When it is your raise, and you do not know what's up, you bet a low chip—the bargaining chip—to find out who thinks they have what. The same applies to any bargaining situation. It keeps you in the game.... Lets you come back with another raise, high or low, or a drop."

Perhaps the bargaining chip has nothing at all to do with poker. Some people think it was spawned in war gaming, which frequently calls for the use of counters or tokens. Other speculators take the "sweetener" line. "A diamond chip," writes Martin Willsted of New York, "as used in settings of wedding rings, might very well have been the sweetener to clinch the sale or exchange." A. J. Gracia of Southbury, Connecticut, works the same side of the street, but with a different chip: "A 'bargaining chip' is that extra consideration one 'chips in' to bring a barter or sale to fruition.... No Yankee worth his salt will ever conclude a trade with an 'outlander' without extracting the extra toll of a 'bargaining chip.' "

Others have put forward a "cow chips" theory, from those dried pieces of manure long used in the West for fuel. Paul Klein, a lawyer of Cold Spring, New York, goes further, suggesting that an Indian word for buffalo is "bahgannah": "Presumably the invading English-speaking frontierspeople, overhearing Indians striking a deal, misheard the throwing in of a 'bahgannah chip' as a 'bargaining chip.' " Mr. Klein is pulling my leg (and readers will kindly refrain from sending in speculative etymologies for the expression "pulling my leg").

Bill Higginbotham, of Fort Worth, Texas, describes it as "the amount of earnest a bargainer was willing to put up as a chip on account. The older phrase was 'bargain penny.' " That merits serious consideration; the *OED* has a 1490 citation of "bargayn peny" with that meaning.

To phrase detectives—and we're all Inspector Javert on this miserable assignment—the most exciting lead was provided by Lewis Anderson, Jr., of Brooklyn, New York, who dug his clue out of the twenty-volume *Century Dictionary of the English Language,* published in 1890. Here is the entry in its entirety: *"bargain-chop, n.* A kind of gambling 'option' on opium to arrive, formerly common among foreign traders in China."

Think about that. Maybe we've all been misled by "chip." The English dialect word "chop" has long been associated with bartering: "To chop horses" meant to trade horses. Also, "chop" in an Oriental context has been used to mean "seal," such as a mark placed on an agreement in Hong Kong. In Hindi, *chapp* means "to print." The change from "bargain-chop" to "bargaining chip" is slight, as is the change in meaning from a futures bet to a negotiating device.

In etymology, nothing beats a printed citation; so far the best we have is that 1890 *Century Dictionary* use. The search goes on, with ever-greater intensity, because the Reagan administration cannot resolutely undertake a new round of SALT negotiations without a firm source for "bargaining chip." (We can reject the nuclear "fission chips," a brainchild of Samuel Beckoff of Monroe, New York.) Are there any Lexicographic Irregulars in Hong Kong who remember "bargain-chop"? I wish we had something to trade for the definitive etymology.

Dear Bill,

On "bargaining chip": A "bargain penny" was paid either by the seller to the purchaser to indicate goodwill or, for the same reason, by the purchaser to the seller, depending on local custom. This custom subsists today in the way people often say, "Let's have a drink on the bargain." The drink in question is in fact the ghost of the bargain penny, but I doubt very much that this is the origin of the phrase that interests you. An origin in poker would be my choice.

Yours ever,
Joe
[Joseph Alsop]
Washington, D.C.

Dear Mr. Safire,

The "chip" is an item of damage. Traders buying various items of ceramic or furniture would carefully inspect for damages. The merchandise would have an established price, but the inspectors, buyers would look for an item of damage and this would open the door to negotiations. It later came into more general usage and a ploy in the retail trades where the customer would look for the "bargaining chip."

Your reference to forthcoming negotiations in the SALT treaty discussions was apropos since there are many "chips" in the existing treaty, and these represent the avenue to negotiation and bargaining.

Very truly yours,
Wilf L. Wood
Cromwell, Connecticut

Dear Mr. Safire,

Your lines on the word "chop" beg a few added meanings. William C. Hunter, an American trader and the author of a wonderful thin volume on the trade, The 'Fan Kwae' at Canton Before Treaty Days *(London: Kegan Paul, Trench & Co., 1882) discusses the word as an example of Pigeon-English (business English) (p.62).*

'Chop,' for instance, is of perpetual occurrence. It is the same as 'chǒ,' which signifies literally any 'document.' A shopkeeper's bill is a 'chop,' so is an Imperial Edict or a Mandarin's proclamation; a cargo-boat is a chop-boat; it does duty also for a promissory note, a receipt, a stamp or a seal, a license for shipping off or to land cargo, a mark for goods, or a permit. 'First quality' is expressed by 'first chop,' and an inferior according to quality is No. 6, 8, or 10 'chop,' the worst of all. When a cooly is sent on an errand requiring haste, he is told to go 'chop-chop.' A 'first chop' man speaks for himself, so does 'bad chop man.'

Yours sincerely,
Frederic Grant, Jr.
Boston, Massachusetts

a barrel of puns

An epidemic of paronomasia has raced around the world. No longer can the obsession to make puns be xenofobbed off with "paronomasia for the paronomasiatics"; the entire English-speaking world is affected.

"The Pun Never Sets on Britain's Empire" was the headline on a dispatch from London by Alan L. Otten of *The Wall Street Journal.* He reported a rash of puns in the British press:

In *The Observer,* a travel piece about staying in private homes on the island of Crete was labeled "Off the Cretan Path," and a news story about film stars running for Parliament in India was headed "Film Stars Want to Lead Castes of Millions."

In the *Sunday Telegraph,* a music reviewer panned a performance as "Haydn Seek," prompting listeners to write, asking about "Handel with Care" and "Black Liszt."

The *Guardian* was not to be outpunned: "Distillery Deal Scotched" was one wry headline, and a story about an economic upturn from Tirana, capital of Albania, was headed "Tirana Boom Today."

Here in the colonies, the grand tradition of *puntiglio*—the Italian word for "wordplay," source of our "pun"—is growing apace. The root of this pace-growing is often a headline-writer's need for quick catchiness, and has resulted in a new tolerance for a long-despised form of humor. (Am I getting hyphen-happy?) As a certified pundit I have been obliged to collect specimens over the years:

The Washington Post is well hooked, from its Style section's "Lettuce

Now Pick Garden Salads" to a front-page headline over a story on the inception of President Carter's short-lived "New Foundation" theme: "Birth of a Notion." A transcendental T was pronounced in "Hatha Yoga Is Better Than None," and a piece on the Aswan Dam's threatened inundation of the Temple of Dendur was nicely double-punned: "Not by a Dam Site."

The New York Times Book Review topped the British "Haydn Seek" with this title to a review of a book about Schubert's songs: "Follow the Lieder." (On literary puns, the name of a cocktail lounge in Tucson, Arizona, comes to mind: Tequila Mockingbird.) A *Times* feature about an electric car was titled "Nuts and Volts," and a piece on psychiatrist Erik Erikson's fears that civilization was threatened by a repression of the urge to have children was headed "Oedipus Wrecks." An Op-Ed piece by the strategist Stanley Hoffman appeared under "New Whine in Old Bottles." And an essay by flamenco guitarist Brook Zern on Spaniards reacting to an American playing their national instrument appeared with this head: "Strum and Drang."

The *New York Daily News,* covering a potential challenge to Ayatollah Khomeini by Ayatollah Taleghani, slugged it "One Ayatollah Too Meini"; along those lines, the congressional aide William Gavin called a confrontation between the leaders of Iran and the United States "Khomeini Grits."

The *Washington Star* editorial denounced "Catching Tuna Without Porpoise," while a letter writer objected to "too many kooks spoiling the broth." The *Los Angeles Herald Examiner*'s analysis of the impact of the metric system was labeled "Take Us to Your Liter."

Magazines have a great fascination for clones: *Newsweek*'s derogation of television's second season was "Send in the Clones," and *The New Republic* reached back to Garbo for "I Vant to Be a Clone." A piece in *Harper's* on the difficulty environmentalists were having on the insect issue was titled "Of Mites and Men."

Individuals are happily afflicted with paronomasia, too. Vic Gold, a writer with an instinct for the jocular, offered "Have Gun, Will Cavil"; former Representative James Symington praised Arthur Burns's "fiscal fitness." Marshall Bernstein of Roslyn, New York, came up with a slogan to those opposed to zero population growth: "Fecund to None." Emil Greenberg of Brooklyn, New York, suggested that a porn purveyor be called a "merchant of Venus," and that the people at Virginia Slims cigarettes send a message to all test-tube tots: "You've Come the Wrong Way, Baby!"

The advertising world, print division, is not averse to puns: A public-service ad for the New York Public Library said, "Read Between the Lions," and an innovative hairdresser in Washington called his relaxing establishment "the most enervative salon in Georgetown."

Poets traditionally play on words: "When I am dead, I hope it may be said: 'His sins were scarlet, but his books were read.'" That was Hilaire Belloc long ago; recently, the poet Peter Viereck made a cushion shot off Samuel Taylor Coleridge with "Ancestral voices prophesying Waugh." That's inside stuff, similar to Vladimir Nabokov's double play in *Pale Fire*: "A curio: Red Sox Beat Yanks 5-4 on Chapman's Homer."

My brother columnist James J. Kilpatrick only a few years ago denounced the revised provisions of the election laws as "a case of hashes to hashes, and crust to crust." I have always been what *Newsweek* called a "punder on the right." My analysis of new Arab wealth was called "a farewell to alms," and a criticism of an early move toward China was "Peking too soon." I have denounced trendy alienation as "anomie-tooism," warned of "future schlock," and, in a Schadenfreudian slip, hailed "urbane renewal." I am ashamed of knocking the President's drug adviser with "What Is Past Is Quaalude," and proud of calling supporters of Jack Kemp's tax-cut plan "Kemp Followers." The Saudi oil minister's ultimatum was sloganeered in these pages as "Yamani or Ya Life," and only an alert copyreader prevented the first name of the leader of the PLO from being followed by "That's My Baby."

Once in a while puns become part of the language: The "funny bone" is a play on "humerus," the bone that extends from shoulder to elbow. Indulge yourself in this worldwide wordplay; there is no more chance of stamping out paronomasia than there is a likelihood of finding a cure for the common scold.

Dear Mr. Safire,

There are some good puns in existence. Tennis star Martina Navratilova, upon her defection to America, asked, "Do you cache Czechs?"

Sincerely,
Billy Weiss
Rego Park, New York

Dear Mr. Safire:

My favorite newspaper headline pun I think appeared in The New York Times. *The article was about a group of people whose job it was to record with stopwatches the exact times of athletes running races. The headline was: "These are the Souls That Time Men's Tries."*

Sincerely,
Michael Feldstein
Teaneck, New Jersey

Dear Mr. Safire:

As I am sure you know, half of the quotations in your "Barrel of Puns" are examples of paronomasia but not puns.

The pun is the use of words with the same sound but different meanings, such as your quotations "Follow the Lieder" and "Oedipus Wrecks." But in many of your quotations (for example, "The Pun Never Sets . . . ," "Birth of a Notion," "Fecund to None") the key words ("Pun," "Notion," "Fecund") are not homonyms of "Son," "Nation," "Second."

These and the others are witty, they are ingenious paronomasias, but they are not puns: fit to praise but not punnish.

Sincerely,
H. W. Liebert
New Haven, Connecticut

Dear Mr. Safire:

I must disagree with your etymology for the word "pun." Puntiglio *translates as "point of honor; spite, pique"; it is cognate with the English "punctilio" (fine point, detail; exactness).*

The Italian noun for "pun" is bisticcio, *or* giuoco di parole; *the verb is* far dei bisticci.

Eric Partridge, in Origins, *says "pun" more likely comes from the Early Modern English* punnet *(according to Ernest Weekley's* Concise Etymological Dictionary, *2nd edition, 1952).*

Any counteroffers?

Ciao,
Esther LaFair
Philadelphia, Pennsylvania

Dear Mr. Safire;

Your article about headline puns reminded me of one that I read in the New York Daily News *several months ago.*

The headline was over a photo of Mayor [Edward] Koch and Governor [Hugh] Carey, who had met all through a weekend to discuss raising funds for the New York City transit system. Early Monday morning Koch and Carey held a press conference to announce the "rejuvenation" of the transit system.

The headline over the photo read: "Sick Transit's Glorious Monday."

John Flanagan
The Bronx, New York

Dear Bill:

You missed one of my favorites, the title of a recent seminar on gold investing "Ingot We Trust" or *the World War II British news story on refugees in the Pyrenees headlined "Too Many Basques in One Exit"* or *the description of a prolonged election in the College of Cardinals "Long Time No See!"*

Surfeited?

Warm regards,
Donald E. Meads
Plymouth Meeting, Pennsylvania

WHAT'S THE GOOD WORD?

Dear Mr. Safire:

I thought you might be interested in these examples from the sports section of the Des Moines Register.

On Monday, following Bjorn Borg's fifth Wimbledon victory, the headline was: "A Legend Is Bjorn."

That same night world heavyweight boxing champion Larry Holmes scored a TKO over Minnesotan Scott LeDoux in the seventh round. With a photo showing LeDoux connecting with thin air, and not Holmes, the Register *punned: "Much LeDoux about Nothing." I was there; it was.*

Sincerely,
Molly MacGregor
Minneapolis, Minnesota

Dear Mr. Safire:

A few years ago, during a particularly bad winter, the New York Daily News*'s center section carried a series of photos of New Yorkers battling the elements. The headline over the pix? "Many Are Cold, But Few Are Frozen." On another occasion the* News *carried a photograph of a group of naked Chinese children in a road race. The cutline under the photo? "All the Nudes Fit to Sprint."*

Sincerely,
Jerauld E. Brydges
Gazette *Staff Writer*
Niagara Gazette
Niagara Falls, New York

Dear Mr. Safire:

Your reference to "Tequila Mockingbird" reminded me that there used to be a bar in the basement of the DuPont Plaza Hotel in Miami called "Chez When." Two puns you may want to add to your collection:

(1) In a primitive Indian maternity ward, two mothers lying on buffalo skins each gave birth to single infants, whereas another resting on a hippopotamus pelt produced twins. The explanation, of course, was, as any high-school-level math student knows, that the squaw on the hippopotamus is equal to the sum of the squaws on the other two hides.

(2) The devoted owner of two porpoises was told by a marine biologist of questionable reputation that they could be given eternal life by putting them on a diet of sea gulls. Returning home from the shore with a sackful of birds over his shoulder, the owner finds a large but sedate cat stretched across the threshold, which he gingerly steps over. Once inside, he is immediately confronted by a police officer who arrests him for violation of the Mann Act. That's right, he had transported gulls across a staid lion for immortal porpoises.

Unashamedly,
William B. Hill
Savannah, Georgia

My dear Mr. Safire,

My only problem with your ideas was that you put all your begs in one ask-it.

Respectfully for puntiglios,
Rev. Francis L. Filas, S.J.
Chicago, Illinois

Dear Mr. Safire,

I hope you have room for one more. This was given me by Elizabeth MacCallum, an editor friend.

In 1843 Sir Charles Napier concluded treaties with the amirs of Sind, thus establishing British possession of the province. Lord Ellenborough, governor-general of India, wrote to London: "Peccavi." The members of the Foreign Office—classically educated all—immediately knew what he meant: "I have sinned."

Yr obdt svt,
David Logan
Cincinnati, Ohio

Dear William Safire:

The Shorter Oxford English Dictionary, *on which I rely, indicates that you have been misled re "humerus"/"humorous"/"funny bone." They derive "funny bone" from the tickling pain that results from being hit on that particular bone, which is part of the elbow, whereas the humerus extends from the shoulder* to *the elbow. I suspect some medical jokester is responsible for the etymology you cited.*

But I do know of one genuine pun in the lexicon, though it involves a little-known word (at least in America). I learned the term "wideawake hat" from A. A. Milne's poem "The Alchemist" (the alchemist is said to put on a big wideawake hat at night and sit in his writing room, writing). I always thought it was a nonce word, a jocular opposite of "nightcap." But then I came across it again in a British book and looked it up, and found (again in the SOED*) that a wideawake hat is a broad-brimmed felt hat, said to be so called because it has* no nap. *Excruciating, what? I guess it's the* pun *that never sets on the British Empire.*

With good wishes,
Marie Borroff
Department of English
Yale University
New Haven, Connecticut

Dear Mr. Safire:

I fear your column about puns contained an error. Newsweek *never called you a "Punder on the Right."* Time *did. I know; I wrote that one.*

Best,
Donald Morrison
Senior Editor, Time
Becket, Massachusetts

Dear Mr. Safire,

I like bilingual puns, such as Geo. S. Kaufman's "Only the brave chemin de fer" or Russel Crouse's complicated one, involving Gloria Swanson's premiere, scheduled for Sunday, postponed for a day because of a flood's wiping out all transport. "Sic transit Gloria mundi," said Crouse.

During my recording of Bolero *the drummer left the studio to get another drum. I told the producer he'd gone for a snare Andalusian.*

And recently, in Monte Carlo, hearing Zizi Jeanmaire described as having no neck, I said she'd borrowed one from the princess, receiving (what else?) the Cou de Grace.

Henri Temianka has just been here to judge the Carl Flesch Violin Competitions. He complained about the difficulty of judging between thirty violinists, all playing the same piece, the Bach Chaconne. Chaconne à son goût, *I suggested.*

I have to confess it: I do a column called "A Yank in London" for a weekly called What's On in London *and have, more than just occasionally, pinched ideas from you.* Is there no end to the vileness of man?*

Still, Kaufman again, "One man's Mede is another man's Persian."

Sincerely,
Larry Adler
London, England

**But always with proper credit.*

Great Ball'Safire,

Using my "Kemp follower" only on loan
Was a certain kind of flattery,
But claiming it as a pun of your own,
Why, that's assault and battery.

Sincerely,
Herbert Stein
Washington, D.C.

battle tank, *see* mod modifiers

bean counter, *see* molar mashers and sob sisters

bear claws, *see* good night, sweet roll

beat up on, *see* upmanship

behind me

Some time ago (as fuzzy a locution as "a number of"—it was ten months ago), I chastised the Chase Manhattan Bank for its advertising theme: "I've Put the Chase Behind Me." Readers had pointed out that "to put something behind you" is not to indicate support, as the advertising intended; rather, the phrase means to forget deliberately, as in "OK, so I was overdrawn a few times, and your computer got my account mixed up with David Rockefeller's, but let's put all that behind us."

Evidently this column has power, clout, swat, and influence, or else a copywriter has had independent second thoughts. Whichever the case, an advertisement has just appeared of a woman holding some papers that look like architectural plans, saying "Ever since I designed my first Off Broadway set, I've had the Chase behind me." The "put" has been recalled; the slogan is now "You Have the Chase Behind You."

That's a good, clear use of the language. As for past disagreement—we can put that behind us.

Dear Saf,

I'll bet fifty or more people must have written Chase or its ad agency about the inanity of its "I put the Chase behind me" campaign. But who's to say it wasn't your straw that broke the beast's back?

On the other hand, you are still using "chastise," which strongly implies a physical beating, when you mean criticize, rebuke, chide, reprehend, admonish, berate, take to task, or dress down. If this be castigation, make the most of it!

Art Morgan
New York, New York

Dear Mr. Safire:

Yes, we read your column. And we listened. Consider our past disagreements dissolved. Thank you for keeping us linguistically lucid. With all good wishes,

Sincerely,
Fraser P. Seitel
Vice-President, Director—Public Relations
The Chase Manhattan Bank
New York, New York

---

belay that

"Their crisp styling underscores their utility," purrs the ad copy for the Century station wagon. "Their plush interiors belie their Buick heritage."

George Mapelsden of Westport, Connecticut, shrugged off that "belie" as a copywriter's poetic imprecision. But he was moved to complain when a front-page story in his favorite newspaper described a witness before a Senate committee in these words: "Slight twitches in his eyes and hands belied his nervousness."

"Belie" means "give the lie to." Twitches would belie a witness's composure, but twitches betray nervousness, just as plush interiors bespeak—and do not belie—a Buick heritage. (Maybe the copywriter meant "underlie.")

Words about deceit can be deceptive. Their smiles belie their fury; I'll never belie to you.

---

best hope on earth, *see* on "of"

---

best shot

"He gave it his best shot."

The locution "best shot," which is punching holes through the language these days, is being used to mean "greatest effort." When used in a slightly different sense, as in "California was his best shot," the two words mean "best opportunity."

Originally this was a military metaphor. In the sixteenth century the "best shot" was that part of any army which could most accurately inflict injury on the enemy—the best archers, for example.

In this century the combat phrase put down boxing roots. Lexicographer Peter Tamony has found a citation in the *San Francisco News* of August 29, 1931: "Smith's blows, though they were his very best shots, didn't feaze Hanna." ("Feaze" is a variant of "feeze," meaning "to embarrass or disconcert," which is now usually spelled "faze.") The way for "best shot" was paved by "get a shot at"—as in the March 13, 1940, use: "Fat Tony Galento gets a shot at Joe Louis's heavyweight championship."

Military phrases ("campaign," "boom," "standard-bearer," "diehard") are always snapped up by politics, and boxing phrases are equally welcome in bloodless combat: "Hat in the ring," "on the ropes," "low blow." With "your best shot," politicians and pundits have found a phrase with provenance in both battlefield and prize ring, which gives the term an especially proud pedigree.

This phrase has not been easy to pin down, but I gave it what used to be called my all.

Dear Sir:

Regarding "best shot," I suggest that you consider the relationship of this phrase to billiards and pool shooting, both of which provide many situations in which the participants must evaluate their choice of shots and select the one that they think will give them the advantage. Indeed, frequently the shot must be called before it is attempted—as no doubt you will recall from personal experience. I believe that it is likely that the phrase was widely used in pool halls and billiard parlors before it came to be applied to boxing.

Sincerely yours,
Winston Wessels
Plymouth, Michigan

big foot

When I climbed aboard the press bus which was following the motorcade of a presidential candidate, a fellow reporter called out, "Here comes another Big Foot!" That meant I had joined the ranks of "media biggies."

Among the boys on the bus, "Big Foot" is a jocular term for a columnist, editor, or journalism celebrity who deigns to mingle with the working stiffs, often to the consternation of a colleague regularly covering the candidate. T. R. Reid, of *The Washington Post,* who sometimes works in the shadow of superstars David Broder and Haynes Johnson, first fixed the appellation in print on *The New York Times*'s chief Washington correspondent, Hedrick Smith, who for some months wore a large cast on a broken ankle.

When Walter Cronkite came aboard, however, "Big Foot" was no longer big enough. "The traveling reporters," wrote Reid, "who have divided political journalists into two categories—junior reporters, known as 'little feet,' and senior political analysts, or 'big feet'—have given Cronkite a designation all his own: 'Ultra Foot.' "

Here's the telltale sign of a Big Foot: The second paragraph of his story, or newscast, always begins with the word "privately." Watch or listen for it. What "privately" really means is: "That first graph is what the bigshot sources are telling the 'Little Feet,' and want printed or filmed on the record. Now here's what they're whispering to me. . . ."

bill stickers, *see* signs of the times

black slang, *see* getting down

blindside

At Senate hearings, a football term was used three times in one day by our nation's leading lawmen. Almost in unison, the all-pro backfield of

Heymann, Martin, Lisker, and Richard snapped: "We briefed the attorney general so he wouldn't be blindsided."

In football, the strategy of approaching an unsuspecting quarterback from behind—from the side he cannot see, or is blind to—often forces the tackled man to fumble. The phrase is bottomed on "blind spot," or area of ignorance, and came into vogue as a verb—"he was blindsided"—in 1975.

The new verb is infinitely more vivid than "surprised." It evokes an image of a frail man with a single digit on his jersey being jumped on ferociously from behind by a monster of a defensive end, with the ball then being jarred loose along with the quarterback's teeth. Excellent new political term—applicable in business, too.

Dear Bill:

Related to your discussion of "blindsiding" is a phrase I've been encountering over the past few months: "I'll eat your lunch." Always used in a business context, it suggests the ultimate in humiliation. ("If we don't improve our product distribution, our competitors will eat our lunch.") But just because it evokes images of schoolyard bullies, it doesn't seem to have any pejorative connotations. Managers will clap their hands with glee after a presentation and exult, "We're really gonna eat their lunch this time!"

Although eating metaphors often relate to "bread and butter" economic issues, the phrase sounds *as if it were coined by a football sportscaster watching a lineman smother a cowering quarterback.*

Cordially,
Ray Boggs
Wellesley, Massachusetts

"bloopies"

Time for the annual Creative Advertising Copy Awards—the coveted "Bloopies," which are five and a half times cleaner than Annys or Grannys. Plus you don't have to go to the dinner.

The Modern Spelling Association gold medal to Time Inc. for its full-page advertisement selling its cover about interferon, the cancer drug: "Its current output of a few hundred milligrams a year is so miniscule. . . ." The old-fashioned spelling is "minuscule," but trendy people are pronouncing it "mi-NIS-kyool," so what the hell. ("Hell," in this sense, is not begun with a majuscule letter.)

The Highly Charged, Plugged-In Vogue Word Award to realtor Shannon & Luchs for its ad for a house in Bethesda, Maryland: "Exciting new contemporary in eclectric, beautifully wooded area." The combination of "eclectic" with "electric" is in the highest traditions, etc.

The Raincoat-by-Any-Other-Name Prize to Barney's clothing store of New York, which called all men to a Burberry's "self-lined gentleman's walking coat," not only creating the first "self-lined gentleman" but introducing the first coat that walks right out of the store.

The Bloodiest Blurb of the Year red sash to *Cosmopolitan* magazine for its teaser on a novel named *Remains,* beginning, "Decimated by the death of her adored and adoring husband ... Joanna is bedeviled by terrifying events." Few heroines are reduced by one-tenth before the story begins.

The Dime's-Worth-of-Difference pointy-headed statuette to ABC News for its headline in an ad picturing five presidential candidates: "What's the Difference Between Them?" The difference among them was never discovered.

The Abel-Bodied Sweetness and Light, Triple-Tiered Sugar Cake to Triumph cigarettes for its proud copy line: "Triumph is raising cane with America's so-called 'low tars' and 'lights.' " Not since Cain slew his brother has this expression been given such a sugar coating. A marked triumph.

The Simple Gold Watch for Candor in Advertising to the Chateau Jewelry Corporation for its ad for "The Octagon Piaget. Simplistically handsome."

The Order of the Shrunken Headhunter to Booz Allen & Hamilton Inc. for its rejection of agreement of antecedents in a person-wanted ad: "The person we want probably spent their early career as a writer ..." All the applicants wasted his time applying.

Runner-up in this category was the Xerox Corporation, which dramatized its recruitment needs with a help-wanted ad that began: "We seek a managing editor that can ..."

The Golden Shard for the Promulgation of Sentence Fragments to Lee A. Iacocca, chairman of the Chrysler Corporation (where he is called "The Iacocca"), for a manifesto which included such sentences as: "The alternative to a loan guarantee is not bankruptcy. For a very simple reason." And: "The loans will be repaid. With interest." Let's not hold. Our breath.

The Ill-Tempered Clavichord Prize to Bloomingdale's for its creation of a new word: "Halston introduces the Well-Kempt Man." The previous opposite of "ill-kempt" was the archaic "kempt"; this new locution will appeal to both the gruntled and the couth.

Finally, the Shoodastoodin Bed Award to Hill TV, of Rochester, New York, for the catchiest correction of the year: "CORRECTION: Due to a Typographical Error in Our Ad in Yesterday's Democrat & Chronicle and Times Union, Our Store Hours Were Stated Incorrectly and Should of Read ..."

William Safire

Dear Mr. Safire:

How come you are so rough on Barney's "self-lined gentleman's walking coat" ("introducing the first coat that walks right out of the store")? You some kind of gerund-grinder? Lose your spending money? Run out of writing paper? Nick yourself with your shaving kit? Were you fleeced by a faulty banking terminal? Chlorinated in a backyard swimming pool? Twist an ankle on the running track? Forget to leave your calling card? Treat your bruises with rubbing alcohol, and you'll feel better in the morning.

Cordially,
Arnold Lerner
Ardsley, New York

Dear William Safire:

Tsk, tsk. Re: Your "Bloopies," you earned a small prize of your own; let's call it the Ill-Tempered & Inaccurately Remembered Clavier *(not "clavichord") Prize, for getting the title of Bach's forty-eight Preludes slightly screwed up (by implication).*

Old J. S. B. was using the German word for any *keyboard instrument, not just the clavichord, a nearly inaudible little instrument largely confined in use to young ladies and polite parlors—probably not much played on by our robust J.S.* or *the pupils for whom he wrote* Das Wohltemperierte Klavier.

Your (rather common) bloopie belongs on the same shelf as other popular misreadings like "gilding the lily," "Pride goeth before a fall," and "transpire" (for "happen"). Let's leave it there, friend.

Fraternally yours,
Ralpn Berton
North Bergen, New Jersey

Dear Bill,

You mentioned "couth" and "gruntled" (in connection with "kempt"), and it seemed to me that it might be time to put these oldies to rest.

If you start from the right end of the word, you encounter gems like "bootless" (whoever heard of something worthwhile referred to as having "boot"?—and "booty," though perhaps worthwhile, is cheating); "feckless" (do you know anyone with "feck"?). How many of your friends have "gorm," yet we constantly encounter "gormless" fools. Tired puns have been made on "(w)reckless" drivers, but drivers possessed of "reck" are few and far between. "Nonetheless" and "nevertheless" are not fair, but it might be useful to observe that both "couth" and "kempt" are "unless."

All the best,
Larry
[Laurence Urdang]
Editor, Verbatim
Essex, Connecticut

Dear Language:

Just among you and I and the lamppost, I think you are going to have to award yourself a special bloopie because you have been hoist in a trap of your own devising.

*You awarded the Dime's Worth of Difference statuette (why the hyphens?) for the wrong reason. "What is the difference among them?" is English if what is meant is: "What is the dispute that is dividing them into factions?" What ABC News meant to say was "What are the difference*s *between them?" meaning, "What are the elements distinguishing them one from another as individuals?" "What are the difference*s *among them?" it should be noted, means "What are their divergent views, some no doubt jointly held, on this or that?" Needless to add (why add it then?), "What is the difference between them?" involves two persons or two factions.*

I trust that all this does not leave you betwixt and between. If it does, you are among the majority (see the appropriate entry in the Stylebook).

Yours faithfully,
Max Lowenthal
Foreign copy desk
The New York Times

Dear Mr. Safire—

Re your annual awards column. Specifically, the award to Barney's for the first "walking coat."

As a retailer in the same business as Barney's, I can assure you that coats that walk out of the store by themselves have been around for many years. Also suits, shirts, and, in fact, any item that a shoplifter can manage to lift.

Very truly yours,
Ruth J. Rosoff
Philadelphia, Pennsylvania

Dear Mr. Safire:

This doggerel in anapestic heptameter from one of your upstate fans proposes a solution to one of the most bothersome problems in our language:

Pronomenclature

When she/he told him/her of her/his three new words
For the pronouns in singular third,
They were sure that this slashing each other could stop,
And the language would be less absurd.

For the words showed no bias in gender at all,
As their letters were chosen with care;
And they rhymed with their plurals for easy recall,
If one only knew "they," "them," and "their."

In the Nom. there was shey, *which has both "she" and "he,"*
While the Acc., shem, *was equally fair*
("m" from him, "e" from her, and the "h" from them both),
And Possessive his/her both in sheir.

So shey gave shem a hug and a kiss on sheir lips,
Just to show shem that shey was aware
That the hermaphroditic neologisms
Were some pronouns the sexes could share.

Apologetically,
Mauritz Johnson
Delmar, New York

Dear Mr. Safire:

You referred to interferon as "the cancer drug." Does this mean it gives a patient cancer? Or is it really an anticancer drug?

Curious,
E. Jimmee Stein
New York, New York

---

bogus titling, ***see*** **loyal apposition**

---

buff up, *see* mediquack

bunk into, *see* New York-ese

bust, *see* words for nerds

card metaphors, *see* take a card

catch of the day

"In London during World War II," writes the veteran broadcaster Edward P. Morgan, "the Fleet Street fare was scrod and more scrod. We spelled it scrod and pronounced it SKROD.

"In Boston three weeks ago, I discovered at least three restaurants—including the Ritz Carlton—where this lowly but nourishing fish was listed on the menu as SCHROD."

Another correspondent, Lynda Morgenroth of Cambridge, Massachusetts, wrote another query about that fish and spelled it both with and without an *h:* "I used to think that schrod was baby codfish. . . . Recently I have been told that scrod refers to a method of filleting a fish. . . . What is scrod?"

Answer: right both times, right with both spellings. A scrod, or schrod, is a baby codfish, or any other young or small, nonoily fish (like haddock). The noun comes from the Middle Dutch *schroode,* meaning "strip," "shred," related to "scroll" or "slip or shred or paper." "To schroode" was to strip a shred from a larger piece, with the same kind of action you use to fillet a fish.

Spell and pronounce it either way in Boston, and you're correct. If you order it outside of Boston, however, the waiter is not likely to know what you're talking about.

Dear Mr. Safire,

"Outside of *Boston" forsooth! Were you thinking of the onetime best seller*

Inside of Asia, *maybe? . . . Or of nineteenth-century outside-of-the-law gunslingers? . . . Or did you simply fall off OF (ugh!) your pedagogic pedestal?*

Yrs, in the Sacred Name of Fowler,
R. D. Darrell
Stone Ridge, New York

Dear Mr. Safire,

Some few years ago, while working in the Washington, D.C., area, I would visit the Lexington Market in Baltimore. One of the major fish stalls there (and unfortunately I can't recall the name of it) had a news article fastened to its wall that described the origin of the word "scrod." According to this story, scrod was the name given to the first catch that the fishing boats would haul in. This was subsequently smothered by the rest of the fish that were piled on top of the first haul during the course of the fishing trip.

When the fishing boats returned to port, the first in was obviously the last out. In the pile of freshly caught fish, this was on top and (as I recall from the article) sold at a discount. For want of a better name, and because it was unrecognizable as anything else, it was referred to as "scrod."

Sincerely,
Fred S. Greene
Freehold, New Jersey

Dear Mr. Safire:

Anent your discussion of the origins of "scrod," you must have heard the old joke, certainly printable these days in a family newspaper:

Boston tourist: Excuse me, Officer, can you tell me where to get scrod?
Policeman: I've heard that question asked a hundred times before, but never in the pluperfect subjunctive.

Larry Josephson
Punnitent
New York, New York

---

caveat, *see* Haigravations

---

chairperson, *see* missing persons

---

chaise lounge, *see* come the millennium

charretting, *see* words for nerds

cheap shots

"That was a cheap shot," said William French Smith, the recently appointed attorney general, responding to criticism about his attendance at a party for a well-known friend of mobsters.

"Cheap shot" is a locution of recent vintage. Stuart Berg Flexner, the slang authority, suspects it may have originated in boxing, but his first printed citation, in *Business Week* in 1971, is about a football player: "Like most cornerbacks, [Lemar] Parrish is a master of the cheap shot." In football, a cheap shot is a tackle or block delivered when the player on the receiving end is unable to defend himself—stretching to catch a pass, for example, or being wrestled down by another player.

The phrase was used in its political sense a year later, again in *Business Week,* in criticism of *A Populist Manifesto,* by Jack Newfield and Jeff Greenfield. The critic wrote of "Gene McCarthy, for whom they reserve most of their cheap shots." The term was picked up by a political reporter in 1976, who asked candidate Jimmy Carter whether he thought a certain barb aimed at President Ford did not constitute such a cheap shot. Mr. Carter replied: "I don't think it was a cheap shot," thus immortalizing the phrase.

Mr. French Smith, not content with the football metaphor, turned to a word long held in favor by denouncers of media attacks: "scurrilous." *The Washington Post* reported: "He labeled news reports questioning the propriety of his appearance at the birthday party as 'nothing less than scurrilous,' repeating the word 'scurrilous' three times, until he finally added, 'Am I making myself clear?' "

To aid our new top lawman in his quest for clarity: The most common definition of "scurrilous" is "obscene, vulgar, coarse," but that cannot be what he meant. Politicians who use the vogue phrase "scurrilous attack" intend the adjective to mean "low, mean," or, if the politician attacked is more literate, "abusive, vituperative." The etymology is from the Latin *scurra,* "buffoon"—a jester who presumably told dirty jokes.

One of the scurrilous cheap-shooters, aghast and nonplussed at the French Smith counterattack, whimpered in print that a man in the position of attorney general "must start acting immediately like Caesar's wife."

That displayed an ignorance of Plutarch even more profound than French Smith's lack of understanding of the requirements of his office. Caesar's wife was Pompeia, who—while participating in a religious ceremony open only to women—was said to have entertained a man named Clodius, her lover. The scandal of sacrilege shook Rome; Clodius escaped conviction in a trial, but Caesar divorced Pompeia, saying "Caesar's wife must be above suspicion." Thus, "like Caesar's wife" does not mean "above suspicion," unless the speaker is artfully referring to Caesar's next wife, Calpurnia, who knew enough to stay away from orgies with the buddies of Roman gangsters.

Let me not mislead readers: One of the obscene vituperators who offended Mr. French Smith was me. The last time I was denounced as "scurrilous" was during the Kissinger administration, when a spokesman at the State Department went on to condemn my "contemptuous behavior." Asked if he did not mean "contemptible," the spokesman recovered quickly with "That, too." To mention his name now would be a cheap shot.

The preceding paragraph's lead sentence ended with "was me." Before firing off a scurrilous postcard, see page 159.

Dear Mr. Safire:

Fine distinctions, like your distinction between Pompeia and Calpurnia, sometimes call for finer ones. Otherwise you are involved in a scurrilous disparagement of philosophy.

The sentence "Caesar's wife must be above suspicion" does not refer to any particular lady. It indicates how Caesar's wife, whoever she be, *ought to behave.*

So the person you criticized did not display ignorance of Plutarch. He recognized a general category when he saw one.

Sincerely yours,
Morris Grossman
Fairfield, Connecticut

Dear Bill:

The evidence seems to point strongly to football rather than boxing as the origin of "cheap shot." This is supported by the earliest citation in our files, also dated 1967:

> *Davidson since has had a reputation among the Jets as a "cheap shot" performer. In pro football jargon, a cheap shot is an unnecessary tackle or*

> *block when an opponent is defenseless. (Dave Anderson,* The New York Times, *December 19, 1967, p. 65)*

The next citation, dated 1968, uses the term in a general context:

> *The movie opened yesterday at the Paris Theater and the Criterion, for the English antiwar cheap-shot satire brigade. (Renata Adler,* The New York Times, *May 29, 1968, p. 20)*

Incidentally, the term and its derivative, "cheap-shot artist," appear in the Second Barnhart Dictionary of New English, *with the date 1967. I don't mean this to be a cheap shot, Bill, but you shoulda looked there.*

Regards,
Sol
[Sol Steinmetz]
Clarence L. Barnhart, Inc.
Bronxville, New York

---

cheese-eater, *see* getting down

---

chello again

A person who signs his name "T. Jefferson, Monticello, Virginia" takes me to task for suggesting that the local townsfolk pronounce his home with an *s*. In fact, he insists, the name in Virginia has always had the Italian pronunciation preferred by the owner of an estate in that area: "Montichello."

The letter is a hoax. I know that because no such town as Monticello, Virginia, exists. The nearest town is Charlottesville; Monticello is the name of an estate once owned by a founding father and is pronounced by Virginians with a *ch*.

Monticello, New York, is a town that pronounces itself with an *s*. All clear, T. Jefferson?

Other shibboleths that have been dribbling in (enough, already) include Marin County, California, which the outlanders call "MAR-in," but the locals floating in their hot tubs call "Muh-RIN"; the cities in Canada that

Americans call "Tor-ON-to" and "Kwa-BECK," but Canadians call "TRON-na" and "Kuh-BECK"; and Wilkes-Barre, Pennsylvania, the last part pronounced "Berry" by outlanders and "Bahr"—as in the first syllable of "barren"—by natives. (But in Vermont, Barre is called "Barry" by natives, and "Bar" by outsiders.)

From Hong Kong, my *Times* colleague Joseph Sterba points out that "Bangladesh" begins with an *ong* sound, as in "Hong Kong." "It is 'Bhangladesh'—not 'Bang,' as in the way the world ends." In a whimper, he adds a note about Afghanistan's Kabul: "It's 'COB-ble,' not 'Ca-BOOL,'" and cautions against an unconscious lisp on the modern name of Siam: "It's 'Tie-land,' not 'Thigh-land.'"

From the *Minneapolis Tribune*'s editor, Charles Bailey, comes a correction: Montevideo, Minnesota, is neither "Monte-vi-DAY-o" nor "Monte-vi-DEE-o," but "Monte-VID-eo." (Place must have great television reception.)

From his ubiquitous camper somewhere "on the road" for CBS, correspondent Charles Kuralt reports: "Beaufort, on the coast of my home state, North Carolina, is 'BO-f'rt.' But Beaufort, another town in *South* Carolina, is 'BEW-f'rt.' It's 'El Do-RAY-do,' Arkansas, but 'El Do-RAH-do,' California."

Mr. Kuralt adds a classic put-down of the arrogance of outsiders: "A man told me that he and his wife stopped for lunch in Mexia, Texas, and unsure of how to pronounce the name of the town, he asked the waitress, 'Would you say, very slowly, the name of this place we're in?' She said, 'Sure. 'Daaairy Queeeeen.'"

Dear Mr. Safire,

Since some of your readers might wonder how, indeed, one does pronounce the name of my hometown, Mexia, Texas, let me say there are three ways. The purists (a dwindling handful) cling to May-HEE-ah; almost everyone else calls it Muh-HEH-ah, and the few who never made it to school clump along with Muh-HAIR.

It was probably this last pronunciation that gave rise to a joke heard in high school about a waitress with a newly dyed coiffure who asked an itinerant customer, "How do you like Mexia?" to which he replied, "It's too damn red."

That didn't exactly kill us in high school either.

Cordially yours,
Michael Brown
New York, New York

Note from W.S.: For the word on shibboleths, see p. 246.

chief executive officer, *see* perils of the fast track

Christian-Judeo, *see* Haigravations II

clothespin vote, *see* kangaroos and clothespins

collective nouns, *see* none are right

c'mon, big boy

The Census Bureau this year is on the alert to avoid "the Philadelphia phenomenon." In 1970 it seemed to census takers that the city of Philadelphia was rife with taxi drivers under twenty-one years of age. That was strange: Pennsylvania law requires all taxi drivers to be over twenty-one.

The people behind the computers "reexamined the data," as they say. It turns out that many Philadelphia prostitutes had listed their occupations as "taxi dancer" in the space provided for occupation; prim census staffers, unfamiliar with dance halls or Ella Fitzgerald's rendition of "Ten Cents a Dance," had interpreted the scrawled "dancer" as "driver" and so entered it in the computer.

Why is a dancer for hire called a "taxi dancer"? Comes from "taxi-dance place," which came from "taximeter motor cab." Harry N. Allen coined the word "taxicab," which he copyrighted in Washington. "The 'cab' part was a natural," he told *The New York Times* in 1974, forty years after the first taxicabs appeared. "The 'taxi' came from a French company that made meters for horse cabs, called 'taximeters.' That means a meter that arranges for the tax. I merely combined the two."

The "taxi" in "taxi dancer," then, comes from the idea of charging a certain amount, or tax, for the time it takes to render the service, or the distance danced. But go try to find a taxi dancer on a rainy night.

Dear Mr. Safire:

In reference to your recent effort to trace the provenance of "taxi dancer," you should have gone a step beyond taximètre. *The meaning does not, as you implied, come from the idea of a "tax" paid, but rather from the Greek root* taxi *which means "travel." Even today in modern Greek "ταξιδεύω" means "to travel" and "ὁ ταξιδιώτης" means "traveler." Thus,* taximètre *was coined as a word meaning a meter which measures (the rate of) travel.*

Truly,
John Czarnowski
Philadelphia, Pennsylvania

come the millennium

"Across the millenia," I wrote in a piece about business English, "the poet warns us to watch out for mentors. Even Homer shook his head."

I was pleased with that conclusion. First, I had used the classic plural ending for "millenium" (just as I stodgily prefer "memoranda" to "memorandums"). Second, I'd made a cushion shot off that classic excuse for errors—"even Homer nodded"—with that tricky "even Homer shook his head." Very suave.

The trouble was, I misspelled "millennia": singular or plural, the word needs a double *n*. "Some months ago," writes Raymond Mullaney of Haworth, New Jersey, "after reading your piece on advertising's bloopie awards, I wrote you to suggest that Elizabeth Arden Inc. be given an award for naming its new product 'Millenium,' misspelling the word in the process. Being a longtime hunter of the misspelled 'millennium,' I was horrified to see the word misspelled twenty-six times in one Elizabeth Arden advertisement and feared that the cause was lost. You can imagine how I felt on reading the mistake in your piece...."

Mr. Mullaney enclosed a photostat of a page from the first printing of the second edition of *Webster's New World Dictionary*, which reads: "mil-len-ni-um ... *n., pl.* -ni-ums, -ni-a [Mod L. (from) L. *mille*, thousand + *annus*, year]." The double *n* was unmistakable, but later in the definition, this highly authoritative source wrote "2000 B.C. through 1001 B.C. is the 2d *millenium* B.C.," misspelling "millennium." The error was caught in the most recent printing.

Armed with these facts, I first spoke to David Guralnik, editor of *Webster's New World* and the Terry Bradshaw of lexicographers. "We got it wrong in the first printing? Well, we're fallible. Three *l*'s in 'fallible.' " I put to him a question from Patricia Salomone, a veiled millennium-corrector from New York City: "Is it possible that this spelling is becoming acceptable? Does this ever happen?"

"Chaise lounge," said Guralnik immediately. I assumed he was barking an order to his secretary for a chair in which he could recline and ruminate, but it turned out that he was giving an illustration of a word that had its correct spelling changed because of persistent error. "Originally that was *chaise longue,* a French term for a couchlike chair," said the lexicographer, "but it was so frequently mispronounced 'lounge' that the *u* was transposed in the spelling in many mail-order catalogs.

"Catalogs," he tangented, "was originally 'catalogues.' At first, the clipping of the *ue* was considered a misspelling, but now it's the preferred form. How many *m*'s in programming?"

"Two," I answered, remembering the two *n*'s in "millennia."

"Theoretically you're right," Guralnik said, "because the last letter is ordinarily doubled as the stress shifts to the last syllable. But in the spoken language—which changes more rapidly than the written language—the emphasis is on the first syllable of the verb 'program.' At last count, the spelling is still most often 'programming,' but 'programing' is catching up."

When does a mistake become correct, and the old "correct" become less preferred? "When enough citations come in from cultivated writers, passed by trained copy editors," the lexicographer replied, "the 'mistake' becomes the spelling."

I then called Paulette Dufault, director of advertising for Elizabeth Arden, to discover if that company's widespread dissemination of "millenium"—with one *n*—was in error or intentional. Miss Dufault, pronounced "doo-foh," explained that Millenium was a product line consisting of a moisturizer, a cleanser, a night cream, and a toner. (An independent, second source informs me that a "toner" is a substance that "tightens the pores" and "completes the cleansing process"—its name strikes the right note.) "We were aware that 'millennium' is spelled with two *n*'s," said Miss Dufault in a moist, creamy-soft, permanently youthful voice. "We spelled our product with one *n* because it would be a trademark." When that was met with suspicious silence, she added tonily, "And we liked the look of it."

Was the company not conscience-stricken at its contribution to error? Did it not consider it to be socially irresponsible for a corporation to corrupt the spelling of millions of innocent schoolchildren and to lead to the embarrassment of language columnists?

"A little poetic license is not bad," Miss Dufault offered. She has a point; the makeup of makeup advertising is blurred—often poetic, sometimes mystical.

As for those nit-picking readers who are reaching for pens to explain with dreary accuracy that the third millennium does not start until the year

2001—you people are going to be a year late for the big blowout on December 31, 1999.

Dear Mr. Safire,

You mention "catalog" as an example of a misspelling that has become acceptable. You will notice, however, that library catalogs, at least in America, are always "catalogs," tended with scrupulous attention to detail by catalogers or catalog librarians. The reason is not, heaven forfend, misspelling. It is a bit of homage to Melvil Dewey, who supported, along with libraries and library education, a range of enthusiasms which included bicycling, feminism, and spelling reform. Professional librarians, while we do not go so far as to refer to the Dui Decimal System, always use the curtailed "catalog"; our influence on the language has been surprisingly small. I stopped at the shopping mall yesterday to see which spelling another great American institution supported, but the saleswoman at Sears could only offer me something called a "Wish Book."

Yours truly,
Eva DeGlopper
New Haven, Connecticut

Dear Mr. Safire:

You were discussing misspellings which have become accepted. One of the examples you used was "catalog" (from "catalogue").

The use of "catalog," especially in libraries, is not a result of misspelling but an intentional shortening of the word by Melvil Dewey. He was very interested in spelling reform and the shortening of words and the use of "catalog" in libraries can be attributed to Mr. Dewey. Many of his other proposed spelling reforms are now in use, e.g., "thru" for "through."

Sincerely,
Carolyn Wolf
Reference Librarian
Hartwick College
Oneonta, New York

Dear Mr. Safire:

"Come the Millenium" reminded me of a recent experience. I noticed that on a package of Granger smoking tobacco there was the statement "Hermetric Seal Pouch." I wrote to the Pinkerton Tobacco Company, makers of Granger, that an hermetic seal is airtight, and wondered whether "Hermetric" connoted a connection with the metric system. Mr. E. D. Wanamaker, their president, replied that "Hermetric" was a deliberate misspelling in order that the phrase could be registered, whereas the word "hermetic" could not. He also said that

they had a number of inquiries regarding this and sent me a supply of Granger in appreciation of my interest.

Cordially,
Curtis I. Kohn
Edmonds, Washington

Dear Mr. Safire:

Did this man really send you a photostat of a page from the dictionary? One does not often see photostats these days, since they must be made by a Photostat machine. I believe they can be recognized by the fact that black and white are reversed from the original. Most often one sees electrostatic copies or thermographic copies, both of which are usually called xeroxes (or is it Xeroxes?) whether or not they have been made on a device sold by the Xerox Company. At any rate, photocopies are made by photographic process, using light on some form of sensitive paper, which must then be developed. The modern dry copy is different.

H. Pinsker
Teaneck, New Jersey

Dear Mr. Safire,

Elizabeth Arden is not the only culprit. Aside from obvious and deliberate misspellings like Diet Rite, Kools, and D-Zerta that will probably stay safely in their own sphere, a certain deodorant springs to mind that has one professor of my acquaintance writing of arrid desert regions.

Very truly yours,
Marjorie Gelus
Queens College
Flushing, New York

Dear Mr. Safire:

Anent "Come the Millenium" I have a comment on your reference to Homer nodding, or shaking his head. My only recollection of any poet mentioning Homer nodding is in Alexander Pope's poem "An Essay on Criticism." Therein he wrote:*

"Those oft are stratagems which errors seem,
Nor is it Homer nods, but we that dream."

Sincerely (with salt),
Benjamin Frank Borsody
Sarasota, Florida

**Anent: "With regard to,"* Webster's New Twentieth Century Unabridged

Dear Mr. Safire:

Re Miss Dufault's spelling "millennium" with one n *for a "trademark":* Don't *be suspicious of that. I used to live on East Fifty-eighth Street and eat at #208—The Girafe Restaurant—with a giant wrought-iron sculpture of a giraffe outside. The owner told me the spelling was bent for a trademark. The Giraf(f)e Restaurant is still standing tall!*

Ad interim,
Alfred Siegel
Commack, New York

---

conditional, *see* craven conditional

---

conservatism, *see* one "v"

---

contact sport

"Contact your travel agent," urges a foreign tourist board on television.

"I always thought if I were to do that, I would have to cover the agent with glue," writes A. Sock of New York. "Isn't that poor word 'contact' badly misused?"

Most of the people who fought the usage fight against the proliferation of "contact" have abandoned that rampart; they can be found fighting a rear-guard action on "hopefully," and will lose that one, too. (Let's all move over to "implement" and "impact on.")

"Contact" is rooted in the Latin *tangere,* "to touch." Everyone accepts "get in touch with"—so what's the big fuss about "contact," which means the same thing? The brouhaha (from the Hebrew "Blessed be he who enters") was stirred by the sudden appearance of the verb "to contact" as an Americanism more than a generation ago and its avid adoption by businessmen. When a new usage, with impeccable etymology, slowly comes onstage, it is tolerated and finally welcomed, but when it comes on like "Gangbusters," it is ridiculed.

The legitimate arguments against "contact" were (1) its vogue use, which always merits chastisement, and (2) its vagueness—did it mean "telephone" or "meet with" or "write" or "have telepathic communication with"? (The argument was mainly with the verb; the noun "contact"—meaning a person of influence with whom the speaker is acquainted—was instantly seen as precise and useful.)

The vogue use has diminished; the people who said, "I'll contact you," just to strut in the verbal fashion, have now turned to "I'll be back to you." The verb "to contact" is still deliberately fuzzy, but no more so than "I'll be in touch with you," its lengthier counterpart. In much the same way that the fuzzy "indicated" is used instead of "said," the verb "contact" is a favorite of lawyers who want their clients to avoid perjury—its imprecision is its value. Similarly, television advertisers may now want their audience to feel constrained to respond in any specific way, and "contact your local travel agent" nicely encompasses "write, telephone, or walk over to your nearest travel agent and grab him by the lapels."

Sorry, Mr. Sock. "Contact" has fought its way into standard usage. The word still lends itself to fads—"Contact!" was the shout to early aviators, and "contact sport" is tossed about today to describe touch dancing on the gridiron. These fade, but the simple expression rooted in the metaphor of individuals reaching out and feeling each other is with the language for good. Use it without shame, and stay in touch.

Dear Mr. Safire:

Your reference to "Contact!" as a fad in early aviation is out of order. In that context the usage was deadly serious.

After the ground crew had turned the engine over several times by "pulling the prop," the pilot shouted, "Contact!" when he closed the ignition switch (making an electrical contact). Thereafter the propeller had to be handled with great care lest the ground crew be seriously injured (or even killed) when the engine started.

Yours sincerely,
J. B. Horner Kuper
Setauket, New York

---

corvine, *see* unacceptable

---

craven conditional

Many academics, diplomats, and television commentators share a favored locution that can be described as "the craven conditional"—the weak-kneed, pompously deferential "it would seem" or "I would say."

A growing number of readers (two this year) have taken offense at this pushy shyness. "I am increasingly annoyed," writes Robert Miles of Brooklyn, New York, "by people in public life answering questions put them by beginning 'I would say that . . .' Well, I would say certain things, too, if I thought they were true. But only if." Irritated by being subjected to the sub-rosa subjunctive, Mr. Miles calls for statesmen with "the courage to use the indicative mood."

Arthur Bruan, also of Brooklyn, the unconditional borough, spotted this statement by Dr. Elliot M. Gross, the city's chief medical examiner: "In a professional office of this type, I would hope that deliberate sabotage would not occur."

Demands Mr. Bruan: "What does the good doctor mean? Does he really hope that sabotage will not occur, or is he just half hoping it? Is he just preparing to hope? Is he just too timorous to indulge in an outright hope? Is he being circumspect or guarded about hoping? How does one ascribe a meaning to his phrase 'would hope'?"

"Maybe and maybe not" is implicit in "would"; the conditional sense has a wish or a worry built in it. "I would say" or "I would think" means, literally, that the speaker would say or think something "if." In recent years, however, this misuse of "would" has become accepted—even embraced—by avid hesitants.

"It would seem" offers a triple helping of mealymouthedness. The construction itself passively attributes responsibility to an indeterminate "it"; the "seem" refers to appearances only; the "would" adds such a further condition as to back the phrase off a cliff. The *Oxford English Dictionary* says the phrase is "used to express somewhat more of hesitation or uncertainty than is expressed by 'it seems.' " I would call it a weasel phrase—and not only would I, I do.

"It seems" is one calibration more tough-minded. " 'It would seem,' " says the *OED*, "is now chiefly used to express a guarded (or sometimes an ironical) acceptance of statements made by others." In a letter to *The New York Times,* William Bowdler, an assistant secretary of state who acknowledges that one of his forebears was probably the editor who published an expurgated version of Shakespeare's plays, stated, "It would seem clear, then, that the junta . . ." Jacques Barzun, author of *Simple and Direct,* points out that "the writer is obviously calling his unnamed antagonists to attention."

Respected usagarians do not agree with me; Professor Barzun thinks "it would seem" is a "useful and acceptable way of expressing doubt." Bergen Evans took a middle position: "The thinking or seeming is first placed in the future and then made conditional or uncertain. It is a very modest way of speaking."

But the modesty is usually false. The commentator acts against the words: The phrase you hear on television is intended to carry great authority, not great doubt. It avoids "it seems to me," which is at least an honest weasel.

"Seems, Madame? Nay, it is; I know not seems." That was Hamlet speaking, and they said he was ambivalent, though I am of two minds about that. Would that his kind were speaking in the indicative unconditional today.

Dear Mr. Safire:

"I should think" = conditional (indicative?)
*"I would think" = subjunctive (contrary to fact)**

I shall *confine my further remarks to the more political realm because I* will *not be deflected from my goal.* (Cf. *"should" vs. "would.") (Or is all this archaic?)*

A "liberal" is a person who confuses and identifies the future indicative with the present subjunctive (substantive volitive); a "conservative" confuses the present indicative with the contrary-to-fact subjunctive. The "liberal" would (should?) have us all support mere hopes; the "conservative," false ideas (of science, etc.) Only the disappearing breed, the "moderate," can help us.

Yours,
David I. Caplan
New York, New York

**If the atomic theory is correct, as I believe it is, then I* should think *that the energeticist school rightly died out, and I* should *further* think *that the theory should be taught more widely.*

If the atomic theory were proved incorrect, then I would *be perplexed indeed and I* would think *that I had been deceived by my teachers.*

Dear Mr. Safire:

I would add—at least it would seem that I would add—one more item to your list of "weasel subjunctives": "it can be said." A typical example, from John Richardson's essay on Picasso in The New York Review of Books: *"Thus the pattern of stylistic infidelity can be said to follow the pattern of amorous infidelity." How about "Thus the pattern of stylistic infidelity follows the pattern of amorous infidelity"? If it can be said, say it!*

Sincerely yours,
Aaron Haspel
New York, New York

Dear Mr. Safire,

You might make a further contribution to language by discussing a feature that could be called "The Probably Definite." It is nearly always spoken, not written. As in "I knew for certain we would probably see him" or "I'm sure all of you probably like peanut butter." You can, I am sure, probably find many better examples and, possibly, an explanation.

Sincerely,
C. X. Larrabee
Research Triangle Park
North Carolina

Dear Mr. Safire:

"Craven Conditional" drew a loud "Aw! Shucks" from me because I had intended writing (to) you on that subject for some time. However, I have another shot in my locker, and I will procrastinate no longer. It is the widespread use of "feel" instead of "think" or "believe." Since it is prompted by the same cravenness as the "would" abuse, it could be called the "craven visceral."

You are surely familiar with this sort of thing: "I feel that the platform is unsound and impractical" and "I feel that we ought to have a big tax cut" or "a crash jobs program." I remember a real beaut from a few years ago. The governor of one of the Gulf states went to inspect the damage done by a ferocious hurricane. Standing in the midst of wrecked houses, downed power lines, thousands of homeless citizens, and a number of corpses, he said, "I feel that this is a disaster area." Why didn't he say, "I think this is a disaster area"? Or "This is a disaster area"? Or even "You bet your sweet life this is a disaster area"?

I suggest that this variety of verbal flabbiness reflects the speaker's desire to escape responsibility for his pronouncement. If you say that you think or believe something, it is yours. It is the result of your personal thought processes, and you must take the consequences. But if you say "I feel," what follows can be viewed as the result of outside forces. Such a declaration gets lumped under the same heading as "I feel sick." You are no more responsible for the pronouncement than you are for the sickness. Thus, the person who says, "I feel that we ought to drop atom bombs on Moscow and Peking," can shrug off the horrid implications of that statement by saying that it was issued without plenary review and consideration. It was just an urge.

(Happily, I have yet to catch anyone saying, "I would feel that . . .")

Yours in the cause of English,
Joseph B. Robison
New York, New York

Dear Mr. Safire:

There is a form of this usage which my brother classed, rather neatly, as the "paranoid they," as in "They won't let you enjoy anything *these days" or "Pretty soon they'll say sleeping is carcinogenic." Perhaps it's time to accord the "paranoid they" its due recognition as an expression of our times.*

Constance A. Sancetta
West Nyack, New York

crowning touch

Vice-President Walter Mondale trotted out a rarely used term to describe the Canadian-assisted escape of six Americans from Teheran: "We had been trying to exfiltrate them safely." "*In*filtrate" is familiar, meaning "to filter in" and, by extension to the military metaphor, "to slip through lines secretly" into enemy territory. "*Ex*filtrate" means "to filter out" and, by extension in the Iranian case, "to slip through lines out of unfriendly territory." Good usage.

California Governor Jerry Brown had a couple of barbs to use on his 1980 campaign trail: "The reason Carter-Kennedy has been yakking about foreign affairs so much is because they don't know what to do about America." The slang term "yakking" is of imitative origin—"yakety-yak" is the sound of babble—but if Governor Brown intends to use "Carter-Kennedy" as a singular subject, he ought not to use "they" as its pronoun.

Governor Brown also belted President Carter with a well-turned phrase: "Carter ran on a platform of love and now he's trying to get re-elected on a platform of fear." But in smacking Kennedy, the rear half of his singular Carter-Kennedy horse, he said, "Kennedy was ready to be coronated four months ago." Wrong. Although *corona* is the Latin for "crown," and a coronet is a small crown, one does not get "coronated" at a coronation. One gets crowned.

Dear Safire—

Wrong on "coronate"—a perfectly legit English word, properly formed from the Latin first declension verb corono *(not from the noun* corona*) with plenty of parallel formations in use (e.g., "rotate" from Latin verb* roto, *not from noun* rota, *or "decorate") and a long, if exiguous, history in English.* OED *cites it from seventeenth and nineteenth centuries; "coronated" is quite common as a botanical term. It does strike the ear as cacophonous, probably mostly because of the comparative rarity of Latin words with (quantitatively) iambic roots.*

Yours,
Sam Abrams
Rochester, New York

crumped, *see* out is in

crump out, *see* out is in

dead cat on a line, *see* getting down

dear madams

On the Op-Op-Ed page of *The New York Times*—that's the page opposite the Op-Ed page—a colleague has explored the problem of salutations to corporations. Now that women are often a part of the corporate structure, is "Gentlemen" enough? Should one try the apocryphal "Dear Sir or Madam as the case may be"?

The editorialist rejected "Gentlepersons" as silly, fretted about using company names, and decided, "We'll reluctantly stick with the traditional 'Dear Sir.' "

That's an editorial "we" that does not include us. The world of business has changed, and the business of communication must change with it. I propose nothing drastic—the suggestion of Tam Deachman of Vancouver, British Columbia, that "Dear" be replaced by "Salu" is far ahead of its time—but just enough to pick up on the tempo of with-it management.

Since a corporation is like a person in the eyes of the law, correspondents should treat it like a person, not merely like a conglomeration of men and women. Certainly the men-only "Dear Sirs" or "Gentlemen" salutations are behind the times.

Helen Gurley Brown—I guess you might say she's that editor of *Cosmopolitan* magazine—agrees. "I think companies might be called by first names," she writes in response to my query, "like 'Dear Bloomingdale's,' 'Dear Citibank,' 'Dear Sardi's,' 'Dear Campbell Soup Company,' etc. Instead of 'Gentlemen,' you'd say, 'Dear Company Name.' "

I like that. Simple and direct, polite, neither arch nor archaic. For familiarity and punchiness, I'd drop the "Company" or "Corporation," and salute with "Dear Ford Motor," or "Dear Pepsico." That applies to noncorporate entities: "Dear Department of Commerce," "Dear Common Cause." Courtesy demands that the full name be given: "Dear Wickersham, Cadwalader & Taft," not a breezy "Dear Wickersham."

Nothing beats a salutation that grabs the audience by the throat, mentioning the name or otherwise accurately describing the object of the communication. Napoleon, addressing his massed troops, knew the way: "Soldiers!"

Dear Mr. Safire:

In reading your comments about the proper salutation in business letters, I am reminded of my uncle Tyler who had occasion to write to The Tailored Woman, the famous Fifth Avenue apparel store. After the usual heading he faced the problem of the salutation—"Dear Sirs" or "Gentlemen" not seeming appropriate. After much thought he came up with this:

The Tailored Woman
Fifth Avenue
New York

My Good Woman:

Helena Frederickson
Little Silver, New Jersey

Dear Mr. Safire:

Anent the problem you have been attempting to solve regarding addressing corporations in these liberated days, I believe I can proffer the perfect solution: "Good Day."

I have been using it regularly for the past number of months, and it has elicited some quite favorable comment. Most people tell me they smile immediately upon opening one of my missives—lovely! Almost all business mail is certainly received and opened during daylight hours so there is little chance of quibbling about the time element. It is indeed a pleasant salutation to either gender—and best of all, it obviates the necessity of saying "Have a good day" again (ever)! Try it on a nice piece of blank white paper and see how good it looks, to wit:

New York Times
229 West 43rd Street
New York, N.Y. 10036

Good Day:

I am really enjoying writing this note to your Mr. William Safire . . .

Betty K. Unger
New York, New York

Dear Bill:

I've always said that a lawyer who defends his client is a fool.

The august law firm of which you spoke is Cadwalader, Wickersham & Taft. You got your Wickershams before your Cadwaladers.

Well, you can't win 'em when the cart's before the horse.

Best,
Morton L. Janklow
New York, New York

Note from W. S.: Mr. Janklow is my lawyer and literary agent. He spots mistakes in my columns, and I spot mistakes in his contracts.

---

desert/dessert, *see* let justice be done

---

dialing back

Newsweek has been dialing back.

Last month the newsmagazine wrote: "As a result, 'Kemp-Roth will be dialed back in the Republican-controlled Senate as well as in the House,' says one well-wired Congressional tax expert."

In the same issue, in a piece on the tax troubles in Massachusetts faced by Governor Edward King, a well-wired *Newsweek* writer used it this way: "King has dialed back on his tax-cut pledges and watched his popularity plummet."

Again in that issue, back in the business section, Representative David Stockman, the Reagan choice to head the Office of Management and Budget, is quoted as saying: "You don't have to dial back on the original public-health protection, but we need to recalibrate all the standards. . . ."

It was as if somebody hollered down the halls of *Newsweek*: "This week, it's 'dial back'!" The expression has replaced "cobble up" (to fabricate, to put together, to emulate the action of a cobbler) as the favored locution at that magazine.

What is the source of the metaphor? According to the reporter who quoted the well-wired tax expert, Rich Thomas (his first name is short for "Richard" and is not intended to distinguish him from a "poor Thomas" on the same staff), the expression is derived from engineering controls: "When you get too much steam in a boiler, you move the pressure dials back," Mr. Thomas explained, adding ruefully, "I've got a hot-water heater."

If you'll dial back on "dial back," fellows, we'll all do what we can to recalibrate Representative Stockman.

Dear Mr. Safire,

Your item brought to mind a word problem I've been having ever since the telephone company installed a push-button phone in my apartment. When the late-night television commercials implore me to "Dial 800" etc., I stare blankly at the dozen little squares on my telephone. And when I am told, "Dial the operator for assistance," what am I to do? Punch the operator? Have you found a way around this developing linguistic anachronism? (Luckily the word problem doesn't pursue me in the newsroom, where I can dial *all the calls I want on my black rotary model.)*

Sincerely,
Ari L. Goldman
Metropolitan Desk Reporter
The New York Times
New York, New York

Note from W. S.: Great idea—"punch the operator"!

Dear Mr. Safire,

Concerning that metaphor "dialing back": I was amused and frightened by the reason set forth for that figure of speech by that tax expert Rich Thomas. You quote: "When you get too much steam in a boiler, you move the pressure dials back." I got big news for you—"moving the dials back" will not get steam pressure down. Usually one opens the pressure relief valve or maybe reduces the flame or fire in the boiler firebox. If he has a hot-water heater, he is lucky, for he will not be able to explode himself into oblivion—but then again if it is a legal installation, his pressure relief valve will save him.

Sincerely,
S. S. Ganick
Boston, Massachusetts

Mister Safire:

"When you get too much steam in a boiler, you move the pressure dials back."

Not once, in upward of thirty years' experience, did I thus relieve a boiler's congested innards. True, it is a minor nit I pick, yet, in that narrow, precise, noisy world, dials only indicate, always; control, never. For the harshest of reasons: clarity. Overstuffed boilers hold an awesome power to ding somebody.

W. E. Wolfe
Petaluma, California

Dear Mr. Safire:

In "Dialing Back," the source of the phrase is certainly not from any engineering control, and Mr. Rich Thomas is very wrong with his "When you get too much steam in a boiler, you move the pressure dials back."

When you get too much steam pressure, the safety valve blows! A pressure gauge cannot be reset or adjusted. It is permanently fixed by safety regulations at 0 to 30 lbs., 0 to 60 lbs., 0 to 100 lbs., etc., etc.

I should say offhand that the term "dialing back" has a linkage with that first clock, the sundial, which indicated time with a pointer on a graduated dial plate.

Sincerely,
Jack Gasnick
Mechanical Engineer
Gasnick Plumbing Supply Company
New York, New York

---

dicey, *see* Haigravations II

---

ding!

From deep inside the Reagan transition team comes word of strange locutions. The people at the power center have already adopted the White House favorites—"in the loop," for those privileged to be "copied" by receiving copies of memoranda, and "the power curve," behind which disaster beckons—and they are bringing along a few of their own.

The verb "to ding" rings bells with Reaganites (or, as the national security aide Richard Allen likes to call them, "Reaganauts"). According to a student of the jargon inside Résumé Arms, "I dinged him" means "I communicated my desire to have this straightened out," or "I let him know this is unclear and he should clear it up," or, the most common meaning, "I made known my displeasure." The verb appears in dictionaries with the definition "to repeat tiresomely," rooted in a Scandinavian word for "hammer"; its current meaning is "prod."

Another import—this one is from business jargon—is the use of "reference" as a verb, as in "I referenced the sinking of the *Titanic* in my report." This means "I made reference to," and is a genuinely silly coinage, since "refer" is already a verb, and shorter than "reference."

When Ambassador Robert Neumann became infuriated at the constant leaking of transition memoranda, he threatened to "salt" them. This does not mean preserve in salt or reference them to the Strategic Arms Limitation Talks. "To salt a memo" means to insert a word in one person's copy and a different word in another copy of the same memo. When the telltale word appears in print, the leaker is identified. (When recipients of leaks suspect that salting is going on, we paraphrase instead of quoting directly from the leaked document.)

One coinage in danger of being picked up and tracked into the White House is "downmouth." Gilbert Sandler of Baltimore sends in this quotation from Walter Heller, chief economist during the Kennedy era: "It's fashionable these days to downmouth economists.... It has gotten so bad that the Polish are telling economist jokes."

"To downmouth" is a blend of "bad mouth" (to derogate) or "poor mouth" (to feign poverty) with "down-in-the-mouth" (depressed) and "downplay" (cable-ese for "play down," or "do not emphasize"), with a soupçon of "downside risk" (the view from the precipice).

Walter Heller is a literate and good-humored economist, which is why I am dinging him on this. Ordinarily I'm a big upmouther of his.

Dear Mr. Safire:

"In the loop" probably has its origins in the field of telegraphy. Morse code telegraph circuits and teletypewriter circuits are constructed as loops. Information is transmitted by one station in the loop's breaking and restoring the loop's electrical completeness according to a specified code (such as Morse). Each time the loop is broken, other stations receive the information because current in the loop drops to zero and electromagnetic devices (such as the "sounders" of yore) cease to be magnetic. Thus, for any station to send or receive information, it must physically be "in the loop." Loop circuits are used with the teletypewriters seen in newsrooms (note that the word "Teletype" is a registered trademark of Teletype Corporation and should not really be used to refer to a type of device). Telephone circuits are also loops in many cases. In fact, loop circuits are associated with all but the most modern of electronic communication methods.

With the close relationship between telegraphy, its descendants, and the media which make new phrases popular, it is easy to see how "in the loop" might have made its way to the Reagan transition team.

Sincerely yours,
Christopher R. Fine
West Chester, Pennsylvania

Dear Mr. Safire:

I agree that it is silly to use "I referenced" to mean "I made reference to" or

"I referred to." However, your referenced article might have come to a kinder conclusion about this word if it had taken the phrase to mean "I cited as a reference."

Yours truly,
Stephen S. Flaum
Brooklyn, New York

Dear Mr. Safire,

In surfboard lingo, "to ding" means "to nick, dent, or damage one's surfboard," as, "I dinged my board on the rocks" or "This guy cracked into me and dinged my board." It is also used to describe a car, "My '40 Ford Woody has a ding in the fender." In the same lingo, a used surfboard or an old car in perfect condition is described as "cherry."

Yours sincerely,
Brooke Alexander
New York, New York

Dear Mr. Safire:

Although your explanation is interesting and amusing, I think the current use carries more reproach than you have indicated. The expression "I dinged him" is synonymous with "I rang his bell" or "I yanked his chain." There is no mistaking scorn and disapproval in the latter two expressions, and it seems this type of pseudocorporate jargon has been modified (at least in tone) for use by the Reagan transition team.

Sincerely,
George J. Cooke
Andover, Massachusetts

Dear Mr. Safire:

Your "student of the jargon inside Résumé Arms" is all wet—but perhaps not wet enough.

"Ding" is a surfing term. A ding (noun) is a dent, bang mark, or bad blemish on the surface of a surfboard. Dings are much to be abhorred.

"Ding" has also become the verb for inflicting dings upon surfboards.

Very truly yours,
Samuel S. Jacobson
Jacksonville, Florida

Dear Mr. Safire:

Your definition and suggested examples of the verb "to ding" lack some depth and limited application. Perhaps your sources are correct, that it derives from some arcane Scandinavian origins, but its survival in America I submit more than likely is from its Yiddish usage, which you did not mention.

My father, who had not a worldwide reputation for doling largess, would say, after we had scrubbed the rooms and performed other weekend chores, upon being asked for an extra two cents for candy, "Ding mir nisht a kup." *We were glad to get the dime and scurry off to the movies, lest that "dinging" made him examine our efforts, which, upon finding same deficient, he often threatened to reject the bargain, with the terse* "Ding zich nisht mit mir." *Do it right, and don't nag or give explanations—the act of "dinging."*

Mr. Safire, the word "ding" implies much more than your very sterile definition—it bears meaning of Orchard Street, the street markets, and two-pants suits. Probably, when Mr. Reagan and associates discover its ethnic connection, [they] will most likely drop it—who knows . . . maybe for another verb that carries some *of its meaning*—hahmper, *to bargain, to deal with in an obstructionist way, argumentive and petty but demanding and whining. Both verbs will, I believe, be the condition when Reagan attempts to* ding zich *with Congress, and they in turn* hahmper *with him, and on in an endless regress.*

Yours sincerely,
Michael E. Zuss
New York, New York

Dear Mr. Safire:

At the University of California at Berkeley, in the Greek letter fraternities, "to ding" means "to blackball, or cast a vote against a membership applicant, or rushee." At my fraternity we actually passed around a box into which each member dropped a white or black marble. Like most slang, "ding" is a simpler, more casual alternative to the ominous-sounding two-syllable "blackball."

Also, in California, a ding is a small dent in an automobile body, sometimes made by a shopping cart or another car's door in a parking lot. Dings are obvious enough to mar the appearance of a nice car, yet small enough to be maddeningly expensive to repair.

Best wishes,
John S. Russell
Kentfield, California

Dear Mr. Safire,

Some time ago I met people who were street hustlers. They used to buy small red, white, and blue bows, then put on soldiers' caps and go out into the streets and subways. They would then pin those bows on men's lapels and ask for donations. Those fellows used the term "I'll ding him" or "I'll ding this side of the street; you ding the other side." I asked them where that expression came from. They explained it came from the old trolley cars. In those days they had a conductor and a motorman. As the conductor took the fare, he would be required to register it by pulling on a small rope which was attached to a bell;

when the bell rang, the money was accounted for. Thus the term "ding." When the street hustlers put a bow on a lapel, the movement is the same as ringing a rope bell; hence the term "I'll ding him." I will admit it is not a formal definition, but it did "prod" people into giving money to those bogus ex-soldiers.

Very truly yours,
Murray Ross
Paterson, New Jersey

Dear Mr. Safire:

After reading your column, I decided to ding you (let you know that something is unclear and should be cleared up) with regard to your discussion of the verb "to ding."

I am a 1980 graduate of Mount Holyoke College. During my four years there, I learned to use the word "ding" in a very specific way. It was a prominent part of the vocabulary of members of the senior class during the manic-depressive months of applying to graduate schools and interviewing for jobs. In its original, most familiar usage, it is a noun, as in the following examples: "Two more dings today"; "I got a ding from Fifty-third National Bank"; "I'm papering the wall beside my desk with dings." (Other uses for dings include: covering doors or bulletin boards; making paper airplanes to fly around dorm dining rooms; cutting up into small squares for telephone messages; using the back to write papers.)

Out of this simple noun there evolved an equally simple verb, e.g., "U. of X. dinged me" or "I got dinged by U. of Y."

I do not know whether there are other schools at which the word "ding" is used in this way. However, the word has such powerful connotations for, at least, recent alumnae of Mount Holyoke that I would be surprised if I were the only one to (in your usage) ding you after reading your article.

Sincerely,
Caroline C. Foty
(who was not dinged by/did not receive a ding from the University of Michigan School of Music)
Ann Arbor, Michigan

Dear Mr. Safire:

We geologists (and possibly other scientists as well) have been using "reference" as a verb (informally at least) for some time. In scientific jargon, to "reference someone" means to include his work in one's list of references. In this usage one goes beyond simply referring to the person.

The scientific community is constantly coining new words and phrases in an attempt to keep ahead of the general public. The other night, as I was playing Scrabble with my wife, I attempted to make a seven-letter word ending in s. *I began to lay down the tiles to spell "linears" when I realized that this spelling would probably not be upheld in our dictionary. Geologists use the word "linears" to describe linear features seen in photographs of the earth's surface taken by high-flying aircraft or satellites. Linears differ from lineaments by being less correlative with known geologic structures.*

Another favorite word of geologists is "surficial," referring to surface deposits of one sort or another. It has its origins in the word "superficial" but lacks its antecedent's more humanistic connotations.

Yours truly,
Thomas A. Baillieul
Pittsburgh, Pennsylvania

---

directly, *see* presently

---

the dotted line

I visited the center of power in Washington the other day—"Résumé Arms," 1726 M Street, home of the Reagan transition staff. On each of the nine floors, men and women guzzle their coffee in paper cups (made of polyethylene), knowing that the days of White House chinaware is only weeks away.

In each key operative's pocket is a table of organization, surreptitiously drawn up by each project chief, all quite different but all with one common denominator: a box at the top with the word "resident" and another box off to the right with the job that person wants, connected by a dotted line.

That dotted line has compounded a new management adjective. In an internal CBS memorandum leaked to me by a linguistic whistleblower, one Bruce Lundvall writes to all fellow department heads: "As chief financial executive of CBS Records' manufacturing operations, [Douglas G.] Sages will have dotted-line responsibility to Sam Burger, senior vice president, manufacturing. . . ."

No, a "dotted-line responsibility" is not the responsibility to get somebody's signature on the dotted line. It has to do with the way that boxes denoting positions are connected on an organizational chart. Since things at CBS and the Harvard Business School are a little busy these days, I called Alonzo McDonald, the management whiz who made order out of chaos at the Carter White House.

"It's business jargon for a nonhierarchical relationship," the no-longer-harried presidential aide explained. "Liaison, exchanges of information, that sort of thing. 'Straight-line responsibility' reports to a boss; 'dotted-line responsibility' could be between executives in the same echelon.

"Hell of a lot of dotted lines over here," Al McDonald added ruminatively, as if he had an organizational chart in his mind's eye, "most of which run parallel and slightly oblique." But that hard-earned wisdom is for the new boys to find out for themselves.

Dear Mr. Safire:

Am I the first to note a glaring error in grammar in your column? The following sentence appears: "On each of the nine floors, men and women guzzle their coffee in paper cups (made of polyethylene), knowing that the days of White House chinaware is only weeks away." The plural "days" is serving as the subject for the singular verb "is." I know of no precedent for such a forced agreement.

If the error is not grammatical, then perhaps it is a confusion of days with the homophonic noun "daze." According to the OED, *the noun "daze" is: "of the mental faculties; a benumbed, deadened condition; loss of virtue or freshness."*

Many would argue that White House china has a way of numbing virtue.

Sincerely,
David Winsper
Instructor of English
Springfield Technical Community College
Northampton, Massachusetts

P.S. Freshman composition teachers have a tendency to become obsessive at this time of year.

Dear Mr. Safire:

I really cannot imagine men and women on each of nine floors sitting in polyethylene cups drinking their coffee. Perhaps you meant that they guzzle their coffee out of *or* from *paper cups?*

Yours truly,
Michael Goldman
New York, New York

Dear Sir:

A paper cup's a paper cup
That's all there is to that.
But, don't put any coffee in
Cups made of polyethylene,
Use cups of polystyrene
—or your hat.

And—
"Is only" is only a singular phrase,
You may use it with "day"
But never with "days."

Very truly yours,
Robert J. Campbell
Avon, Connecticut

Dear Mr. Safire,

While I often drink coffee from *a polyethylene cup, I would probably feel a bit cramped if I tried to fit inside, in order to guzzle my coffee* in *a paper cup. I wonder how many transition staffers can squeeze into a (polyethylene) paper cup? Or, for that matter, how many angels guzzle their coffee while dancing on pinheads in "Résumé Arms"?*

If the days of *White House chinaware* is *only weeks away, might we predict that prosperity* are *just around the corner?*

Sincerely,
Jason Gari Umans
New York, New York

Dear Mr. Safire:

"The days are" or "the day is," but "the days is" isn't good grammar. Sometimes I suspect you drop one of these mistakes in deliberately on occasion just to see how many close readers (and admirers, certainly, in my case) will write you. Many, I hope.

Sincerely,
Diana Riggle
New York, New York

---

downmouth, *see* ding!

---

down with "one"

I have thrown an irrational hate on the formal pronoun "one." One has to lift one's pinky to refer to one's self in the spoken language—why, then, must one use "one" in writing prose? The form is standard British usage, but it has not traveled well; the only American writer who can get away with it, one must add, is William Buckley, who likes to skewer his opponents' rodomontade in a deliberately high-sounding style.

In an age when writing is becoming more personal—more one on one—it makes no sense to strain to retain the impersonal "one." If it makes you feel awkward, you don't have to use it—which comes more comfortably to the pen than "If one feels awkward, one does not have to use it." When a relaxed style is out of place or when informality makes meanings fuzzy, change should be resisted—but when the colloquial voice is suitable and just as precise, there is little reason to hang onto the formal form. The lusty "Write so that people can understand you" is better than the stilted "One should write so that the reader can grasp one's point."

If we've just dumped the impersonal "one," what do we do about the impersonal "they"? "They say" has been tracked to a Ben Jonson play of 1637, and "they" is widely used as an indefinite pronoun to mean "people"—it's a livelier and more forceful construction than the passive "it is said that."

But the singular-made-universal "they" bothers careful writers. "Why do Americans use 'they' so much," writes John Pope of the New Orleans *Times-Picayune/States-Item,* "as in 'They're going to have a sale'?"

Professor M. Stanley Whitley of West Virginia University has studied the blurred singular "they" as used in sentences like "Does anyone want their coffee black?" and "Either Hal or Mary sank their teeth into my apple." These are called mistakes because noun and pronoun do not agree, but they are attempts to avoid the "his or her" awkwardness. Moreover, "Either Hal or Mary sank his teeth into my apple" is, Professor Whitley writes, "not just sexist, but downright bizarre."

The professor gets tough: "Grammarians have shown fits of academic apoplexy, inveighing against what they perceive as ... a deplorable lack of agreement. As a replacement for the impersonal uses, they insist on 'one,' a rather formal pronoun which, despite a strenuous campaign in its favor, has never quite attained the idiomatic and free occurrence among the folk that its foreign cousins—French *on,* German *man,* and Spanish *se*—have."

Let's deep-six "one." I don't care what they say.

Dear William Safire:

A poet and translator, born and raised in the "unconditional borough" of Brooklyn, "Down with 'One' " gave me pause.

Two or three points need to be made about "one."

1. *It is, at times, the best way to translate the German* man *and the Swedish* man *(I'll confine my remarks to those languages from which I*

translate), which are not invariably used "idiomatically." Man, *in both German and Swedish, can be used formally and/or evasively, just as "one" can in English.*

2. *I do not want to open the can of worms labeled "Formal/Informal & Singular/Plural Forms of 'You,'" but those worms coil around my pen and crawl onto my typewriter keyboard when they hear (if worms can hear) of the possible abolition of "one." Translators lose quite enough without also losing "one."*
3. *One might add (translate to read: "I must add") that "one" is often used, evasively, as a stand-in for "I."*

With all due respect,
Rika Lesser
Brooklyn, New York

---

dribble-off constructions, *see* nature boy

---

dwindles, *see* mediquack

---

ee!

Carter White House aide Jack Watson, according to *The Wall Street Journal,* referred to Cubans seeking asylum in the United States as "asylees." This is undoubtedly based on the analogy of "escapee."

"I am interested in the use of the noun 'escapee,'" writes Russell Drumm of New York. "I have always believed that the one who does the action is an *er,* and the one who is acted upon is an *ee.* [The word to be used here should] be 'escaper,' yet the 'escapee' designation is universal. Could you, the explainer, explain this to me, the explainee?"

Sorry, pal, idioms is idioms. The double *e* came from the French ending of words receiving action and was popularized by English lawyers: Someone to whom something was entrusted became a trustee, and the person to whom a matter was referred was a referee. The lessor leased the house to the lessee.

With logic, the practice was extended to the one to whom mail was addressed (addressee), the one who received honors (honoree), and celebrities who were nailed to the wall by sensation-seeking reporters (interviewees). An appointee was happy, a draftee was not, but both were on the receiving end of an action.

While this *ee*-ing was going on, another bunch of words trooped in from the French reflexive verbs, with its devotees using the double *e* to mean "one who is." My favorite is "debauchee," which can denote an absentee employee who is a refugee from morality. From this reflexion comes "escapee" and "standee," and that is what caused the confusion.

If English were neat and tidy, fun would be had by debauchers, freedom by escapers, and standing room only by standers. Fowler's *Modern English Usage* grumbles that "we already have at least three suffixes for that purpose (-er, -or, and -ist) and to add one whose natural meaning is the opposite is gratuitously confusing." (In that sentence, "gratuitously" is uncalled for.)

My advice to would-be escapers from the illogic of idiom is: Consider yourself rounded-up escapees. The language is what it is, and not what you want it to be. When the double *e* construction is overused, it looks silly—the headline calling the Afghan people "invadees" was dropped in a later edition—but I disagree with my colleague Red Smith, who insisted that " 'standee' is the one stood upon."

Gentle ridicule is the best way to discourage rampant use of any form. Neil Simon, who wrote *The Goodbye Girl,* put a line in the mouth of a recent divorcée that did the trick: "I myself am a recent dumpee."

Dear Mr. Safire:

The ee *suffix is not as illogical as may seem at first glance. Its use seems to imply "affected by an action" and as such can include both subject of an intransitive verb and object of a transitive verb, respectively "escapee," "returnee," and "employee," "draftee."*

Grouping these two cases together into one "affected" or "patient" case is a common phenomenon in English. We do the same thing with compounds: Examples of verb and object include "pickpocket," "chewing gum," "skyscraper," "blowgun," etc., whereas intransitive verb and subject include "crybaby," "glowworm," "blowfish," "workman," "go-cart," etc. Secondly, notice how many verbs in English are used both as transitive and intransitive with "affected" nouns: "bakes the bread," "the bread bakes"; "sink the ship" and "the ship sinks"; "open the door" and "the door opens."

There are languages in the world (e.g., Basque, Eskimo, and some languages in the Caucasus) which place this object of a transitive and subject of an intransitive in one grammatical case (the "absolutive") as opposed to the subject of a transitive verb (the "ergative"). It makes sense if you throw out our concept of subject and use instead a case characterized semantically as being affected by the action.

Incidentally, a couple of exceptions to such use of compounding: "hangman," in which "man" has to be the subject of a transitive verb, and "con artist."

Sincerely,
Jonathan Seely
Center for English as a Second Language
University of Arizona
Tucson, Arizona

---

effect/affect, *see* the affect effect

---

eight hundred pound gorilla, *see* taking over

---

emergency situation, *see* nature boy

---

ending with "gry"

Everybody in the language dodge gets a query, sooner or later, from a member of a strange cult dedicated to driving crazy the members of the language dodge.

The seemingly innocent question these cultists ask is: "Aside from 'angry' and 'hungry,' is there another word in the dictionary that ends in *gry*?" They usually add—as does headhunter Dianne Hanson, of Stamford, Connecticut, this week's cultist—"A friend assures me that there is; she can't remember it and I can't conjure it up."

It's a hoax, designed to provoke hours of useless brainracking. Lexicographer David Guralnik, editor of Simon & Schuster's *Webster's New World Dictionary,* gets hundreds of these queries, and replies that there are no other "native English words" ending in *gry.* Here are three imports:

"Puggry," more often spelled "puggree," occasionally "puckery," is a noun for an Indian turban or head covering, and is also a useful word used to denote the scarf wound around a sun helmet and falling down behind to shade the neck. (Wear your puggry, Beau Geste, or you'll get a neckburn.)

"Mawgry" is the state of being regarded with displeasure. The word comes from the Old French *maugré*; in English, "mauger" means "ill will." If you are afflicted by mauger, you're mawgry. It's obsolete; forget it.

"Aggry," also spelled "aggri," to assure readers they have not read a typo for "angry," is the word to describe colored glass beads worn by Africans, thought to be of ancient Egyptian manufacture.

That's three. No follow-ups permitted. If you're hungry to be angry, cultists, you can flap your puggry over your aggry beads and stand around mawgry.

Dear Mr. Safire:

There is a word "gry," which appears in Webster's Unabridged Dictionary *(Springfield, Mass.: G & C Merriam and Co., 1889, p. 594).*

1. *A measure equivalent to one tenth of a line.* Locke.
2. *Anything very small, or of little value.* obs.

Sincerely yours,
Renee Schlesinger
Rutherford, New Jersey

Dear Mr. Safire:

Your mention of words ending with gry *reminded me of something that has been bothering me for years and years. I was once told there are ten words in the English language which end in* dous.

Diligent research by me only came up with five—"horrendous," "stupendous," "hazardous," "tremendous," and "jeopardous." All my reading has been colored by my subconscious urge to find more.

Lo and behold, your column provided me with the know-how to solve my problem, grown ugly with the years. I wrote to your friend Mr. Guralnik, and that gentleman came up with the other five—none of which I had ever heard of before. They are: "vanadous," "molybdous," "decapodous," "gastropodous," and "isopodous." He also listed eight other "highly arcane" words also ending in the elusive dous.

Now I can go back to other things, including worrying over whether Jimmy Carter ends in dous *as in "horrendous."*

Yours,
Alexander L. Milch
South Orange, New Jersey

exacerbate, *see* Haigravations II

farewell

As one who rarely ingratiated himself at the Carter White House by commenting on Carter oratory, I am impelled to cough up a bit of praise for his farewell address. A solid job was done by the speechwriter Hendrik Hertzberg, with help from Gordon Stewart, a fellow speechwriter, and the pollster Pat Caddell, based on a detailed outline by Jimmy Carter.

The outgoing President wished the incoming man "Godspeed." That struck me as curious; usually "Godspeed," a contraction of "God speed you," is wished to one going off on a journey, not one coming in. I checked with Hertzberg. "My roommate, Michele Slung, warned me: 'Safire's gonna get you on that,' " replied the speechwriter. "So I looked it up in the *OED*—the British use is for people departing, but the American usage is the more general 'good fortune.' " (Roommate? "OK—in the Reagan administration, she's my fiancée.")

The speech featured what speechwriters have come to call "the Sorensen antithesis," after Ted "Ask Not" Sorensen. Said Carter: "America did not invent human rights. . . . Human rights invented America."

With some daring—since President Carter has occasionally stumbled over the pronunciation of "nuclear"—the phrase "nuclear conflagration" was part of the speech. (I would have avoided the mispronunciation "nukeular" and fallen flat into the error of "conflag-aration." Putting those two words together asks a lot from a speaker.)

The best metaphor was about the nuclear shadow that this generation has lived with: "Our minds have adjusted to it, as after a time our eyes adjust to the dark."

The best example of speech structure was the use of Jefferson's "life, liberty and the pursuit of happiness" in this fine summation of Carter's three themes: "For this generation, ours, life is nuclear survival; liberty is human rights; the pursuit of happiness is a planet whose resources are devoted to the physical and spiritual nourishment of its inhabitants." That was the most skillful line of the Carter presidency and had its genesis in the mind of the speechwriter's mother, Professor Hazel Hertzberg of Columbia University.

A nitpick: "I will work hard to make sure that the transition from myself to the next President is a good one." That was an unstylish, though not incorrect, use of "myself"; the better word is "me." Use "myself" as an intensifier (I myself prefer "me"), as a reflexive ("I misspoke myself," as press secretaries say), but not as a cutesy turning away from the harsh "me."

The high point of Carter's farewell address was the last word. Every speechwriter dreams of concluding a concession speech with a direct "I concede," or an acceptance speech with a ringing "I accept!" But not since Lincoln's speech at Springfield had we heard a man elected President end a farewell address properly. "Thank you, fellow citizens," said Mr. Carter, "and farewell."

Dear William Safire:

Messages of tentative congratulations have been trickling in to Rick (Hertzberg) and me. However, he and I have been discussing it—and, in my opinion, he really didn't have his terminology correct.

In the Carter *administration I would have been a "fiancée"; in the Reagan era, with its dusting off of so many ideas that have been sitting on the shelf, I think "mistress" might be a better translation.*

With best wishes,
Michele Slung
Washington, D.C.

Dear Mr. Safire:

Sorensen's device was not antithesis.

It was chiasmus.

Rhetorically yours,
Richard P. Hunt
New York, New York

fascinoma, *see* mediquack

fashion lingo, *see* neatness counts

fast food, *see* hashslinger slang

fast track, *see* perils of the fast track

feaze, *see* best shot

flea, *see* mediquack

for attribution

A noun that modifies another noun is usually singular: A brush for the teeth is not a "teethbrush," but a "toothbrush"; a case for books is not a "bookscase," but a "bookcase"; a factory that produces automobiles is not an "automobiles factory," but an "automobile factory."

Not only that, points out Hal Niergarth of Westfield, Massachusetts: Even when a noun is modified by a number that would logically push it toward a plural form, it hangs grimly onto its singular status when it modifies another noun. A plan now being considered in Moscow is a "five-year plan," not a "five-years plan," which is an economic system we would not touch with a ten-foot pole, not a ten-feet pole. (Even a two-year-old kid—not a two-years-old kid—knows that.)

Despite that traditional tendency of attributive nouns to inflect for the singular.... (What is this, a grammar text? Start over.) Despite our habit of using singular nouns to modify other nouns, we are faced with a new wrinkle—a recent trend toward breaking that habit. Mr. Niergarth acknowledges some old exceptions to the singular rule—"civil liberties union" and "honors list"—but points to the tendency now to use the plural: "weapons system," "enemies list."

What's going on here? Do we go to an "antique dealer" or an "antiques dealer"?

My special consultant on attributive nouns, Sol Steinmetz of Barnhart Books, says we are not to worry. He advises us to make the choice of singular or plural depending on the meaning. For example, I would say "antiques dealer" because the alternative, "antique dealer," could be confused with a very old and rickety dealer.

"A college's 'studies program,'" says Steinmetz, "is not the same as a student's 'study program.'" On "enemies list," he likes the plural: "An 'enemies list' can only mean a list of enemies, whereas an 'enemy list' is more likely to mean a list belonging to the enemy, like 'enemy country.'"

The need for technical precision is the cause of the rise of plural attributives. "An 'earth-resources satellite' gathers data on the earth's resources (not just one resource), a 'systems analyst' analyzes systems of all sorts, 'operations research' is research into all manner of complex operations, and an 'incomes policy' has to do not with the government's overall income from taxes but with the multitude of incomes embracing wages and profits which the government seeks to regulate."

The noun that modifies another noun should be singular unless clarity demands it be plural. Think about that the next time you go to a singles bar.

Dear Mr. Safire,

An exception to the rule that the "noun that modifies another noun should be singular unless clarity demands it be plural" is the term "gay bar." Should this be "gays' bar" or is the popular usage only indicative of the demise of gay as meaning anything other than homosexual?

Very truly yours,
Don E. Watt, Jr.
San Antonio, Texas

Dear Mr. Safire:

Adverbs *modify their verbs.*

However, adjectives, *and nouns used adjectivally,* qualify, *not modify, their nouns.*

Yours didactically,
Leslie McBride
Grosse Pointe, Michigan

Dear Mr. Safire:

Is the use of the possessive case forbidden at Barnhart Books? My special consultant at Random House tells me that a list belonging to the enemy is "the enemy's list." I agree, and believe, further, that only a jargonaut *would refer to such a list as an "enemy list." That person is then likely to vitiate your distinction by using "enemies list" to refer to a list belonging to the enemies.*

It seems to me that "enemy list" makes more sense, and is more likely to be interpreted correctly, when it refers to a list of enemies. Or does Mr. Steinmetz believe that a "guest list" is a list belonging to a guest (like "guest room") and that a "book list" is a list that is part of a book (like "book cover")? While the English language is glorious for its flexibility, the development of rules based on purely subjective criteria can lead to total confusion.

Yours truly,
Marvin P. Epstein
Montclair, New Jersey

fubar, *see* glitch

fulsome rushes in

"That was a fulsome answer," said Ronald Reagan to a questioner in Brooklyn, New York, last month; "I hope you don't think I was filibustering."

It was not his long answer but his use of "fulsome" that was fulsome. The word is not the adjective form of "full"; it is not a synonym for "complete," though Reagan's misuse of it is widespread.

"Fulsome" is related to "foul"; one meaning is "loathsome" or at least "offensive." A related meaning—and here's where the confusion starts—is "excessive." The frequently used phrase "fulsome praise" does not mean "lavish praise"; rather, it means "praise so excessive that it is obviously insincere and fawning."

The distinction is worth preserving. If you mean "lengthy," use that word; if you want to go a step farther (or further; either is correct), say "overlong"; beyond that, you can accuse a speaker of logorrhea. But if you want to say, "That turns me off because it's just too much, and I think he's laying it on that thick because he knows it isn't true"—and you want to put it all in one word—use "fulsome" to describe an introduction, or oratory, or praise, or even blame.

"Lavish" is a word awash with abundance, and means "unstinting" and "generous"—but it does not have that clank of falsity that resounds around "fulsome." Let's protect our insults.

fungo

"Origin unknown," say the dictionaries. Does anybody have a good theory about how the word "fungo" came to be? The word is baseball lingo for a lazy fly ball hit for fielding practice, and some aging outfielders think it may have had to do with the type of wood used in fungo bats. In *High and Inside,* a new guide to baseball slang, Joseph McBride speculates that it may come from "one go, two goes, fun goes."

William Safire

Dear Mr. Safire:

Concerning the origin of the word "fungo," I think Joseph McBride's speculation has substance. Fungo was a children's street game, dating back some ninety years, in which a player catching a certain number of fly balls qualified to replace the batter. "One go, two go, fun-go."

Also, when I have had enough of some person's prattle, I have found that telling him to "Go shag a fungo" does the trick.

I look forward to the fungo consensus.

Yours truly,
Joan P. Locke
Colorado Springs, Colorado

Dear Mr. Safire:

Concerning the word "fungo" since I first heard it, which was anyhow fifty years ago—from a rural origin that was my provenance—the word means nongenuine, not bona fide, lacking in real character. Fungoes are not real, dyed-in-the-wool fly balls because the man hitting them tosses the ball in the air and also hits it. Thus it is no real challenge to him, and with a bit of practice, he can about make it do what he wants except to get it really to drive slam-bang into the outfield so a fielder has any trouble running it down.

Among rural folk, the term relates to "fungus," which lacks the character of being a real plant. Instead of getting its roots in the ground as it should, it prefers to "graft" off a log or an old stump; it has no green leaves, and as often as not it is poisonous. It has no flowers and lacks vigor or strength and so crumbles if one tries to pick it up. The notion is a pejorative one, somewhat as fungoes are a whole lot less than real baseball flies.

Respectfully yours,
Stephen V. Fulkerson
Santa Paula, California

Dear Mr. Safire,

I asked my husband, an avid baseball fan, if he knew the origin of the word "fungo." "Of course," he replied. "On the days when Van Lingle Mungo wasn't pitching, he enjoyed hitting fly balls to the fielders during practice. Van Lingle did this regularly, and after a while his teammates would say to anyone batting to the outfield, 'Mungo me a few.' One day a player (who may have been standing out in the Ebbets Field sun too long) somehow twisted his tongue and said, 'Hey, fungo me a mew.' "*

When I suggested that his explanation seemed like a fable, my husband admitted, "Well, I'm not really sure, but how's this? . . . Van Lingle Mungo used to 'fungo' in Durango while eating a mango and dancing the tango."

None of this information answers your question, but I thought it might tickle your "fungo" bone!

Humourously yours,
Elsie Plotkin
The Bronx, New York

**Pitcher for the Brooklyn Dodgers in the 1930's.*

Dear Bill:

While my fat old Webster *calls the origin of "fungo" uncertain, it defines the word to include any case where the batter throws the ball up himself and hits it, including infield practice as well as long fly balls.*

This implies that it's the self-service that constitutes fungoing. Therefore the word could very well come from the Latin verb fungor, fungi, functus *(whence "function"), meaning "to serve, to produce, to execute."*

*The batter is doing all these things, hence fungoing. The bat has a specific shape, long and thin, different from those used in a game, but I believe it got its name from its function [*sic*!], rather than the other way round.*

Cordially yours,
Art Morgan
New York, New York

Dear Mr. Safire—

Questions about the origin of "fungo" have been asked as long as I can remember (which means the 1930's), and I have never come across a definitive or even convincing answer. But there is no doubt that in ordinary baseball usage, it seems to be attached to the implement—the "fungo bat"—and not to the act or the result. A coach says, "I'll hit some fungoes (fungos?)," meaning he will hit practice drives (grounders as well as flies) with a special narrow-handled bat, tossing the ball up himself rather than having it thrown to him by someone else. It became a verb well within my memory—let's say, the 1950's or 1960's—but whether or not it was a verb long before that (and maybe even before special bats), I don't know. The essential feature is that you toss the ball yourself *in order to hit it, regardless of what bat you use or what kind of drive you hit.*

Leonard Koppett
Palo Alto, California

Dear Mr. Safire:

In a substantial amount of this century's earlier English literature, especially some humorous things by P. G. Wodehouse, there is reference to the warm-up for cricket matches involving "fun goes," i.e., practice strokes before the game began in earnest. I have always taken it as a fact of life that "fungo" represents a shortening of this English usage.

Yours truly, in extreme haste,
Frederick L. Smith
Short Hills, New Jersey

Dear Mr. Safire:

My grandfather, who Knows All Things About Baseball, had no trouble fielding your query about the origin of "fungo." In fact, Grandpa claims he was present when the word was first used. "It was one o' them tough managers of a cellar club, son"—he sometimes forgets that I'm his grand*son*—*" 'bout 1910—coulda been '20. I think it was Connie [Mack]—coulda been McGraw. Anyway, he was disgusted with his outfielders, who muffed three flies the day before. He grabbed a bat the next morning, sent the stumblebums out in the field, and yelled, 'Here're some flies* F*or* U N*o-*G*ood* O*utfielders.' A nearby news guy noticed that the first letters made a word, 'fungo,' put it into his paper, and there it is, son."*

Thinking it over, Grandpa added, "There's them that hold that the word comes from great outfielders like Johnny Cooney and Willie [Mays], that they liked to chase fly balls even in practice, and that the word stands for 'FUN for G*ood* O*utfielders'—but don't you believe it, son. It was Old Casey who used it first, jest as sure as that my Mets are gonna cop the flag."*

Sincerely,
Edward Tobias
Brooklyn, New York

My dear Sir:

"Fungo" is derived from the Latin fungos, *meaning "spongy or soft as a sponge." In baseball (practice sessions only) a ball is tossed lightly into the air by the batter himself (or herself) and struck as it descends by means of a fungo bat, which is lighter (also softer), longer, and narrower than the customary bat. The implication in this practice session activity is that the ball is batted* softly *to the fielders with a bat which is* softer *—i.e., more spongelike—than the bat used in active competition.*

Perhaps the aging outfielders who suggested that "fungo" is derived from the type of wood used in fungo bats had a point well taken!

Sincerely yours,
Cassius M. Plair
St. Albans, New York

Dear Sir,

As a hard-core baseball buff let me offer my version as to the origin of the word "fungo."

In the early years of major-league baseball, Hillerich & Bradsby with their Louisville Slugger bats practically had a monopoly on baseball bats. But the lighter and less sturdier bats used for hitting practice flies were put out by another company.

The trade name stamped on the bats was Funco, short for the company name. I'm not sure of the actual full name of the company (something like "Fun Things Co." or "Fundy Co."). When a player said "Funco bat," it sounded like "Fungo," and they were eventually called that.

Yours truly,
Ted Berkelmann
The Bronx, New York

Dear Mr. Safire:

Dolph Fungeau was an assistant coach of the New York Highlanders from 1905 to 1909. He was married to Shahageen Singh, a girl considerably younger than himself, whose family had emigrated from Bombay to Trinidad during the great mango famine of 1890.

Dolph was particularly adept at hitting fly balls a long distance, and his wife often accompanied him to the old Polo Grounds, where she enjoyed racing around with the professional ballplayers trying to catch the old horsehide. Not only did Dolph, who subsequently ran a Reo dealership in Lancaster, Pennsylvania, give rise to the word "fungo," but unbeknownst to all but a very few, his wife gave rise to the term "shag," which means to catch a fungo.

Sincerely,
George D. Clahr, M.D.
New Milford, Connecticut

Etiology of "Fungo"
by Miles Klein, Optometrist,
English Major in NYU Class of 1952, and All-around Wordsmith

The word "fungo" comes from Van Lingle Mungo, a Dodger pitcher of the pre-World War II era, who enjoyed hitting flies to his outfielders with a weighted bat. If you don't believe that one . . .

The word "fungo" comes from the French fungeaux, *which means "eaters of mushrooms, truffles, and other fungal plants." They believed that men who hit balls with sticks, ran bases, and caught and threw the balls were suffering from some kind of hallucination, as though they had eaten some type of hallucinogen . . . or . . .*

The word "fungo" is an acronym for "For Use in Nurturing Green Outfielders"—no further explanation is needed. Should you find that none of my three explanations is adequate, I'll be glad to supply more.

Sincerely,
Miles Klein
Staten Island, New York

Dear sir,

A fungo is a ball hit for fielding practice with a fungo bat. If one tries to hit many such balls with a regulation bat, he soon becomes arm-weary, as well as raising a blister on his little finger from friction with the handle. The original fungo bat was a lightweight bat of willow, the handle of which, instead of ending in a flat button, ended in a mushroom-shaped knob, that fitted nicely into the palm of the hand. It was this knob that gave the bat its name.

Very truly yours,
John Dardess, M.D.
Chatham, New York

Dear Mr. Safire:

With respect to the etymology of "fungo," let me suggest something more plausible than "one go, two goes, fun goes." The Scots are better known for their fairways and greens, but they also have given us "fungo." According to The Scottish National Dictionary, *the verb "fung," meaning "to pitch, toss, fling," was in use in Aberdeen as early as 1804: "Ye witches, warlocks, fairies, fien's! / Daft fungin' fiery pears an' stanes." The connection with "fungo" is clear, the game being one in which a batter tosses a ball in the air before hitting it with a bat. (The ball so hit, the bat, and the game itself are all called "fungo.") As for the* -o *ending, its use as a hypocoristic suffix is well attested in such other games as "bingo," "beano," "bunco," and "keno," and it is doubtless regularly employed on playgrounds all over the country.*

A second Scottish mean of "fung," "to fly along at a high speed with a buzzing noise, to whizz," is not unrelated to the American game—at least for good fungo batters. An 1845 quotation, "Thick past my lugs [= ears] the rackets fung'd, / Hard stanes, auld turfs" (also from the SND*), establishes this usage well in advance of the earliest quotation for "fungo" (1867), reinforcing the theory of a Scottish origin, if not identifying the etymon itself.*

Judging from the evidence in the DARE *files, hitting fungoes is chiefly a northern pastime and seems to be declining in popularity, at least as a casual backlot sport. Our written sources come from New York, Illinois, and Washington; one lone* DARE *informant from New Jersey (aged eighty-two at the time of the interview) admitted to "batting fungoes" when asked about bat and ball games for just a few players.*

I fung this your way, hoping it will put to rest those left-field speculations about tropical woods and all the fun that has gone. Your aging outfielders have caught many a fly ball, but as etymologists they strike out.

Sincerely,
Joan H. Hall, Associate Editor
Dictionary of American Regional English
Madison, Wisconsin

---

gandy dancers, *see* molar mashers and sob sisters

---

gel-o again

A relatively new verb is coming into more general use, elbowing its way past "take shape," "form," "solidify," and "crystallize." The word is "gel."

"New Yorkers are waiting for something," wrote columnist Mary McGrory about President Carter, "some event or action, that will gel their ambivalent feelings about him and the election."

I am of two minds about "ambivalent," but the use of "gel" as a transitive verb strikes me as an aid to clarity. The word is the first syllable of "gelatin," from the Latin *gelare,* "to freeze." In a gelatin, one substance is chemically suspended, as if frozen, inside another. As everyone knows who has mixed a box of Jell-O with hot water, and then added a bunch of ice cubes, there comes a time when the thing congeals, or changes from liquid to a gelatinous mess. It is the perfect metaphor for the mysterious formation of an opinion.

But why is the new verb spelled "gel," and not "jel," as in "jelly"? Early on, as the British say, jelly was spelled "gelly," as befits a derivative of "gelatin," but along in the sixteenth century the feeling began to take shape that the word's sound was best expressed in print with a *j.* Perhaps the *g* looked as if it called for a hard pronunciation, so the *j* took over, along with "Jerry," not just for Jerome, but for many people named Gerald. The French still serve it up *en gelée.*

Like "crystallize," the word has its origin in chemistry; the coiner was the Scottish chemist Thomas Graham, who came up with the verb "gel," to change to a more gelatinous colloid, and its opposite, "solate," to change from a gel to a sol. (When public opinion dissolves, and people are wondering what to think, their opinions may be said to "sol"; that is the first time that verb has been used, and probably the last.)

To my mind, "crystallize" implies a fast hardening; "set" connotes the slow merger of ingredients, as in dough; "gel" fits nicely in between, denoting the coming together at a given moment, with the result still quivering and likely to revert to a liquid if the atmosphere changes.

The word has already been misused. Chastising Director of Central Intelligence Stansfield Turner at a Senate hearing, Senator Richard Lugar of Indiana said, "All of this just won't gel together." In the Senate report, the word was spelled "gell," which is a rare variant, and if you like the second *l*, you're better off going all the way to "jell." Also, "gel together" is redundant; "gel" means "come together into a solid form."

The new verb has been kicking around in my file for a few weeks. But when a senator misused it and misspelled it, suddenly the item seemed to—I don't know, one minute it was all over the place and the next minute it had a beginning and an end and just seemed to coagulate nicely.

Dear Mr. Safire:

I can't believe you devoted half of your column to a "new word" ("gel") that I and most of the people I know have been using all our lives, only spelling it "jell." We use it mostly to describe ideas, thoughts, images, etc., coming together, taking shape, e.g., "the plan began to jell." We also use it to describe what happens when gelatin congeals. The latter is the literal usage; the former, an analogous extension. The only times I've seen "gel"—spelled that way—is as a noun. It describes jellylike substances and is often used in the names of cosmetics, e.g., face gel, hand gel. It also describes a medium like agar used to grow things in Petri dishes. It also describes a colored filter for theatrical lights.

Sincerely,
Barbara Novack
Laurelton, New York

Dear Mr. Safire:

You espouse "the use of 'gel' as a transitive verb," but imply that one is not *"better off going all the way to 'jell.'" Well, why not? The question sent me all the way to the* Random House *unabridged for reassurance that "jell" is a perfectly fine intransitive verb ("The plan didn't begin to jell until a consultant was called in").*

Why shouldn't "jell" get the nod for double duty as a transitive verb as well? Since the two forms are pronounced the same, the issue resolves itself to a question of Simplified Spelling. Could it be that Mary McGrory's proofreader just goofed? Senator Lugar spoke, not wrote, his verb; could it be that the Senate report's "gell" was a typo for "jell," not "gel"?

The Random House, *of course, also reports the use of "gel" as an intransitive verb. Nonetheless, in the race for honors and recognition as the transitive form, I'm rooting for "jell." The* j *affords quicker recognition of the sound of the initial consonant, and the vast majority of English monosyllables that rhyme with it are spelled with a double* l.

What the hell. Give a yell and ring the bell—for "jell."

Sincerely yours,
Charles E. Selinske
Port Chester, New York

Dear Mr. Safire:

The verb "jell" is in my 1971 Webster's Collegiate *and in my 1961* Webster's New World, *but not in my 1936* Webster's, *which contains "jellify" to convey the same meaning. I suspect some writers use the spelling "gel" because they don't know how to spell "jell" and can't find it in the dictionary—much the same as they can't find "faze," but they write that it doesn't phase them.*

Very truly yours,
John Fries
Cleveland Heights, Ohio

Dear Bill,

*Perhaps others have already written to you about "gel." But in case they haven't, I draw your attention to "jell," which is far from a recent invention. It may have been coined by Louisa May Alcott (*Little Women, *1869). Mathews's* Dictionary of Americanisms *gives in addition two further uses, dated 1890 and 1949, one of which states that dictionaries don't include "jell." But the big* Webster *No. 2 (1934) has it in its lower depths as "American colloq." and nowadays the* New World Webster *and the* American Heritage *both list it as an accepted back formation.*

Best regards to you and Peggy Miller.

Yours,
Jacques B.
[Jacques Barzun]
Charles Scribner's Sons
New York, New York

---

gentlepersons, *see* dear madams

---

get on my case

When the pandas in the National Zoo once again refused to mate, a *Washington Star* editorialist suggested that the animals might be making a rational decision—that they had been "repulsed at the idea of accepting the responsibility for raising a panda which, when told in some future year to take out the garbage or mow the cage, will scathingly inform its parents that they are corrupt representatives of a decadent civilization and to get off his case!"

The teenage locution "Get off my case" is on the rise; it is apparently a variation of "Get off my back," which originated among welfare recipients who directed the remark to social caseworkers.

In a related terminological development, students who wish teachers would get off their cases have taken to calling more studious students a variety of new terms. "Grind," which replaced "bookworm," has been replaced by "squid" at Wesleyan, "throat" at Tufts and Johns Hopkins, "wienie" at Yale, and "tool" (or "power tool" if especially bookish) at Bowdoin. For this information, old grinds are indebted to Helen E. Kelly of New Haven, an avowed nonwienie.

Dear Mr. Safire:

Re " 'Get off my case' . . . is apparently a variation of 'Get off my back, [sic]*' which originated among welfare recipients. . . ."*

If the volume of your correspondence has run high about the erroneous comma, I suppose you're wishing the readers would get off your case. Who ran afoul of the restrictive/nonrestrictive rule—you or the typesetter?

The sentence provides a perfect example of the rule, for teaching purposes: With the comma present, the sentence means exactly the opposite of what you presumably intended. It now says that "Get off my back*" originated with welfare recipients; I believe you meant that "Get off my* case*" originated there.*

True, without the comma the reader has to pause a moment to fathom out the meaning. Better than the same sentence without the comma would be a recasting; e.g., after the semicolon, "it apparently originated among welfare recipients, who directed the remark to social workers (perceived to be hostile), and is a variation of 'Get off my back.' "

Up the language.
Paul L. Klein
Cold Spring, New York

---

getting down

One of the joys of American English is black slang. Inventive, humorous, evanescent, its coinages are here today and abandoned tomorrow—unless the meanings are taken into general usage. Most Americans now say "to make it" when they mean "to succeed," and know that "kicks" means "pleasure"; those locutions, from black slang, are now in the general slang vocabulary. A few black slang words—"jazz," for example—have been doing their gig long enough to become part of standard English.

"If any *racking splibs* want to help me *get down,*" I wrote recently in this space, "my *tude* is neither *bent* nor *Flash Gordon.*"

"Racking" means "studying," presumably from the suffering of a student stretched on the rack. A "splib," according to Clarence Major, author of the *Dictionary of Afro-American Slang,* is "a black person"; however, Rosetta James of New York adds that "terms of endearment when we use them among ourselves become the height of insult when used by others."

Getting down is a *serious* coinage. "*Serious* is not to imply that something is grave or worrisome," wrote Jacquelyn Powell in a piece entitled "Basic Black" in *The Washington Post*; "rather, that it warrants highest merit. Like your mother's cooking may be *baad*—i.e., very good—but your grandmother's cooking is *serious.*"

But to get down to *getting down.* The expression may be bottomed on "get down to brass tacks," meaning "reduce to essentials," but it has gained a black-slang meaning of "achieving a sense of brotherhood." My *New York Times* colleague Karen DeWitt suggests: "*To get down* means 'to no longer be distracted by status.'" This idealistic phrase should not be confused with *to get off,* "to achieve satisfaction," or *to get back,* "to reconsider."

"My tude is neither bent nor Flash Gordon." *Tude* is short for "attitude," and means exactly that—mindset or outlook. *Bent,* as used here, means "old" or, by extension, "old-fashioned"; the word also can mean "drunk," "stolen," or "homosexual" ("not straight"). And *Flash Gordon,* from the comic-strip character by way of "flashing money around," means "grandiose," from which flows the slang verb *to grand.*

My snappy advertisement did not meet universal acclaim. "I do not think you know anything about black slang," writes Pam Smith, a member of Lois Weiner's class at Malverne High School on Long Island, New York, "because we do not use or understand the words up here that you wrote there. Some words that are used in black slang here are: *chill out* (stop acting foolish), *looking chilly* (looks nice), and *crib*—means 'home.'" Her classmate Lateshia Holland added *that's deaf,* which she defined as "nice clothes," and Bruce Welburns contributed the verb *to zeke,* meaning "to make a mistake."

Other slang authorities confirm that the noun *crib* has replaced "pad" as the current slang synonym for "domicile"; that the verb "cool" has graduated to *chill,* and that *deaf*—a mispronunciation of "death"—is the current superlative. (In topsyturvytalk, *death* is the liveliest and *baad-baaader-baaadest* is the equivalent of "good-better-best.")

A person dressed spiffily is said to be *clean* and, in some areas, *pressed.* He will take out his *hamma,* or *sleek lady,* sometimes used derogatorily as the opposite of *foxy lady,* who may become his *main squeeze.* You are *tight* with your best friend, with whom you may use rhyming lingo: "Take it slow, Bro," while rolling in your *ride* or *mean machine.* The verb *hang* may mean "compare"—as in "How do that hang?"—or may mean "stay home," perhaps from a clipped version of "hang around," as in "I'll just hang this evening." A *world* is a life, as in "It's your world, I'm just a spear carrier." When your world is unbeatable and you're feeling *joint-joint,* a television term expresses the feeling best: *all the way live.*

Old-fashioned slang used mainly by blacks has held its place over the years: *Onliest* is useful when "only" needs emphasis, and there is no worry as worrisome over a long period as a *worriation.* Finality is expressed with *That's Law.*

Some black slang is alliterative; you head for a party to *get some grins* and express your satisfaction with *sure shocks.* Some is descriptive: *Face* is used as a salutation when you remember the face but not the name—"Hey, Face, what's goin' down?"—and may have led to the change of "whatsisname" to "whatsisface." Some slang improves an adjective: A "murderous look" has become a *murder-one look,* which you get from someone contemplating murder in the first degree. And some varies with inflection: *I hear ya* can mean "I understand," or "I agree," or "Now go away," depending on the tone of voice.

Black slang, as I use the term, is distinct from "black English," a dialect that J. L. Dillard holds is rooted in various Creole and West African languages. Other linguists argue that such dialect usages as the perfective *done*—as in "I done told her"—grew out of Middle English. This controversy has led to claims that dialect forms like "I be sure," rather than "I am sure," are "not incorrect" and should therefore be accepted in schools.

That's a mistake. A dialect is useful for communication within a group, but in dealing with the outside world, a knowledge of the larger community's language is needed. Contrary to an alarmed impression held by many educators, Federal Judge Charles B. Joiner did not tell Detroit teachers that black English is acceptable; rather, he held that teachers should learn the rudiments of black dialect so as to better teach standard English to black students. That makes good sense to me; it would be just as foolish to treat any dialect as if it were gibberish as it would be to insist that any dialect should be treated as standard English.

Are there any words that are "basic black"—coined by, and used mainly, by blacks only over a long period of time? Thanks to the *Dictionary of American Regional English (DARE),* the most exciting linguistic project going on in the United States, we may soon find out. Associate editor Jeffrey Hirshberg reports that some fifty words and phrases have been found that qualify as long-lived black vocabulary and are well beyond the street-hustle vocabulary most commonly quoted. Among them:

Airish, inclined to put on airs.
Behind a dime, absolutely anywhere, as in "I wouldn't trust him behind a dime."
Cheese-eater, one who tries to ingratiate himself; a toady. (Does this come from "rat"? Or from one who says "cheese" to appear to smile?)
Excuse, or **skusin,** to mean "except for," or "not counting." An 1887 citation: "The greatest gent'man in the county skusin him ..."
Fat-mouth, to talk too much. Perhaps an intralingual calque of "poor-mouth" or "bad-mouth."
Foreday, the earliest morning hours.
Jackleg, amateur, as in "jackleg preacher."
Later, to mean "good-bye." A 1954 citation in *Time* magazine reports this "catchall word for 'I'll be seeing you.' " Today "lay-tuh," from "see you later," is the vogue farewell on most college campuses.
Natural, an Afro haircut: "There's a lean young cat wearin' a natural," reported *Ebony* in 1969.
Nose open, to be obviously in love.
Ticky, exacting. Probably from "particular."

One black expression that puzzles the researchers at *DARE* is *dead cat on a line,* which means "something suspicious." If anybody can figure out where that is comin' from, alert the troops at *DARE*, University of Wisconsin, Madison, Wisconsin 53706.

This column will surely offend some people who think any discussion of slang derogates its users or who feel de meaning is demeaning. Take it slow, Bro. Dialects flow in and out of the mainstream of English, enriching the mixture all the time. That's Law. Or as more current black slang puts it: That's Word.

Dear Mr. Safire:

Your words today on black slang were serious. Your onliest 'stake was 'bout "the def," which my household bros assure me derives not from "a mispronunciation of death" but is rather an abbreviation of "the definite," as in the def*inite best.*

As a suburban liberal mother I have discovered that one of the long-term benefits of busing has been that my teenagers have acquired a whole new esoteric language with which to baffle me and never have to resort to pig Latin or Obby Dobby talk, for which I would have been somewhat prepared. They carry on elaborate conversations, seemingly in English, and I barely understand anything they say. My only defense is to hit them with the Yiddish with which my parents used to baffle me. The children, of course, think that I, with a language of my own, am the def!

Louise Wollman
White Plains, New York

Dear Mr. Safire,

Over the years, my response to your political views has generally been summed up in the current phrase "That's dead," and my assumption has been the same about you personally: "He be dead."

"Getting Down" changed that. If you have succeeded in overcoming some of the ignorance about black nonstandard English among teachers by what you wrote, thank you.

Some things that are current, but which you missed, include the usage of "dead" above, which will probably begin popping into hip white talk soon. Others include "set" (a party, usually where you pay to get in), "clean" (which you note, but don't do justice to—a male in a three-piece suit, soft shoes, and a white fur overcoat merits the compliment "He be clean" in a way that draws out the adjective to denote admiration), and "my fault," currently a standard answer to any correction. "Dead," by the way, is the superlative of "boring."

The study of American English will probably become more exciting in the coming generation because racial prejudices about black nonstandard English are being overcome. Mencken has been discredited (at least on this score) and western and southern Africa is moving from self-rule to self-consciousness. As it becomes possible for those of us interested in the language to study the African languages more, the importance of intonation and certain structural differences will become more clear.

At the same time, however, we shouldn't overlook the contribution made by the Irish, English, and Scottish lower classes who came to America and lived and worked among the slaves. Unfortunately there are very few written records of how these classes of English-speaking people actually spoke *200 to 400 years ago. However, a few examples should do:*

1. The pronunciation of the verb "to ask" in Mississippi and in black Chicago is "axe." If you refer to your Oxford English Dictionary *(Vol. I, p. 489) you will note the following: "1803: Pegge* Anec. Eng. Lang. *114, 'A true born Londoner, Sir, of either sex, always axes questions, axes pardon, and at quadrille axes leave.' . . ."*

2. One of the most reliable writers for reproducing lower-class English dialect is Dickens. All of the later works are filled with it. Magwitch, for example, in Great Expectations *(Chapter 39), says, "Here's the boy again, a looking at me whiles I eats and drinks. . . ." It is also reported that Magwitch was married by jumping "over the broomstick" (a custom that went unnoticed until* Roots *brought it back into people's minds). When he returns to Pip, Magwitch asks Pip to show him to his "crib." It would do well for someone to pursue Dickens further in this regard, since the roots of black English are not simply Creole and*

West African, but lower-class English as well. As it now stands, I find Dickens useful in teaching students in the ghetto because he does such a good job with dialect and because there is no discrimination in the characters in this regard (i.e., a good man can speak badly, e.g., Joe, while a bad man can be a gentleman, e.g., Compeyson). An added value is that Dickens is recognized, almost an icon, among English teachers, so that there is less tendency to put down our students when Dickens can be cited as authority for their speech. (I agree with you that we have to teach standard English for both reading, writing, and formal speaking, but we shouldn't in the process negate the richness of the dialect or the value of the people who speak using it.)

I also encourage you to pursue these questions. Perhaps he not be dead after all.

Yours truly,
George N. Schmidt
Chicago, Illinois

Dear Mr. Safire:

You say "over a long period of time." Isn't that redundant? Wouldn't it be better to say "over a long time" or "over a long period"?

Nell Lewis
Chicago, Illinois

Dear Bill:

As the white boys ask, "How are you?" as the white boys with soul and the brothers ask, "What's sup?" or, equally as effective, "What's the deal?" Did you get down with that fine-looking "babe" the other night? Not to "brass tacks," but to a brass bed. "I hear you," so you did "get over" (to get over, to have done well). She's got a pretty "saaarious joint" (I prefer this over "crib" or "pad.") You sure "faced" her "old man." The roots of "to face" or "being faced" are within the interstices of the asphalt of urban basketball courts, as a substantial amount of black slang is. To use the term "face" in its original setting: First you "burn" someone with a nice move; then swish; then you say "face job." Why? Because you shot the "rock" in their eyes. If you hog the rock, "you best be" giving it up—the basketball, that is.

Back to the fine, foxy lady, her "old man" is a big "dude." You "dig my rap"? Now if you didn't, you might say, "Put a chill on your rap." Well defined in the article. However, "take it slow" is antiquated or better yet uncool. To sound smooth, you best be saying "take it light." Now if her old man start giving you a lot of "sheeeit" and the "sitcheeeation" (these pronunciations are extremely important) be such that you might get beat, since we be tight and you be my "blood" (not in the relative sense, but in the friendship sense, i.e., "You are my 'ace' "), "I got your back," (i.e., "I'll be there with the second"; in other words "I'll help you fight"). The help would be forthcoming in light of the fact that you did me a "solid" (a favor) the other week by lending me your baaaaaad "box," a box being one of those big portable radio/cassette players the bros carry around.

By the way, I'm glad you didn't go out with that other lady; she was "nasty"-looking. "Nasty" is sometimes fungible with "funky," when "funky" is used in the negative sense as opposed to the musical sense. The best way I can think of learning contemporary black slang is by hanging out at the basketball courts or going to a predominantly black urban public high school, both of which I have done.

"Later" (as written here this term means "good-bye"; however, there are variations, e.g., "much later" or "later for your face," both of which have obvious negative connotations). How about "say whaat?" in place of "what did you say?"? Supra, *please replace "lady" with "brickhouse," one of the best I have to offer. The Commodores, a soul group, created the term "brickhouse" and composed a song of the same name. Darryl Dawkins of the Philadelphia 76ers says he is from Planet Lovetron where the brothers be bad and the "biddies" be brickhouses. The rock is also a disco dance of which Michael Jackson composed a big hit, "Rock with You." Ask Annabel, she probably knows these songs.*

Later,
Jeff
[Jeffrey Cylkowski]
New York, New York

P. S. Being called a "brickhouse" is a compliment; in other words, if you've got yourself a little brickhouse, you are in good shape and she probably has a good shape.

Dear Mr. Safire,

"Dead cat on a line" may refer to a trick used by dog thieves, at least in books and movies. Perhaps burglars, seeking to suborn watchdogs or children, hoping to cause a commotion, do it, too. "I borrowed a dead cat and tied a string to it, legged it to old Nickerson's garden after dark, dug a board out of the back of the shed, and shoved my head down and chirruped. The dogs came trickling out, and I hared off, towing old Colonel Cat on his string. . . . Hounds picked up the scent right away and started off in a bunch at fifty miles an hour. Cat and I doing a steady fifty-five. Thought every minute old Nickerson would hear and start blazing away with a gun, but nothing happened" ("Ukridge's Dog College," a short story by P. G. Wodehouse). The trick has been described by Mark Twain and many others, and probably does actually happen, though I have never seen it. It is clear how suspicious it would be to see such a cat, dead "yet in death alive," mysteriously animated by a twitching string, leading to an unseen plotter.

Sincerely yours,
Douglas Stahl
Princeton, New Jersey

Dear Mr. Safire,

I was surprised to learn that "jackleg," for amateur, is "black slang," as I remember its being used long before it became the "in thing" for academics to use such expressions as "Right on!" The definition, however, is correct. The definition in Webster's, *2d, which makes "jackleg" synonymous with "blackleg," which has connotations of corruption and criminality, does not conform to any usage I have ever heard. "Jack," I think, frequently has connotations of amateurism, particularly in relation to a "jack," a servant or subordinate, who picks up his knowledge, such as it is, by attending and watching a skilled practitioner. E.g., "Jackeroo," Australian slang for a "new chum" working as a "station hand" to learn something about stock raising.*

"Natural" means a good deal more than the so-called Afro haircut, which is both unnatural and un-African. It also means something that is complete of its kind, even superlative. A "natural man" is a "man in full." See Sterling Brown's poem, "Strange Legacies," with its tributes to Jack Johnson and John Henry: "So if we go down/Have to go down/We go like you, brother,/'Nachal' men. . . ." Or my own poem, "Ballad of Adam Payne," Seminole Negro bad man whose head was shipped to Washington: "President was lookin' / at de head on his desk, / wid de Sec'try of War / an' all de rest, / When it speaks up: 'White folks, / look while you can— / you's lookin' in de face / of a natural man!' "

Sincerely yours,
Kenneth Wiggins Porter
Professor Emeritus of History
University of Oregon
Eugene, Oregon

Dear Mr. Safire:

Your mention of "jackleg" recalled to me another bit of vocabulary learned in my oil field days in the early thirties.

I wonder if this is not "Jake Leg," which I was led to believe was the name applied to one who, by virtue of taking on too much Jamaica ginger, temporarily lost control of his leg muscles and gave all the appearances of being plastered. Perhaps he was.

Very truly yours,
W. E. Schroeder
Sharon, Connecticut

Dear Mr. Safire:

After reading your recent piece on black English, I wondered whether you have encountered the word "sadit."

I first heard the term while working as an English teacher at a predominantly black high school here in Durham. A "sadit" is a snob—specifically an upper-class black person not in touch with the average black language, style, and experience. As "saditty," the word is also an adjective, and was used to describe, for example, the teacher who played classical music rather than jazz as background for a creative writing assignment.

I have never seen the word in print. It is pronounced "sah-dit" and is accented on the second syllable. Black friends from the South know and use the word, but when I ask northern blacks about it, I get puzzled looks.

I never heard the word used to describe a white person, even though the school had its share of white snobs, too.

Sincerely,
David C. Stevens
Durham, North Carolina

Dear Mr. Safire:

I suffer gladly an occasional egregious misspelling, repetitious redundancy, or grammatical solecism. But your "Getting Down" piece . . .

"Racking." In the forties I attended a then all-white, all-male, obscure but fully accredited liberal arts college in Williamstown, Massachusetts. We were unaware of black argot, to say nothing of "black" qua "Negro." But we did "rack it," which in terms of severity of study was somewhere between "hitting the books" (in-room study) and "hitting the libe" and could mean either or both. "Racking" comes from "book rack," of course, except when we "hit the rack," a term, courtesy of the navy, meaning "hit the sack" or (again, then) "hit the pad." Neither use had anything to do with students' stretched suffering. Kind sir, are you perchance putting us on?

"Whatsisface" is similar to "whatsername." Both are old New England terms I learned at my WASP father's knee.

"Dead cat on a line" is meaningful to most everyone who has lived in Belize or on some off-the-path Antillean islands where voodoo is still practiced and believed. Incidentally, it works when it's laid on a believer. If you awaken to find a dead cat strung up by the neck, it's time to pack. Aleurophiles can take heart: Where cats are in short supply, a chicken will do.

Much "topsyturvytalk" is of dubious origin. "Onliest" and "sour up" ("sweeten up" or "be nice") were Appalachian contributions to the all-white World War II army combat arms.

Sincerely,
Thomas de Forest Bull
Boston, Massachusetts

Dear Mr. Safire:

I am not generally shockable, but I was a little surprised at The Times *when I read your column because in my school, among my black students, "getting down" is a synonym for sexual intercourse. I am an English teacher at a large Queens high school that has about 35 percent black students, and I questioned Eric Johnson and Everett Johnson in my sixth-period class today. When I showed them your column, Eric giggled (being sixteen years old), and Everett wanted to know what kind of dirty magazine I was reading.*

Upon further questioning I was told that "to get down with" is used almost as a euphemism: "I get down with my girlfriend because I love her," or "I was getting down with Sonya when my parents came home." When talking to another man, a young man might use more explicit language. Perhaps your explanation of "reducing to essentials" explains it since sex is so important and basic.

Another note concerning sex and my kids, white and black. The current general term for "making out," engaging in sexual activity, is "fooling around." "Do you and Joe fool around?" It is amusing that fooling around (kidding around, goofing around) as I remember it is referred to as "fucking around": "We didn't get any homework done because we were fucking around."

Sincerely yours,
Greta Singer
Rockville Centre, New York

Dear Mr. Safire:

You speculated on the derivation of "cheese-eater." It is more scabrous than you suggested—related to "cutting cheese" as an expression for farting and being roughly equivalent to "ass-licker."

Both expressions, "cutting cheese" and "cheese-eater," were in use in the army in the mid-1960's.

I can offer no written evidence of this derivation, but that certainly was the sense of the terms, and it tallies with its current use as well.

Sincerely,
Robert C. Hahn
Journalism Librarian
University of Missouri—Columbia
Columbia, Missouri

P.S. Partridge does refer to an old use of "cheeser" to connote "a strong smelling fart."

Dear Mr. Safire,

You listed the word "cheese-eater" as a representative of the "long-lived black vocabulary." I first heard the word in a 1971 viewing of a 1954 film, On the Waterfront, *in which Johnny Friendly (Lee J. Cobb) used it to describe Terry Malloy (Marlon Brando). The latter character has testified to the crime commission about Johnny Friendly's crooked union; he has ratted on his former pals and is, ergo, a cheese-eater.*

Alfred Lea
Doylestown, Pennsylvania

givebacks

An unfamiliar word churned up by the New York City transit strike is "givebacks," defined in *The New York Times* as "nonwage concessions, involving reductions in benefits and increases in productivity."

Up to now the lingo of negotiation has been dominated by "demands" by unions and "concessions" by management; now, however, the employers are beginning to make demands that unions give back some previously received concessions.

The union official Victor Gotbaum recalls that the term "givebacks" was used in the municipal employees' negotiations two years earlier. "In 1978, Mayor Koch said that in order to bring about a productivity change, there had to be a work-rule change. He prepared a list of sixty items, including everything from vacation time to surplus mothers-in-law. He referred to these as 'givebacks' in the interest of productivity. This became a very emotional issue."

Mayor Koch informs me he did not coin the term, but merely popularized it; obviously it was coined on management's side of the table. Says Al Zack of the AFL-CIO: " 'Givebacks' is a management term. We call them 'takeaways.' " This is in accordance with organized labor's traditional resistance to any term that puts it at a propaganda disadvantage; for example, "right to work" laws were called "union-busting laws" by union officials. A neutral term—in the no-man's-land between "givebacks" and "takeaways"—is "buybacks," which connotes purchasing rather than snatching.

" 'Givebacks' is a new word of the seventies," says Jonathan Grossman, librarian at the Bureau of Labor Statistics. "The concept is old—in the 1870's there was the issue of the 'green hands,' an attempt to reduce the number of masters and increase the number of green apprentices." Sure enough, one of the issues in the New York strike was management's desire to hire more part-time employees, which the old contract restricted it from doing; the idea was to get the union to "give back" that concession. The hands would not necessarily have been green, but management felt they would be more productive.

Labor skates—old-timers—are shaking their heads. They find the idea of givebacks as puzzling as some lexicographers find "labor skate" obscure.

SHAME ON YOU SAFIRE:

Your claim that organized labor objects to the term "right to work" laws because it "puts it at a propaganda disadvantage" is certainly true, but you overlook the fact that it is an obvious misnomer Laws which prohibit or interfere with employees' right to organize for purposes of collective bargaining have nothing to do with "right to work," whatever that means.

Sloppy thinking is incongruous in a column devoted to clear and proper use of language.

Peter Thor
East Norwalk, Connecticut

---

glitch

Herbert Berman, treasurer of the World Jewish Congress, came out of a White House meeting with President Carter to tell reporters of his puzzlement not only with policy but with a word.

"We were told there was a glitch," he said of the President's explanation for the mistaken vote by the United States in the United Nations condemning Israeli settlements. "I haven't been able to find a definition of what a glitch is."

A glitch is a mechanical or electronic failure which—when it afflicts political campaigns—can cause great mischief. Mr. Carter remembers the word well; when he first traveled abroad as President in December 1977, he whispered a suggestion to Secretary of State Cyrus Vance that he send "a cold, very blunt" letter to the Indian prime minister upon their return. The conversation was picked up by an open microphone nearby and caused a small diplomatic flap.

The malfunctioning—or, in that case, the functioning at the wrong time—of the machinery was defined in the *Washington Star* as a "glitch." An editor, unfamiliar with the relatively new slang term, changed the word in the second edition to "snafu," a well-known acronym from World War II armed-forces jargon, "situation normal, all fouled up" (euphemistic version). In most uses, a glitch is not as serious as a snafu. Recently "foul-up" has overtaken "snafu" and carries the same weight of confusion as its root. ("Tuifu"—"the ultimate in foul-ups"—may be the origin of the noun.)

The man from the World Jewish Congress should not have been so puzzled at President Carter's use of the term. "Glitch" probably originated in the German and Yiddish *glitschen,* meaning "slip" and, by extention, "error." According to the *Polyglot's Lexicon,* the term entered the language on gremlinlike feet in 1966, denoting a false signal or minor mishap in spacecraft.

Dear Mr. Safire:

As to your military acronyms, you missed two. FUBAR, for "fouled up beyond all recognition," and the character familiarly named SOL TATAO, to whom one was sent if the chaplain wasn't available. Using another euphemism for the first word, this translated into "Surely outta luck, things are tough all over."

With regard to a fellow Syracusan,
Ted Lustig
Carlstadt, New Jersey

Dear Mr. Safire:

The first time I heard the word "glitch" was in 1941 in Worcester. I got a job there as an announcer at WTAG. When an announcer made a mistake, such as putting on the wrong record or reading the wrong commercial, anything technical, or anything concerning the sales department, that was called a "glitch" and had to be entered on the Glitch Sheet, which was a mimeographed form. The older announcers told me the term had been used as long as they could remember.

"Snafu" I first heard in the army in 1942. It was used at first smirkingly, with nods which meant, "Do you know what this means? Situation normal—all fucked up." We were demurer then and didn't say it around girls. Then a B'way play named Operation Snafu *came along and made it general. Not that it was ever caviar.*

Best wishes,
Tony Randall
New York, New York

Dear Mr. Safire:

Now that I've learned what a "glitch" is, I think I'll start a collection of the verbal variety—such as "extention," which appeared in your column on the subject.

Cordially,
Rosemarie Williamson
Basking Ridge, New Jersey

Godspeed, *see* farewell

---

going to the well

Well, here goes.

I interviewed Ronald Reagan and came away with the impression that he begins every answer with the word "well." The interjection of a meaningless word or phrase to help a respondent fill the sound vacuum as he arranges his thoughts is hardly new: In 1968 one presidential candidate began many answers with "golly" while the other preferred "Let me say this about that." President Carter eschews all this verbalized throat clearing, preferring a straightforward, if immodest, "I and my advisers." (Unlike his opponent-to-be, Mr. Carter doesn't dig "wells.")

"Well"—originally "it is well"—is the only exclamation or interjection capable of expressing a range of emotions from satisfaction to puzzlement to indignation to resignation. To confirm the suspicion that a Reagan presidency would be studded with "wells," I have analyzed a *Wall Street Journal* interview with the candidate and can report that Governor Reagan uses the interjection with all its nuances:

- The well that says, "Now hold on a minute." To the *WSJ* question about a large tax cut, Mr. Reagan replied: "Well, I would want a lot more study of that."
- The well that pleads, "Give me a second to get my thoughts in order." If you couldn't get a spending cut, would you still want to cut taxes? Reagan: "Well, to begin with..."
- The dry, "I understand your question" well. *WSJ*: "Would you give direct aid to the Somalis?" Reagan: "Well, now here again, you're running the risk..."
- The "Gee, now, you've got me all wrong" well. Asked about a blockade of Cuba to retaliate for Soviet moves in Afghanistan, he replied: "Well, I've suggested that hypothetically..."
- The exclamatory well that asserts, "Now hear this." To a question about how we can help our allies who are dependent on Middle East oil, Reagan welled up with a strong "Well, maybe we could be of more help to them than we are right now."
- The abandoned well that says, "I'm sorry I ever showed up for this interview." Asked if he had ruled out a running mate who did not support his tax-cut position, he said, "Well, let me say ... I regretted saying it."

In all the above, the transcriber punctuated the deliciously varied "wells" with a comma, which was a disservice to the reader. Different "wells" have different spells:

- "Well!" The exclamation point gives a harrumphing quality to the ejaculation. (That's right, "ejaculation"—it's not a dirty word. Never feel guilty about expostulating either.)
- "Well?" The question mark turns the word into "So? What's next? I'm standing here patiently waiting for a complete explanation."
- "Wellwellwell." The run-on says, "Imagine that. Who'd a thunk it?"
- "We-e-ell . . ." This stretched version says, "Now you're getting into sensitive areas, and it's inappropriate for a member of the Appropriations Committee to confer approbation . . ."
- "Wa-all." Western version: "Shucks, partner, I'm too modest for that. . . ."
- "Well." The period turns the word into a door-slamming sentence: "We're finished. That's it. Mail me the cat."
- "Well . . ." With the dotty ellipsis trailing despondently behind, the word conjures up the vision of a statesman walking around the circular park behind the White House, contemplating the loneliest job in the world. This is the "well" of loneliness.

Dear Mr. Safire:

Wellwellwell. Imagine that! Who'd a thunk that Mr. Language himself would trail with dotty ellipsis (as opposed to ellipsis of the undotty variety)?

Since I am a member of the famed Redundancy Squad (Squad Squad), I find it my duty to question your judgment.

According to Webster's New World Dictionary, *Second College Edition, the second entry for ellipsis is as follows:*

> *Writing and printing a mark (. . . or formerly ***) indicating an intentional omission of words or letters or an abrupt change of thought, lapse of time, incomplete statement, etc.*

So isn't "dotty ellipsis" redundant? Well, you're the expert.

Yours truly,
Lisa D. Corbin
New York University
Society of Professional Journalists
New York, New York

Dear Bill,

Going back to the "wellwellwell," a word that takes on almost magical powers through repetition is "there." This commonplace word, when repeated nine or ten times in a row, has the power of stopping the sobs of a distraught woman or child. The word must be uttered, however, while hugging the afflicted person and patting him or her on the back. If "theretheretheretherethere-theretheretherethere" doesn't stop the tears after the fourteenth or fifteenth "there," the comforter should switch to "now." A few "nownownownownows," with continued backpatting, usually does the trick. Maybe you or one of your millions of readers can tell me how "there" and "now," when repeated, take on these curative powers.

Sincerely,
Sid
[Sidney Goldberg]
New York, New York

---

gomer, *see* mediquack

---

good night, sweet roll

I had my mouth fixed for a prune Danish—nothing else would do—when a letter came from William Boring, of the English department of the Garden City, New York, High School, asking: "How about variations on pastries? In Texas, everything is a roll."

Pastriotism is the first refuge of a newly awakened scoundrel. However, when the pastriot wakes up in a strange city and calls for his Coffee Regular (there's a good name for a movie star), he may find it difficult naming what he wants.

What's the difference between a Danish and a sweet roll? A doughball and a huffle-duffle? A jelly doughnut and a jelly roll, a turnover and a pocketbook, a Bismarck and a bear claw?

These and other dialectical variations were put to the man from *DARE:* Dr. Frederic Cassidy, editor of the *Dictionary of American Regional English,* the great linguistic project cooking at the University of Wisconsin. It turns out that one of *DARE*'s national interviewing questions has been "What names are used around here for fancy rolls and pastries?"

We are not talking here about breads—hard rolls and soft rolls. Sweet (or "fancy") rolls are yeast cakes with fruits or nuts baked in, often with a sugary glop on top. Northerners call that topping "frosting"; southerners call it "icing." (A more substantive difference is that frosting is soft and icing is hard.)

On the West Coast, "bear claws" are a favorite—fan-shaped cakes, with the fruit filling oozing up between what looks like fingers of dough. In the Northwest, the oblong maple bar is the sweet roll in demand. From the Rockies to Michigan, a term used mainly by older people is "pocketbook," for a folded-over cake. A "fantan," a yeast roll that opens like a fan when baked, is also middlewestern. In Pennsylvania and western Maryland, a "fasnacht" is popular—the Pennsylvania German "fast night" is the origin—along with a "fat cake," from the Pennsylvania German "fett-kuche." Another term for a similar product is "Bismarck," probably named after the Chicago hotel in which it may have originated.

"Jelly rolls" are deceptive. They are not always flat cakes, smeared on top with jelly, then rolled up and sliced. In the South, the phrase is often a code word for copulation: the "Jelly Roll Blues" is a far cry from a passion for prune Danish. More often, a jelly roll is a "jelly doughnut," fried dough with jelly inside, familiar on both coasts but less in the nation's interior.

Now we're into "fried cakes," the yeast-leavened, fried dough that you have during a coffee break in the north-central states. The original doughnut gained its name because the dough was shaped into a nutlike ball; later a culinary genius conceived the toroidal shape, which enabled the cake to float in the frying fat so that it could be flipped over easily and not stay all soggy inside.

"Fried bread" is a bread dough fried in deep fat and is called "Baptist cake," "dough ball," "huffle-duffle," "morning glory," and "spider bread." Confusingly, "fried bread" is the term used by South Carolinians for pancakes and by Marylanders for French toast.

In New York and New England, the fried word is "cruller," from the Dutch *krul*, or "twist"—root of "curl." "Glazed doughnuts" (also spelled "donuts") are popular there; when the doughnut is long and straight, it takes on the name of underwear: "long johns."

When uncertain about ordering a Danish or a sweet roll, ask for a bun. Hot cross buns are an Eastertime favorite, and "honey buns" are thicker and taller than most breakfast pastry (in Philadelphia, say "sticky buns"). Be careful about asking for a tart, as a prostitute may appear at your door: a "jam tart" was a sweet pastry in England, and the term was soon applied to a feminine sweetie.

What does the nomenclature of pastriotism teach us? First, that the diversity of our taste resists all regimentation in rolls, and second, that even when we eat the same thing, we insist on our local terminology. Homogenization is for milk, not for dialect.

Final swallow: When in Copenhagen, use the word the Danes use for Danish pastry: *Wienerbrot.* That means "Viennese bread." When in Vienna, say, "Send up a prune Danish."

William Safire—

As a charter (and dues-paying) member of the new elitist intelligentsia, I hereby take offense at your purloining phraseology "Good Night, Sweet Roll" (pure Hollywoodese) and the cavalier manner in which you exclude that all-American cruller, the infamous *and much beloved "Mae West." How could America's beloved Mae West be forgotten?*

Not by those West Side veterans still young enough to recall those dear old days (when men were men, and imitations were nonexistent), [when] "coffee and a 'Mae West'" was an endearing cry to us of the waterfront fraternity.

Mr. Safire: How could you?

Yours,
Lawrence Miller
Brooklyn, New York

Dear Mr. Safire:

You left out the two I expected most to see, common here, yes, here, in New York: "bow ties" and the notorious "Mae West."

Sincerely yours,
Daniel Jennings
New York, New York

Dear Mr. Safire:

As faithful perusers of your column and transplanted midwesterners, we feel obligated to point out that in some areas of the Midwest (notably Wisconsin and Minnesota) "Bismarcks" are "jelly doughnuts."

Having grown to adulthood in part as a result of consuming quantities of Bismarcks, a.k.a. jelly doughnuts, we shudder to think that readers all over the country are consuming their "fancy rolls and pastries" under the misconception that jelly doughnuts are unfamiliar to natives of the interior.

Yours truly,
C. A. Kern-Simirenko
M. L. Stark
Syracuse, New York

Dear Mr. Safire,

In "Good Night, Sweet Roll" you gave the correct definition for the English slang term "tart" for a "sweetie," but you didn't say that "tart" was derived from "sweetheart." In the north of England haiches *are almost always dropped, so "sweetheart" is pronounced "sweet'art." It is only in the south of England that "tart" indicates a whore. North of Birmingham it can mean any female who might be available.*

Other terms used in England are "pusher" and "party" (in the southeast). The Cockney term for a prostitute is a "brass."

Sincerely,
Tristan Jones
New York, New York

You missed the "snail," which I remember from Seattle as being very like a sweet roll in Chicago ◎ and frosted with glop. Very good, too.

Norman Israel
Birmingham, Alabama

Dear Mr. Safire,

Although there is a wide variety of regional usage in Britain, as in the States, we would never say just "a Danish"—which would elicit the question "a Danish what?" In England one must always say "a Danish pastry." What you call "jelly roll" is in England, for some reason, "Swiss roll"—another of the many examples of the way foodstuffs are called after foreign countries which would not in fact recognize them. ("Russian cake," in England; "English muffin" here). And in England, "fried bread" is usually fried in bacon fat or something like that and is served with eggs or sausages or bacon at breakfast, especially in institutions like boarding schools. I imagine that all the "fried breads" you listed are sweet.

Finally, you say that a jam tart was a sweet pastry in England. It still is and is very common in cheaper bakeries, being usually nowadays a factory product. All this reminds me of a well-known English ballet critic, some years ago, seeing a Danish ballerina as Carmen and remarking that she was more like a Danish pastry than a French tart.

Yours sincerely,
Oleg Kerensky
New York, New York

Dear Mr. Safire:

As someone who was born in "LAN-cuh-ster," Pennsylvania, and ate fastnachts every Shrove Tuesday for many years, I must disagree with both the pronunciation you attribute to us natives (notice the* uh *which you omitted) and the category in which you place the "little pillows" (that's what fastnachts look like). I no longer have the pastry column, but I believe you put fastnachts and bear claws in the same paragraph. No. No. Fastnachts are made with a yeast dough and they are deep-fat-fried like doughnuts. They are eaten plain or sprinkled with powdered sugar, and they are very much a one-day specialty in the same way that hot cross buns should be eaten only on Good Friday.*

Incidentally, outsiders refer to my hometown as "Lan-CAS-ter" and call the "Ah-mish" "Ā-mish."

Sincerely yours,
Josephine Feagley
New York, New York

***Note from W. S.: For more on pronunciation, see "shibboleths."**

gorked, *see* mediquack

gridlocks

Rarely does a member of journalism's Thumbsucking Corps get a call for help from a deadline-driven ace reporter. Therefore, when Peter Kihss of *The New York Times* got on the line with a linguistic query, I was eager to help.

"Gridlock," he said, putting the story in the lead. "Where's it from?"

"You mean *gravlax,*" I said instantly, "one of the 'power lunches' served at the Four Seasons. It's a Swedish word for a dry-cured salmon, marinated in salt, sugar, and spices, but without a wet marinade containing oil or vinegar or juices. The 'lax' is akin to 'lox,' as in 'belly lox.' "

"Gridlock," said Kihss, whose power lunch at his desk that day consisted of a tuna on rye and a side of slaw. "It's a word they're using to describe a possible massive traffic jam in the transit strike. See what you can find."

From my post at the Washington bureau, I proceeded to roust bureaucrats out of linguistic lethargy. At the Department of Transportation, traffic specialists and highway engineers checked technical dictionaries; no luck.

Stan Byington, chief of the systems and evaluation group—which combines the vogue words "systems," "evaluation," and "group" to form the most forgettable moniker in the Federal Highway Administration—came to a screeching halt to offer this explanation.

"A grid, in highway engineering, is any layout of streets—usually applied to the cross pattern in cities." That checked out: The 1922 edition of the *Encyclopaedia Britannica* wrote of trench warfare being plotted "from a 'grid' or network of lines printed on a map," the image rooted in electrical circuitry.

"A lock," continued Mr. Byington, "refers to an intersection blockage which causes backup—disrupting the flow of traffic in all directions. A locked pattern in an east-west corridor will result in a backup that will eventually block the north-south corridors. It's like a radiation effect." This is called a "spillback," leading to a chain reaction that ultimately freezes all movement.

"Gridlock" is to highway engineers what "meltdown" is to nuclear engineers—a panic inside a nightmare inside a worst case. Instead of going with the traffic flow, everything stops and every frenzied driver leans on his horn. My brother Len Safir once wrote a piece for *The Times* suggesting steps to be taken toward the ultimate traffic jam: making the Long Island end of the Triborough Bridge a dead end, for example, or making all north-south avenues on Manhattan Island one way—downtown.

Washington credits the word to New York, but who coined it and when? According to Samuel I. Schwartz, assistant commissioner of the city's Department of Transportation, he first heard the term used around the office in 1971, when an ambitious "Red Zone" banning all autos was being planned: "We were worried that it might overload the connecting streets and the grid would lock, so we talked about a 'gridlock.' Then, in 1980, we put it in the transit-strike contingency plan, and all of a sudden it was all over the papers."

Such a word cannot miss. When a baby was born in a taxi that was trapped in traffic, Police Commissioner Robert J. McGuire could not help saying, "We're checking out a rumor that the baby was born out of gridlock."

Gridlock is a fine neologism for the automobile's Armageddon, and I am pleased to pass this on to the news department only three weeks or so past the deadline.

Dear Sir:

Your discussion of the word "gridlock" as a twentieth-century neologism was quite interesting. However, I can cite a much earlier use of the word "lock" as specifically applied to an unmanageable horse-and-carriage traffic jam. In Chapter VII of his Autobiographic Sketches *(first published in* Tait's Edinburgh Magazine, *1834–40), Thomas De Quincey describes his experience of entering London in an "open carriage" in May 1800:*

> *All that I remember is one monotonous awe and blind sense of mysterious grandeur and Babylonian confusion, which seemed to pursue and to invest the whole equipage of human life, as we moved for nearly two hours through streets; sometimes brought to anchor for ten minutes or more by what is technically called a "lock," that is, a line of carriages of every description inextricably massed, and obstructing each other, far as the eye could stretch. . . .*

De Quincey goes on to say that, at least, the lock would from time to time "thaw," and traffic would flow again. Maybe the modern term "gridlock" communicates a much more ominous sense of utter immobility and powerlessness.

Sincerely,
John H. Johnston
Professor of English
West Virginia University
Morgantown, West Virginia

Dear Bill:

More on "gridlock."

It was first used as a literary theme by O. Henry, who employed what he termed a "street blockade" as deus ex machina in his story "Mammon and the Archer." His description of traffic coming to a complete halt in midtown Manhattan is all the more poignant because most of the vehicles were horse-drawn.

Sincerely,
N. Brust
[Norman Brust]
New York, New York

gross distortions

As an apoplectic service during the height of the political season, we present herewith an interview with Christopher Q. Gross, president of Gross Distortions Inc., on the art of the red-faced response.

"We're having a run on 'reckless disregard for the truth,'" said the expert on ripostes challenging veracity. "It seems to have overtaken 'a deliberate prevarication on the part of my opponent,' which television advisers have told their clients is stuffy."

I was sorry to see "prevaricate" go—the term is rooted in the Latin for "to walk crookedly," and has come to mean "to stray from the path of truth"—but it comes across as hifalutin (itself an altered form of "high-floating," with a vowel intruded to make fun of pomposity). Is this because the *r* in "reckless" lends itself to infuriated rolling?

"*R*'s and *f*'s are the favorites in appalled responses these days," said Mr. Gross. "'Fast and loose with the facts' has those two *f*'s that can be spat out, and 'arrant falsehood' takes a good degree of umbrage. 'Arrant,' a variant of 'errant,' is a hearty synonym for 'notorious,' and 'falsehood' has an old-fashioned flavor but still is not stuffy. My personal preference, if the *r* sound is required for its snarling quality, is the more modern 'no relation to reality.' That's good because it imputes a zonked-out craziness to one's opponent, but you have to be careful—a politician recently changed that to 'Unreal!'—which is more of a confirmation than a denunciation."

Does the word "falsehood," now considered old-fashioned, carry the sting it once did? "We don't consider it a Gross Distortion," ruled Gross. "It's like 'untruth'—the word carries no sense of deliberate, willful twisting of the facts. It's like meekly saying, 'That's just not so.' These days, the shocked responder has to get off the defensive and carry the battle to his enemy—without using the one little word that turns people off."

That little word never used, of course, is "lie." Why do politicians shy from "lie"?

Gross winced at my cavalier use of the word. "That's beyond the pale, below the belt, and just too shudderingly mean. You can excoriate a person as a 'master of mendacity,' but you cannot call him an outright, uh, 'liar.' Try something like 'dissembler'—which can be played with, as in 'He is turning out his speeches on a dissembly line.'

" 'Dissemble,' " Mr. Gross explained, "shares a root with 'simulate'—it means to pretend something that is not. It's a mild shot, usually spoken with sad amusement, as: 'I fear my opponent is dissembling.' That's OK for an intellectual audience, but I wouldn't recommend 'dissemble' for the stump—too many people think it means 'disassemble.' Not bad, though, if you want the audience to think your opponent is taking himself apart."

What about something stronger—not neutral, like "falsehood" or "untruth"—but not so naked an accusation as "deliberate deception"?

"Try 'fabrication,' " said the apostle of the appalled. "The only adjective that goes with it is 'outright,' which seems to have replaced 'total.' If you need a clean shot, implying that your opponent deliberately made up his charge, or constructed it from nothing, use 'outright fabrication.' It can be sputtered in high dudgeon, which helps, but it's still not mean."

What about "made of whole cloth"? "We're not cutting whole cloth anymore," said Gross. "If you're into that archaic stuff, try 'canard'—it's a falsehood that has a connotation of trickiness. The only acceptable adjective is 'base,' which shows you how dated it is. Still, a 'base canard' has a ring to it, especially in diplomacy. A canard is the French word for 'duck'—*canard rôti à l'orange* is delicious—and the word's mendacious image comes from the expression 'to half-sell ducks,' or to trick the buyer. Big in foreign-affairs arguments—try it on Brzezinski."

Is it true, I baited him, that imputations of intended deceit are going out of style? Did not Adlai Stevenson once say, "He who slings mud loses ground"? Are we, perhaps, coming into a new era of gentle reproof where polite adversaries will merely admonish opponents for being "in error" or "mistaken"?

"That hypocritical misstatement is a malicious misrepresentation," blazed the founder of Gross Distortions. "Business has never been better. We invite countercharge accounts. Our motto is 'Never Say, "Lie." ' "

Dear Editor,

Being a lover of parenthetical comments (which, in some of my correspondences have involved brackets [for parenthetical comments within parenthetical comments (and sometimes even parenthetical comments within parenthetical comments within parenthetical comments)]), I was quite impressed with one of the few analogous instances I have ever seen of quote within a quote within a quote in William Safire's column (" 'Our motto is "Never Say, 'Lie' " ' ").

Sincerely (or better yet,
Yours very truly),
Richard D. Putter
Dix Hills, New York

Dear Mr. Safire,

You, or perhaps Mr. Gross, defined "dissemble" as "to pretend something that is not."

On the contrary, "to dissemble" is to pretend that what is *is* not *true. The word is opposite to "feign," among others.*

You could look it up, starting with the Latin simulo *and* dissimulo.

Yours truly,
Christopher Kerr
New York, New York

Dear Mr. Safire:

At long last I find some small matter to add to your essay on untruth.

What of "duplicity" and "duplicitous" and "duplicitously"? And for those steeped in Indian lore, what of "speaking with a forked tongue"?

By the way, we judges and lawyers are continuously struggling with the difference between "findings of fact" and what is "truth." Also, what is the difference between "a preponderance of the evidence," "clear and convincing evidence," and "evidence beyond a reasonable doubt"?

Millard L. Midonick
Judge
Surrogate's Court
County of New York
New York, New York

Dear Mr. Safire,

Shame on Christopher Q. Gross, president of Gross Distortions! He is obviously president of Gross Omissions as well.

Otherwise, how could he fail to recall Winston Churchill's famous definition of untruth in 1906 as "terminological inexactitude"?

Sincerely yours,
Fred B. Charatan, M.D.
Syosset, New York

grub, *see* words for nerds

-gry, *see* ending with "gry"

gurney, *see* mediquack

Haigravations I

A new linguistic form called "Haigravation" is rearing its head in Washington. It is the tendency of the new secretary of state to change the state of parts of speech—from noun to adverb, from noun to verb.

The new top man at Foggy Bottom, General Alexander Haig, studded his testimony at confirmation hearings with locutions like "I'll have to caveat my response, Senator," and "I'll caveat that.... "

"Caveat," as used by generals like Julius Caesar, is the third-person singular present subjunctive of the Latin *cavere,* "to beware." Standing by itself, *caveat* in Latin means "Let him beware"; in English, the word is a noun synonymous with "warning." It is also part of the Latin phrase *Caveat emptor,* "Let the buyer beware," the new slogan of the consumer-protection movement.

Until now, "caveat" has been a noun; in Haigravation, it has become a verb. "I'll caveat that" means, presumably, "I'll say that with this warning." (I'll caveat the reader that this locution will soon be followed in literary circles with "I'll asterisk that.")

Not to be outdone, Senator John Glenn asked the witness, "Will you burden-share?" This is a heavy new verb formed from "burden-sharing," diplomatic jargon for "My taxpayers won't kick in any more until yours do."

But Glenn is not in Haig's verbifying league. "Not in the way you contexted it, Senator," was a four-star reply about immorality in high places. To context something, in this lingo, is "to place it in context." Somehow, the verb form rips the noun out of all perspective.

Haig has a history of this sort of thing. In hearings last year, the general said something like "There are nuance-al differences between Henry Kissinger and me on that." The exact quotation cannot be found, because "nuance-al," or "nuansle," was expunged from the written record of the hearing by some unknown hand, and "differences of nuance" put in. But reporter Charles Mohr, a nuancenik, remembered.

Linguistic whistleblowers at Foggy Bottom are encouraged to keep a close watch on the new secretary of state and to send along other abuses of powertalk.

Haig has been caveatted. (There are two *t*'s in "caveatted.")

Dear Mr. Safire:

You must now include me among your persistent critics.

You indicate that "Haig has been caveatted" and add, parenthetically: "There are two t*'s in 'caveatted.'"*

On the contrary, Mr. Safire—no more than there are two l*'s in "marveled."*

> *Rule: All verbs ending in a single consonant preceded by a single vowel (or by a double vowel which is not diphthongal, and permits each to fall into a different syllable), and stressed on that single vowel (or, if two vowels, if stressed on the second of the two), will, on adding a suffix beginning with a vowel, double the aforesaid consonant (to maintain said vowel's sound).*

"Caveat"—as my dot below indicates—is stressed on the first, *not the second,* a, *and therefore, not having the stress on the vowel immediately preceding the final consonant, cannot involve the latter in doubling, on picking up the suffix.*

If, however, you mean to remonstrate that you were *stressing the second* a *in "caveated" and that, therefore, the* t *did need doubling, I must again chide you for misplacing the stress (and, consequently, for misspelling the word in question). For where, pray, can you instance a verb whose stress shifts on changing from one tense to another? On changing from verb to noun, or vice versa: yes—as in "prọgress (noun)," "progrẹss (verb)." In fact, even the syllabification changes: "prọg-ress," "pro-grẹss." But in a tense shift? Never.*

If you agree (as you must) that "caveat" bears the stress on the first a, *then you may not derange the stress in the present perfect tense, passive voice.*

Cordially,
Hyman Yudewitz
New York, New York

My dear Mr. Safire,

I don't want to belabor the case of Secretary Haig, but I am compelled to recall a moment as memorable as any you wrote about in The Times. . . . *Fed up with references to the dead issues of Watergate, the new secretary complained about the senators' determination to (and here, disdaining the simple "revive," he reached haughtily for "disinter," fumbled hastily in the wrong bag and alas! snatched out . . .) "reincarcerate."*

On another day, according to a friend of mine, Archie Bunker, who couldn't tear himself away from the televised hearings, the secretary began one of his ripostes with the qualifier "epistemology-wise."

Archie, who himself has a way with words, reported that a flicker of unmistakable respect crossed the faces of the senators.

Cordially,
Carroll O'Connor
Malibu, California

Haigravations II

The red alert flashed here a few weeks ago—warning of incoming semantic missiles from the new secretary of state, Al Haig—turned out to be on target and calls for follow-up. A man who uses "caveat" and "context" as verbs must be eternally vigilanted.

In his first press conference at Foggy Bottom, General Haig quickly reversed the flow of history by speaking of "the Christian-Judeo values" of Western civilization. These values had hitherto been called "Judeo-Christian, " with the *o* a combining form; if Judaism is placed at the end, the phrase should be "Christian-Judaic," or perhaps "Christo-Judaic." But I would stick with "Judeo-Christian" because the phrase reflects the chronology, going with the flow of Old Testament to New.

The new secretary is becoming a master of the art of the almost correct word. "I have no finite plan for my own travel," he stated. "Finite" means "with measurable boundaries"; a word he might better have used was "specific." Perhaps a current use of "finite" to mean "tangible" influenced General Haig; the possibilities are infinite, but there is a big difference between "finite" and "definite."

Vogue words are his specialty: The academic joyword of the seventies was "exacerbate," an exasperating way of saying "aggravate," "irritate," or "annoy." The secretary said he hoped that the Soviets would do nothing "to exacerbate the kind of mutual restraint that both sides should pursue." (He meant "lessen"; in vogue lingo, only tensions get exacerbated.) A newer vogue word—pioneered by David Stockman, the budget hawk—is "hemorrhaging." Terrorism, said General Haig, was "hemorrhaging in many respects throughout the world." This two-*r*, two-*h* term—Greek for a burst blood vessel—is going to lose some nice kid the title at the National Spelling Bee.

Another vogue word that is a favored Haigravation is "dicey." (I am indebted to Charles Zaug of *The New York Times*'s recording room for catching Haig's "It was a dicey game. . . .") "Dicey" is a British colloquialism, meaning "risky" or "chancy," from World War II use when RAF pilots talked of "dicing with death"; it was picked up quickly ("early on") by Americans who "go on holiday" rather than "take a vacation."

Redundancies abound. Those who suspected his "an additional number of augmentees" to be redundant were mistaken, but there is no defending Al, my old colleague, on his reckless locution: "the most careful caution." (The "augmentees" are people who augment the staff already on the job, and are therefore properly "augmenters." Haig compared his augies with "in-place pros," a phrase that is out-of-place poetry.)

Although the Associated Press transcript of Haig's remarks read: "Let me clarify one prospect of your premised question," I think the secretary must have said, or at least meant to say, "aspect" rather than "prospect." Come to think of it, he meant to say "one premise of your question."

It is not wholly fair to grade the grammar of anybody's spoken language, because few of us speak as carefully as we write—when we write, we get a chance to edit. But when words are deliberately used to stand meaning on its head, the speaker deserves some censure. Haig on human rights: "There will be no deemphasis but a change in priority." If "a change in priority" is not a "deemphasis" of what had been top priority, what is it? Because of too much careful caution, his meaning is hemorrhaging.

Not all Haigravations call for criticism. When it comes to a trope, he is no dope: Asked about Europe, he referred to Poland as one of a number of "watchpots." A watchpot is, presumably, a pot that bears watching to make certain that it does not boil over— a good trope that belongs in diplomacy's hot-stove league, coined on the analogy of "crackpots." Good coinage on "watchpot," Al—now just be certain it does not become "a watchpot situation" or "in a watchpot mode."

A generation ago the historian Oliver Jensen dealt with another military man's lingo in a classic parody about the Gettysburg Address as Eisenhower would have delivered it. ("I haven't checked these figures, but 87 years ago, I think it was, a number of individuals organized a governmental setup. . . .")

As soon as the Haigravation reached Great Britain, a parody was called for, and an editorialist for the *Guardian* wrote:

"Haig, in congressional hearings before his confirmatory, paradoxed his auditioners by abnormalling his responds so that verbs were nouned, nouns verbed and adjectives adverbised. He techniqued a new way to vocabulary his thoughts so as to informationally uncertain anybody listening about what he had actually implicationed. . . .

"If that is how General Haig wants to nervous breakdown the Russian leadership," concluded the *Guardian,* "he may be shrewding his way to the biggest diplomatic invent since Clausewitz. Unless, that is, he schizophrenes his allies first."

Dear Mr. Safire:

Humpty Dumpty was an early and enthusiastic champion of Haigravation, as in this exchange with Alice: "They've a temper—some of them—particularly verbs, they're the proudest—adjectives you can do anything with, but not verbs—however I can manage the whole lot of them! Impenetrability! That's what I say."

When Alice asked what he meant, Humpty Dumpty replied: "I meant by impenetrability that we've had enough on that subject, and it would be just as well if you'd mention what you mean to do next, as I suppose you don't mean to stop here all the rest of your life."

I read Alice frequently, because—as a character in a St. John Gogarty novel says, explaining why he stops for a drink at every pub he passes—"It helps."

Jack Hooley
Washington, D.C.

Bill—

I was alarmed at your column which says, "The red alert flashed here [about Al Haig] turned out to be on target and calls for follow-up."

That's a metaphor mangled almost beyond recognition.

It's not the "Alert" that was on target; it was Haig's missiles into the fortress of correct usage. (I think that's grammatically incorrect, but you grasp my meaning, I am sure.)

At any rate, in our paper it will read: "The red alert flashed here . . . turned out to be correctly triggered and now must be reactivated."

Yours in love for the language.

Doug Smith
Buffalo Courier-Express
Buffalo, New York

Dear Bill:

I've heard "Judaism" pronounced by public and private speakers as "Judah-ism," "Juday-ism," "Judy-ism," "Ju-dism," and even "Judo-ism."

My Webster's *says it's pronounced "Jud-i-ism" with the* a *sounded the same as the* i.

I'm an old man now and have been learning English from the cradle through college and for decades thereafter. Nobody can master the language completely. It makes no sense as it stands. Change it please.

Sincerely,
Ed Morse
Port Washington, N.Y.

Dear Mr. Safire,

I was pleased to find in your "Haigravations" several references to the word "hemorrhage." For the past couple of years I have been aware of a different usage of the word, one that could easily be applied to General Haig's paper-shredder language.

I first heard this usage at Pomona College in California, but the speaker was from Brooklyn. The general idea was that "to hemorrhage" was to say something stupid. My friends and I were intrigued by the word and spent many a late dinner (putting off our studies) exploring its meaning. With all the academic rigor we could muster we came up with the following definition:

> *A "hemorrhage" is a social blunder made during some form of communication interaction, whereby the person committing the blunder says or communicates something so stupid, confused, meaningless, or out of place that those around this person judge him or her to be a fool, idiot, dolt, or schmuck.*

The word conjures up an image of the speaker lying on the ground and bleeding to death in front of the crowd, in a figurative sense, of course. Most of General Haig's "Haigravations" certainly qualify as hemorrhages, and I'm sure that in the future we will have Haig "hemorrhaging in many respects throughout the world." He will not be the first, though. President Carter's "joke" about Montezuma's Revenge was a hemorrhage of international proportions, with deep influence on relations between the United States and Mexico.

One of my colleagues and I have developed an in-depth analysis of the hemorrhage from the point of view of social psychology, but I will spare you all that, as you can see the results when our paper is published. He is very intrigued by the causes of the Hemorrhage Prone Personality (HPP), another question on the influence of environment and heredity (an interesting question in Haig's case). I would like to study cultural variations in the duration of the Post-Hemorrhage Pause, that awkward silence that often follows a hemorrhage. I'm sure that the world will be panting to hear about our pioneering researches in the near future.

I hope that you have found this note concerning hemorrhages helpful. Should there be any questions about classifying future comments by General Haig as hemorrhages, I would be happy to make available further results from our research.

Sincerely yours,
Eric A. Myers
New Haven, Connecticut

P. S. We borrowed "communication interaction" from a psychology text. It's spinach, to be sure, but it makes it seem we know what we're talking about.

Dear Mr. Safire,

I was so very glad to read your column about Alexander Haig's rather interesting English. I had wondered if I was the only one who noticed. A few weeks ago, he was reported saying, "I'd like to clarify the air . . ." I was not sure if he wanted to clear the air or clarify an issue, but as he expressed himself, I had a vision of a man trying to stir egg whites into a large pot of boiling air to clarify the broth. I wonder if he uses cheese cloth to strain it afterwards?

On another subject, am I the only one in the world who is horrified at the growing use of the word "snuck"? I seem to be on a one-woman crusade, and I'm losing badly. Everyone knows the past tense of "peek" is not "puck," so why do they think the past tense of "sneak" is "snuck"? Twice within this month I've seen the word in print, once in a national magazine, and I heard it on the radio the other day. Perhaps it is just a personal peeve of mine, like fingernails on the blackboard.

Very truly yours,
Betty A. Bishop
Chester, California

Dear Mr. Safire:

I believe, though I am not certain, that the verb "to dice," meaning, more or less, "to be in a close contest with," came originally from European Grand Prix auto racing in the years before World War II, whence RAF personnel adopted it. Most Grand Prix drivers were not British, which suggests the possibility of an origin in some other language. Alas, I can't prove it.

I am distressed by what you say about "exacerbate." With respect to language I am a bit of what a jazz fan would have called, in the 1930's, a Moldy Fig—a person of possibly excessive conservatism—but I really do think that you're wrong when you describe that verb as "an exasperating way of saying 'aggravate,' 'irritate,' or 'annoy.' "

Surely to exacerbate is to aggravate, to exasperate is to irritate or annoy. Ignoring for the moment Marine's First Law of Written English ("No Two Words Mean the Same Thing"), words like "exasperate," "irritate," and "annoy" refer to an initial effect; "exacerbate" and "aggravate" refer to a heightening, usually a worsening, of the effect. One's skin is irritated, perhaps by a rash or minor wound; one aggravates or exacerbates the irritation by scratching it.

As a corollary, a person *can be exasperated or (at least metaphorically) irritated, but only the irritation itself can be aggravated or exacerbated. "Mr. Weinberger's testimony exacerbated my irritation about the amount of money spent for armaments."*

Cordially,
Gene Marine
Berkeley, California

Dear Mr. Safire:

Granted Mr. Haig has some problems with the use of words to express what is on his mind: "exacerbate" does not mean "lessen" and "finite" does not really mean "specific." But perhaps a man who uses "caveat" and "context" as verbs should be included among the venerable giants of our language. What I am getting at is that this morning, while skimming C. Hugh Holman's A Handbook to Literature, *I came across the term "antimeria" which is defined as "the use of one part of speech for another, as in 'But me no buts.' 'But,' which is a conjunction, is used in this sentence as first a verb and then a noun." Mr. Holman then goes on to say, much to the delight of Haigiographers everywhere, "Shakespeare used 'antimeria' often, as in 'His complexion is perfect gallows'* (The Tempest, *I,i) and 'The thunder would not peace at my bidding'* (King Lear, *IV,vi)."*

In his emulation of Shakespeare Mr. Haig has comeuppanced us language snobs.

Sincerely yours,
Eileen H. Gorman
Yorktown Heights, New York

Dear Mr. Safire:

After reading your entry I murmured to my husband, "Haig is going to have a contract out on Safire's life." Then the mutations began: "Haig is going to contract Safire's life. He will contractualize it. Safire will be contracted."

Sincerely,
Diantha Horton
Alfred Station, New York

Dear Mr. Safire:

I must say I take exception to the way you treat H. E. General Alexander Haig. You seem to forget, Mr. Safire, that the General was selected to perform duties which, I humbly believe, are not as engrossing, captivating, and rewarding in terms of brilliancy as may be the case with linguistics. His, I imagine, is a job that calls for intelligence, a great sense of responsibility, experience, action, and imagination. Even if you refuse to concede the first four qualities, you simply cannot deny him credit for the last.

I admire the hair-splitting way you dissect his verbs and nouns and all the booby-trapped tools of the language we all know you master with such scholarly perfection. I even have many a hearty laugh when I read your column! But, excuse the personality, do you honestly think it is cricket to attack him on your own palaestra? If *you were to take his place, I am sure that etymologies and punctilious propriety of language would be of little use to you.*

I think you should stop picking on him. Remember that General Haig has barely started his thorny way. Remember that "noblesse oblige," Mr. Safire, and remember to criticize him as a Secretary of State, not as a linguist!

Sincerely,
Cora González-Torrado
Santo Domingo,
Dominican Republic

---

hashslinger slang

The mechanization of food service—the speedup at the fast-food counter—has led to greater efficiency and more uniform portions, but has cost us a lingo that was evocative of hometowns, youth, night, and the moon.

"Poached eggs on toast," you would say to the counterman, or soda jerk.

"Adam and Eve on a raft!" he would holler to the hashslinger.

"Better scramble the eggs," you would say, on second thought.

"Wreck 'em!"

"I'll have a cuppa cawfee."

"Draw one!"

"And my friends here will have a malted, a large Coke, and a chocolate Coke."

"Burn one! Stretch one! Drag one through Georgia!"

"And a bacon, lettuce, and tomato sandwich on toast, to take out."

"BLT down on wheels, hold the mayo!"

The hashslinger in the kitchen would yell back, "Eighty-six on the BLT!" That meant, we knew, he was out of bacon—an "86," for "out of it," was as famous as "87½" for "There's a good-looking girl out front," and the real insiders knew that a false order, barked, "Fix the pumps!" meant, "Get a look at this girl in a sweater." That was sophisticated, but even the squares knew that "Squeeze one" called for an orange juice, and that "Stretch sweet Alice" was an order for a large glass of milk.

What has become of these terms of yesteryear? The airplane designer who, as a thirsty kid, used to stretch sweet Alice applied the term to his lengthened versions of giant aircraft, and now we have a stretch DC-9 with forty extra windows. "Hang a draw," or "Hang a forty-four," which meant "One large root beer, please," has reappeared in the surfers' "hang ten" (to grip the edge of a surfboard with all ten toes) and the skiers' "hang a left" (to make a left turn).

Soda-fountain lingo persists in some modern slang, but the argot has disappeared as an art form because both soda jerk and hashslinger have lost direct contact with the customer. Not enough time to talk. I got on line at a fast fooderie and for a wild moment thought of saying. "A cluck and a grunt on a burned British," but bit my tongue and dutifully murmured, "Egg McMuffin." That's progress.

Aloha Mr. Safire!

Your assumption that the phrase "hang ten" derives from "hang a forty-four" doesn't hold water. And your description "to grip the edge of the surfboard with all ten toes" is as soft as wax. "Hanging ten" means just that. Walking to the front, or nose, of the board, while riding a wave and hanging all your toes over the front edge, or rail. Toes over the nose.

For those less skillful, there's hanging five. Somewhat easier because one foot is kept back, so your weight is more evenly balanced. Simply put, these terms derive from nothing less, or more, than a precise description of whatever's being done. Certainly not from some ancient soda-fountain lingo.

Sorry, Mr. Safire, but your references to surfing terminology hold up as well as a three-foot close-out grinder pounding on dry reef! You wiped out. You took gas. You ate your lunch. Paid your dues. You got axed. Nailed. Picked off. You had a bad go-out. You got caught inside a ropey wave, got sucked up the face and went over the falls. You bounced off the bottom and had a coral sandwich. Your stick was broken in half. You were drilled so hard for so long you were going numb from lack of oxygen, and when you finally found the surface, and gulped some air, the second wave of the set was closing out even harder, and you were sitting right in the impact zone for this one, too!

Hell, you should have asked. I could have told you that break was no place for a gremmie!

Keep surfing,
Dave Zito
Stone Harbor, New Jersey

Dear Mr. Safire:

Add to waiters' slang, shortcut for orders:

"Sweep up the kitchen"—corned beef hash, 1910–1913, but bread pudding in CCNY, 1913–1917.

"Fishes eight eyes"—tapioca pudding.

"Croton highball"—a glass of water.

"Customer wants to take a chance"—beef stew.

Faithfully yours,
W. C. O'Brien, Sr.
Riverdale, New York

Dear Mr. Safire,

You might be interested in my favorite bit of hash-house slang. I found it (or it me) in about 1967 in New York.

The order was "radio Christmas."

Its origin: Since toast is "down" (presumably because the bread must be pushed down into the toaster), tuna salad on toast is "radio" (tuna down, or tune-it-down).

"Radio Christmas" proved to be tuna salad on toast but hold the lettuce: "Noel" (no L*).*

Since that day I have gotten all my food from vending machines.

Scott Parker
Washington, D.C.

---

hassle hustle

" 'Hassle' is a gorgeously descriptive word," wrote *The Saturday Evening Post* in 1946, "which lately has won wide usage in show business." A year earlier *Down Beat* magazine used the word to mean "arguments" and spelled it "hassel."

The noun became part of the protest movement of the sixties, and took on a verb shape meaning "to annoy, harass, beat up on, make life difficult for." The verb "to bother" was overwhelmed.

As pushing around persisted, so did the word, and it is now firmly placed in most dictionaries. Both *Webster's* and *American Heritage* speculate that the word may have come from a combination of "haggle" and "tussle"; that seems farfetched to me. Thorndike-Barnhart's *World Book Dictionary* guesses at a derivation from a southern dialect verb, "to hassel," meaning "to pant, to breathe noisily," but my tongue isn't hanging out over that one either.

"Hassle's" origin is a mystery, which is a pity because the coinage is recent and the word is in the process of spreading its meaning over another popular new verb. Leslie Sawyer of the RKO Radio Network sent me this Associated Press dispatch, which was filed from the island of St. Martin: "Rolling Stones guitarist Ron Wood and his girlfriend have been deported from this Caribbean island after spending five days in jail when police found cocaine in their apartment. 'I think we were victims of a hassle,' said Wood just before leaving for California. . . ."

The meaning of "hassle" in that use seems to have gained an additional overtone of "deception, ploy, trick, frame-up"—in other words, to have merged partway with the noun "hustle." The old slang verb "to hustle"—"to gain money dishonestly, as by prostitution"—includes a meaning of "jostle or shove" which intrudes upon the meaning of "hassle." In effect, "hassle" is being hustled.

This merger of hassle ("to harass") and hustle ("to defraud") should be resisted. Each lively locution should stand alone. Hustlers and hasslers alike should guard against pollution of the one by the other.

The Lexicographic Irregulars are urged to plumb the etymologies of these terms of the subculture; the earliest known use of "hustling" as "robbery" was tracked by the *Oxford English Dictionary* to 1751. Research, especially on "hassel" in the South, is called for.

Letters complaining about wastes of time, or berating me for dignifying the substandard, are not solicited; we know what *they* are.

Dear Sunday Safire:

You write that tracing "hassle" to a blend of "haggle" and "tussle" seems farfetched to you.

Actually that etymological speculation which a couple of dictionaries seem to advance was quick-fetched.

I fetched it myself—one day in the summer of 1948, as I remember—when a word scout from Webster *got on my office telephone at* Time.

Webster's *man (or woman—I forget) said they had been keeping cards on "hassle" and had some occurrences in* Variety, *but here it was in* Time, *after running that well-known gauntlet of editors and female researchers and copy desk characters.* Webster *had learned from the head of research that I had written the word into a writer's copy in my role of senior editor.*

—And what did I think it meant, and what might it derive from?

One doesn't like to keep Webster *waiting or to appear in silly uncertainty. Replied quickly.*

The next edition of Webster's Collegiate *offered my meaning and, speculatively, that haggle and tussle business. With* Webster's *insertion, "(spec.)."*

I was scanning Variety *myself in those days.*

Sir.
Jack Tibby
Port Washington, New York

Dear Mr. Safire,

When I first heard the word "hassle," in Pearl Harbor during World War II, I was told it was a combination of "hustle" and "wrastle" (for "wrestle"), which sounds quite logical.

Sincerely yours,
Robert Scott Milne
New York, New York

Dear Mr. Safire,

I remember "hassle" as a southern word from my thirties childhood spent partly in Virginia and think it was both noun and verb. It doesn't appear in my OED, *but the 1967* Random House *unabridged has:*

> *hassle N. INFORMAL. quarrel; squabble. [var. of obs. HARSELL to irritate <MF HARCELL(ER), deriv. of HERSE harrow; see HEARSE]*
>
> *hearse N. . . . 2. a triangular frame for holding candles, used at the service of Tenebrae in Holy Week. . . . [ME HERSE <MF HERCE a harrow, candle frame <L HIRPICEM acc. of HIRPEX harrow]*

I also remember it used by black civil rights campaigners here in the early sixties, which makes me think of it, again, as a southern word since the people I knew tended to use speech patterns from their childhood rather than fashionable forms. Too, I do not think "hassle" was then fashionable; it was just used to describe something that wasn't big enough to call a "struggle."

Sincerely,
WMWeaver
Rahway, New Jersey

Dear Mr. Safire:

You appeal to the Lexicographic Irregulars (shades of Sherlock Holmes?) to consider "hassle." I think you should take a look at the coverage given to that word in American Speech, *Vol. 35 (1935), pp. 143-45. I think it provides the best treatment of its origin.*

I may add that the Random House College Dictionary *derives it from an obsolete* harsell, *"to irritate," from an old French word,* harceller, *"to harrow."*

If you consult Eric Partridge, Dictionary of Slang, *you will find him unreliable. He guesses at both "haggle" x "tussle" and "haggle" x "wrestle" and calls it a Canadianism. The* Dictionary of Canadianisms *does not list it at all.*

As for "hustle," which you also brought up for further explanation, a definitive origin is listed by Reddall, Fact, Fancy and Fable, *that it was originated by Mr. A. J. Wagner during the Civil War and has been used along the Mohawk Valley ever since. However, there are pre-Civil War citations to refute this Wagner, whoever he was.*

Yours sincerely,
David Shulman
New York, New York

Dear Mr. Safire:

After reading "Hassle Hustle" I have to hassle about your definition of the slang verb "to hustle"—"to gain money dishonestly, as by prostitution," unless *you meant to invoke the obscure* sense of the word "dishonest" which is "shameful, unchaste."*

Wouldn't "to make strenuous efforts to secure money as by prostitution" be less of a hassle to hustlers?

Sincerely,
Stella Croker
Greenwich, Connecticut

**No evidence of use since 1755, when noted by* Merriam-Webster.

heathen Chinese

"In an Oriental context" was a phrase I used to discuss the possibility that "bargain-chop" might be the origin of "bargaining chip."

That raised some Western eyebrows. "Oriental," it was pointed out, is starting to become an ethnic slur—a word applied by whites to the yellow race. The preferred term, according to hypersensitive wordwatchers, has become "Asian."

In Latin, *oriens* is that part of the horizon in which the sun first rises. That is always the east, of course, and "orient" came to mean the East.

It is a beautiful word, more of a rise-up than a put-down. As a verb, "to orient" has been overworked lately (the assistant secretary of state for East Asian and Pacific affairs is Orient-oriented), but as an adjective "Oriental" has delicious overtones of mystery and spice. I'll continue to use it; if I ever substitute "Asian," it will be by occident.

Dear Mr. Safire:

"Asia" is etymologically from a Semitic root meaning "rise"—as in "sunrise"—and therefore has the same meaning as the Latin-based "Orient." Likewise, "Europe" may be from the Semitic root meaning "pass" or "set." All of which lets us know where people were standing when the world was named.

Sincerely,
Harvey Minkoff
Associate Professor
Hunter College
New York, New York

Dear Mr. Safire:

The word "Oriental" is objectionable to us Asians not so much because it is an ethnic slur—although some people may intend it as such—as because like "Far East" or "Far Eastern," it is Eurocentric.

When the word "Oriental" or "Eastern" is used, our first reaction is to ask, "East of what?" Upon hearing the term "Far East" or "Far Eastern," we wonder: Far from where?

The answer, of course, in terms of the origins of these words, is "East of Rome" and "far from Rome," which was then considered (by Europeans) as the center of the world, or at least of the civilized world.

Aside from our wish not to be placed on the periphery of civilization, we Asians have a different perspective—or orientation.

When we Filipinos wish to go to the United States, for example, we fly eastward. But we call the land beyond the Pacific not the Orient, but America, and the people who inhabit it not Orientals, but Americans.

When Americans fly from California to Manila or Tokyo or Peking, they go west. But many of them insist that they are going to the Far East.

Because the world is round, the East or the West is not a definite place. It all depends on where you are standing and in what direction you are going.

This is why we insist on being called Asians rather than Orientals. To us, East Asia is not the Far East. It is not far at all. It is where many of us live. And we would rather say "West Asia" than "Middle East."

This insistence arises not from hypersensitivity but from a desire for logic and geographical precision.

Sincerely yours,
Rodolfo Severino, Jr.
Consul General of the Philippines
Houston, Texas

Dear Mr. Safire:

Much like an alcoholic who takes a drink to deal with his drinking problem, you have attempted to justify usage of the word "Oriental."

You write, "'Oriental' has delicious overtones of mystery and spice." We Asians do not think of ourselves as mysterious. You demonstrate the meaning of ethnocentrism by your projection of that inaccurate image onto us.

Your association of "Oriental" with "delicious" and "spice" is equally revealing and, to me, disheartening. It is disheartening when, upon meeting people, I hear them suddenly rave about a meal they had recently in Chinatown. (How would you feel if Asians, upon meeting you, were to start raving about McDonald's?) We Asians, contrary to your Oriental image, are more than a culinary people.

Language reflects and reinforces a people's thinking, however accurate or inaccurate such thinking may be. "Oriental" reflects an inaccurate image. Its continued usage, which you advocate, would reinforce the inaccuracy. As a fourth-generation American, I am no more mysterious than a white American. And I would like to be thought of as an expert on Chinese food as much (and as little) as a white American would like to be automatically labeled as an expert on McDonald's. Continued usage of "Oriental" causes me to be seen not for the individual I am, but for the mysterious culinary expert I am not.

Anthropologists talk about ascribed status and chosen status. We choose to be Asians. You ascribe an inaccurate image to us. I think you're being unfair. What we would like to be seen as is a matter for us to decide. After all, we know more about ourselves than others do. In fact, you admit that to you, we are "mysterious." Even though "Oriental" may be a beautiful word, as you claim, its beauty does not make up for its harmful consequences (however unintended they may be). Asian Americans have suffered from positive stereotypes. We work harder for less pay, for example. Or consider that we are compared against blacks, Asians being the "model" minority (the implications regarding blacks being insidious). The positive image of "Oriental" architects, engineers, and physicians has caused our presence in the arts, humanities, and social sciences to be seen as anomalous. The good intentions you have for perpetuating the usage of "Oriental" does not make up for these harmful consequences, all of which stem from the "Oriental" image.

I hope you will reconsider.

Sincerely,
Allen Lee
Cambridge, Massachusetts

Dear Mr. Safire,

It is not Westerners who cringe at the use of "Oriental"; it is Asians. And it is not starting *to become an ethnic slur; it* has *been for well over thirty years—at least, when we went out to Japan in 1952 for a four-year stay, it was already unacceptable. I think this is because it suggests the stereotypes of Chinese in the early twentieth century—slanty-eyed, pig-tailed, pidgin-speaking Chinks. To my ear, it is much like using "Hebrew" as a general term for "Jew": "I was talking to this Hebrew the other day." It is not as bad as "kike," but nevertheless, it sounds both old-fashioned and somewhat illiterate, and this is the same feeling that the use of "Oriental" conveys—where have you been all these years? Every article in* The New York Times, *every book on the subject, every specialist in the field, not to mention every person with a general interest in the Far East, not only use "Asian" but have used it ever since I first tuned in way back in the fifties. There is nothing wrong with "Oriental" in the abstract—but you could make the same argument for "Hebrew." I hate to come down so hard on you, but today, with every group's sensibilities rubbed so raw, I do not think we can afford the luxury of choosing ethnic names which we ourselves prefer.*

Yours sincerely,
Peggy Munsterberg
New Paltz, New York

Dear Saf,

You're still being solipsistic when you use "Oriental" instead of "Asian."

So it means "where the sun rises." Standing where? Standing in Washington? But China isn't where the sun rises when you're in New Delhi.

You have oriented the world from a Western standpoint . . . and that's what's wrong with calling Asians "Orientals."

Yours faithfully,
Arthur J. Morgan
New York, New York

hemorrhaging, *see* Haigravations II

hit list, *see* list to this

hit the ground running

The cliché that landed on its feet and then took off like a bat out of hell is "hit the ground running." This is the metaphor of the early days of the Reagan administration, which hits the ground on January 20 but has been running for some time.

I sent out a search party for the origin of this expression while on the *Larry King Show*, an all-night extravaganza for the nation's insomniacs, and several callers offered these explanations:

1. Paratrooper lingo. One former paratrooper recalls this as the instruction given by the jumpmaster before the troopers reach the drop zone; another former paratrooper called to say the first guy didn't know what he was talking about.
2. Airborne assault-unit terminology. A small helicopter sweeps down and hovers a few feet off the ground; its passengers disembark hurriedly, keeping in motion to avoid enemy fire. This theory is shared by Anthony Dolan, the Pulitzer Prize-winning reporter on the Reagan speech-writing staff whose legs are churning in the transition air.
3. Navy-marine slang. A former naval person in North Carolina recalls "hit the deck running." The treasury secretary, Donald Regan, told a television interviewer that as a former marine he used the expression "hit the beach running." Throughout the military and naval usages, there is the constant combination of the verbs "hit" and "run"—could it have anything to do with "hit-and-run driver"?

4. Cartoon-character imagery. In a variety of *Tom and Jerry* and *Road Runner* animated cartoons, one of the animals is dropped from a great height, or leaps high in the air, and begins running furiously before he gains traction on the ground. At that point, he takes off in a cloud of dust.
5. Hobo lingo. I have no citations to support this, but it seems to me that when a hobo was stealing a ride on a freight train and saw a "cinderbull" (railroad detective) approaching, he was tempted to leap from the moving train. In that case, to avoid a bad fall, he would pump his legs in the hope of maintaining balance when he hit the ground, or at least until he could roll into a soft spot.

Whatever its origin—other speculative etymologies are welcomed—this figure of speech has earned early retirement. In a few months, Reaganauts may be searching for the origin of "screech to a halt."

Dear Mr. Safire:

While preparing an article for The Times Magazine *during the Eisenhower-to-Kennedy transition, I heard the phrase so often in Washington that I made an effort to find out who began its use. I traced it to Roger W. Jones, then chairman of the United States Civil Service Commission, who, in an article in the* Civil Service Journal *in late 1960, pledged the Civil Service to help the new administration in 1961 to "hit the ground running." I mentioned these facts in my article, "Problem of the Interregnum," which was published in the* Magazine *on October 2, 1960. So the modish cliché of the present transition is, alas, a hand-me-down.*

Sincerely yours,
Henry F. Graff
Department of History
Columbia University
New York, New York

Dear Sir:

If, as you suggest, you hit the ground running when you jump off a freight car moving into the yard, you'll add your own speed to the momentum imparted to you by the train. As the train is still going at a good clip, you'll fall head over heels—possibly onto the tracks. I hope that no novice riding the freights has followed your reckless suggestion.

Remember, if the Democrats ever force you off a press car, push back as you leave the step, and hit the ground braking.

George Turitz
Washington, D.C.

Dear Mr. Safire,

Did you intend the line about Donald Regan to be taken literally (he used the expression only after leaving the marines), or did you mean that Regan is a former marine who uses the expression? I believe you meant the latter, since "used" is in the past tense and Regan is not.

If you are a language maven, I am a language maven troubleshooter.

As always,
Bill Weiss
Rego Park, New York

Dear Bill:

I can provide a skimpy clue for your search party seeking the origin of "hit the ground running."

It goes back at least as far as, or predates, the professional football career of the great Green Bay pass catcher Don Hutson. (Note that I did not use the bogus title "Green Bay Pass-Catching Great Don . . .")

I know this because, about twenty-five years ago, I was doing research for a sports article on outstanding professional players of the past and looked up newspaper clippings written when Don was playing. (He played end, by the way, but today he would be a wide receiver.) I vividly remember reading a clipping dated during the peak years of his professional career that said the secret to his success as a pass receiver was that "he could jump, catch the ball, and hit the ground running."

My too-faulty memory tells me that the date on the clipping in which I read that phrase was 1939. Hutson, who played college football for Alabama, was a Packer from 1935 to 1945. I'd bet that the phrase was used as a football cliché prior to the World War II military uses that you suggested as possible origins.

But the bottom line *is that Hutson has long since been retired, and so should the cliché, and I am*

Sincerely yours,
Tom Wark
Philadelphia Inquirer
Philadelphia, Pennsylvania

Dear William Safire:

I figgered I'd better "hit the ground running" with this before any more of them effete easterners pass off any more bullonee on you.

It is a western saying that originated years before World War II. When I was a little kid, my grandmother used to tell me about a great-uncle who rode in the Pony Express system and always "hit the ground running" for the fresh mount that would carry him on to the next change station. It was also said that sometimes he rode with "blood in his boots" because of an arrow he picked up en route.

When I was older, I listened to the cowboys at a rodeo. Some horses were known as "killer broncs." When they pitched their rider, they would try to stomp him on the ground. The cowboys used to say, "If'n that one throws you, you'd better hit the ground running."

Sincerely,
Joe Alexander
Aptos, California

hogwash

"What flatulent balderdash!" wrote Andrew Reed of New York to the editors of an eminent newspaper last month. "Sometimes I wonder if the editors of *The New York Times* live in the same world as I do."

That was a forceful expression of opinion and deserved its publication in the Letters column. "Flatulent" is an acceptable adjective in polite discourse, meaning "windy, pretentious," though many people know that the windings originally referred to gas in the stomach. "Balderdash," in the sixteenth century, meant "froth"; a century later it became the name of a fiery concoction of booze—still with beaded bubbles winking at the brim—and the frothy word was taken up in 1890's American slang as an exclamation of shock that would not in itself cause shock.

That's the trick in the language of high dudgeon—to say a word that sounds explosive but is otherwise innocent, or is presumed to be. An unknown nonadmirer of my political views sent me a laundry bag from a shop in the Fanueil Hall district in Boston with the word "Hogwash" printed on it. That's a nice bit of wordplay—suggesting that hogs, too, have problems disposing of soiled linen—based on the expression rooted in "swill," or the garbage fed to pigs.

"Fiddlesticks!" is the favorite term of Sara Miller Cutting, a State Department aide, when she wants to heap disdain. According to Stuart Berg Flexner's *I Hear America Talking,* "fiddle-faddle," "fiddlededee," and "fiddlesticks" all refer to the sounds emitted from homemade fiddles, or noisemakers called "horsefiddles," in the 1800's.

If "fiddlesticks" seems old-fashioned, dudgeoneers often try "malarkey," sometimes spelled "malarky," which comes from an Irish source nobody has been able to identify solidly. Perhaps it is a cousin to "blarney," from the stone which supposedly conferred gifts of eloquence; that term is useful, too, but has remained within Irish dialect.

"Baloney!" has been enjoying a vogue since Al Smith said in 1936 of some Rooseveltian rhetoric, "No matter how thin you slice it, it's still baloney." (Clare Boothe Luce later internationalized it with "globaloney.") Though the name of the Italian city and the delicatessen delight came into use in the twenties as a slang expletive for "nonsense," it has gained and held a political flavor. The word is spelled "baloney," "bolony," "balony," "bologna," and several other ways, but no matter how you spell it ...

Dear Bill:

My own favorite expression of emphatic disbelief is "Bullfinch!" To which is added, of course, "That's pure mythology."

Best regards,
Monroe
[Monroe H. Freedman]
Washington, D.C.

Dear Mr. Safire:

You stated that flatulence "referred to gas in the stomach." Support for such a statement might be obtained from the dictionary, but from a physiologic standpoint "flatulence" refers to the movement of gas or expulsion of gas. Gas in the stomach usually produces a sensation of fullness, whereas excessive gas in the small bowel may rush through this organ and, when mixed with fluid, will produce borborygmi—often referred to as "one's stomach talking." Gas in the colon will produce distension and often results in the passage of flatus. Thus, in medical parlance, "flatulence" refers to small intestinal or colonic gas rather than to stomach gas.

Most cordially,
Stanley H. Lorber, M.D.
Professor of Medicine
Chairman, Department of Gastroenterology
Temple University
Philadelphia, Pennsylvania

honing out

Columnist Mary McGrory recently honed in on campaign clichés—from "negatives" (formerly "minuses") to "volatility" ("The damn voters surprised us again") to "skewed." ("'Skewed' began appearing on Kennedy managers' lips early on," Miss McGrory wrote, presumably using the voguish Briticism "early on" ironically. "The Iowa results were 'skewed' by the hostage situation.")

Then she came to my favorite: " 'Honing in' is having a good run. George Bush, having had a brief and passionate attachment to 'Big Mo' [momentum] after Iowa, belatedly began to 'hone in' on the issues. The press has recently been 'honing in'—formerly known as 'zeroing in'—on Reagan's cavalier way with facts. Kennedy was extremely grateful that reporters were diverted in this wise. For several months, his slips of the tongue and pauses had undergone a 'honing in' of exceptional severity."

The noun "hone" comes from the Greek word for "cone" and refers to a whetstone, a material used for sharpening knives and tools. As a verb, the word means "to sharpen." Emphasis can be added with "hone down," a phrase President Carter used in a recent press conference: To "hone down" is to "sharpen up."

The phrase "to hone in on" is a mistake. The confusion is based on "to home in," or "to home in on," used by pilots or radio operators who wish to follow an electronic beam or signal to a destination.

You can "hone," or sharpen, your arguments, or you can "home in"—with an *m*—on an issue, but you cannot "hone in on the issues." The expression is a hopeless mishmash. Evidently Mr. Bush wanted to say "home in," or to use the rifle term "zero in," and mixed it up with "honing down," or refining, his points of view. Out came "hone in on," and nobody asked what it meant. Sounded good.

I hate to horn in on the fun, but be it ever so humble, there's no phrase like "hone in on."

Dear Mr. Safire:

One of the most difficult ideas to lodge into a college student's head is that the English language does not "come from" Latin or Greek, but from Anglo-Saxon. You do not give us teachers much help when you write that "the noun 'hone' comes from the Greek word for 'cone.' . . ." The noun "hone," as the OED *entry makes quite clear, was in use in English in the tenth century and couldn't possibly have come from the Greek. Were you perhaps misled by the* American Heritage Dictionary, *with its reference to a* ke- *root? But the root demonstrates that the English word is cognate with, not derived from, a Greek (or, as the case may be, Latin) word. In general, the relation of English to Greek (apart, of course, from deliberately borrowed words like "ecclesiastic" or "psychology" or "cybernetics") is not that of son to father, but of cousin to cousin. Both languages come from a common ancestor.*

Sincerely yours,
Carl Niemeyer
Union College
Schenectady, New York

horrors

"The advance-decline figures on the New York Stock Exchange are a horror show," declared a stockbroker on the day in early December that the exchange's composite index took its second-deepest plunge in history. He meant that few issues advanced compared to the number of issues that declined.

The brooding broker used an interesting phrase to mean "disaster." Although "chamber of horrors" has been taken from old wax museums and applied to any farrago of threats or list of good examples (Eric Partridge's pseudonymous "Vigilans" used that title for a book about jargon), the metaphoric extension of "horror show" is relatively recent.

Popularizer of the phrase was Anthony Burgess in his book and movie *A Clockwork Orange.* In that work of fiction, a band of futuristic goons terrorizing the populace used "horror show" as their term to mean "terrific" or otherwise to express cold-blooded jubilation. Novelist Burgess is also an eminent linguist: He was playing on the Russian word *horosho,* which means "OK." Thus, what was horrible—"a horror show"—was considered good. The irony was lost on the stockbroker.

how come?

Ian Bell of London's *Daily Telegraph* has rapped my knuckles for using the phrase "how come" in a recent column. He is not alone. "The chastisements of my fourth-grade teacher for the use of that phrase," writes Judith Feldman of New York, "are still vivid in my memory. After all these years, am I to learn that 'how come' is an acceptable substitute for 'why' after all?"

The phrase's provenance was first treated by John Bartlett in his 1848 *Dictionary of Americanisms:* "How-come? Rapidly pronounced huc-cum, in Virginia. Doubtless an English phrase, brought over by the original settlers, and propagated even among the Negro slaves. The meaning is, How did what you tell me happen? How came it?"

How did "how come" come to be? Ted Bernstein, in *The Careful Writer,* cited a parallel use in Shakespeare's "How chance the roses there do fade so fast?" But he condemned "how come" as "out of place in good writing."

Usagist Bergen Evans dismissed it as "used in speech but not in writing," and the *Harper Dictionary of Contemporary Usage* gives it a hard shove: "Acceptable as Informal idiom. It is not acceptable in Formal speech or writing."

How come? What do these usage authorities have against a perfectly good, deliciously archaic-sounding, widely used form of putting a question?

I like "how come." It belongs in formal writing when it conveys a skepticism or challenge not necessarily found in the word "why." You can ask, "Why?" in all innocence, but you put a slight edge of distrust in your voice or writing when you ask, "How come?" The distinction is valid. I would use "how come" to connote doubt, but would not use it as a substitute for a neutral, nonskeptical, trustingly inquiring "why."

"Why" is nice; "how come" is nastier. As for you, Miss Feldman, how come you use "after all" twice in one sentence?

Dear Mr. Safire:

Have you ever noticed that we use another, quite awkward substitute for "why"? The "what are you doing" query.

> *"What are you doing, tipping the waiter twenty-five percent?"*
>
> *"What are you doing, opening an umbrella indoors?"*

Sincerely,
Father Cronan Kelly, OFM
New York, New York

---

huffle-duffle, *see* good night, sweet roll

---

hustle, *see* hassle hustle

---

hype

"We live in a world of hyperbole," editor Samuel Vaughan of Doubleday told his book-publishing brethren recently, bemoaning the inflation of expectations caused by supersalesmen. "Hyperbole has become so common that we now refer to it by a cozy contraction. We call it 'hype.' We decide to apply it, as if it were a wax compound for shining up a car."

Here's how "hyperbole" came about: A little kid playing stickball in ancient Greece surprised his teammates by becoming a two-sewer hitter. This was *hyperballein,* from *hyper,* meaning "over" or "beyond," and *ballein,* meaning "throwing a ball." Combined, the two words meant "The kid hit the ball too far," and has come to mean "intended excess"—as in "That book is a blockbuster."

However, the notion that "hyperbole" gave birth to "hype" is folk etymology. "Hype" comes from "hypodermic needle," such as the one used by narcotics addicts; to be "high" was to be "hyped up." Billy Rose, in a 1950 newspaper column, carried that euphoria a step away from drug lingo in writing about a movie: "No fireworks, no fake suspense, no hyped-up glamour." It was a short leap from the compound adjective "hyped-up" to the noun "hype" and its most current compound noun, "media hype."

Curiously, both "hyperbole" and "hype" now mean "exaggeration"—the first intended, the second as a result of sensational attention. "Hyperbole" tries to fool nobody, as I've told you a thousand times—"There is a book with legs!" points to a book that figuratively walks out of the stores, not one that has real legs. But "hype" means "artificial, phony," as if in a dream induced by drugs.

To say that "hyperbole is as riveting as a page turner" is hyperbole; but to say that " 'hyperbole' is the root of hype" is pure hype.

Dear Mr. Safire:

I think you used just a little hype to let us know how "hyperbole" came about. Maybe those little kids played stickball in Greece, but when I played, which was in the Bronx some time ago, there never was a two-sewer hitter in our stickball league. We used a different measure.

The standard measure of distance in stickball was the pole, not the sewer. In Brooklyn, where they didn't know about stickball and played punchball instead, the sewer was the accepted measure, but in the Bronx, where stickball was the major sport, the distance between telephone poles was standard. The pole was the equivalent of a sewer and a half, and a two-sewer hitter would be popping up to the second baseman because second base was the sewer cover. "Two poles," or "three sewers," wasn't too much of a hit either.

Any decent stickball player could hit three poles, which was where the other fielder played (we had only two outfielders). Hell, we could throw two sewers.

Sincerely,
Harold Kocin
(A three-pole hitter)
Tiburon, California

if my aunt had wheels, she would be a teacart, *see* if wishes were horses

if wishes were horses

In a commentary on a primary election, Jack Germond wrote a paragraph that seemed to have an out-of-place sentence at the end:

"It is no secret that many of the moderate Republican leaders who have remained neutral would have been quick to line up with Gerald Ford if he had run, or with Senate minority leader Howard H. Baker if he had survived those early primaries." The paragraph concluded: "If my aunt had wheels, she would be a teacart." (In H. L. Mencken's *A New Dictionary of Quotations,* this is rendered as "If my aunt had wheels, she would be an omnibus," and is described as a German proverb. Others include an English proverb: "If my aunt had been a man, she'd have been my uncle." An American version: "If a frog had wings, he wouldn't bump his backside every time he jumps.")

Was that last sentence the work of a typo prankster, like the person on the *Boston Globe* who surreptitiously removed the headline "All Must Share the Burden" and replaced it with "Mush from the Wimp"?

No. According to the *Star*'s executive editor, Sid Epstein, Germond was dictating his copy by telephone. When he came to his speculation—a line with two "ifs"—he could not help mocking himself with an aside to the dictationist. The person taking it down did not realize Germond was commenting on his own commentary, and wrote down his delicious illustration of iffiness: "If my aunt had wheels, she would be a teacart."

Big Foot Germond probably wishes he had kept his thoughts to himself, but—in the seventeenth-century English predecessor to this construction—if wishes were horses, beggars would ride.

Dear Bill:

You were misinformed. It was not *a dictationist's error. I wrote it that way, on purpose. So sue me.*

Yrs. for accuracy in media,
Jack Germond
Washington Star
Washington, D.C.

Dear Mr. Safire,

The item concerning teacarts and omnibuses brought to mind an especially interesting variant. Perhaps a genuine bit of southern folk wisdom, it first came to my attention in the screen version of William Faulkner's The Sound and the Fury. *In that less than perfectly faithful adaptation, one character mocked another's wishful thinking by remarking, "If pigs had wings, they could fly to the moon." The necessity of an atmosphere for winged flight adds a dimension of scientific speciousness to the device, which depends primarily on a fantastic supposition.*

Students of linguistic phenomena might wish to trace the relationship between these perversions of the logicians' stock "If a, then b" construction and a genre of comic insults, viz., "If my mother-in-law lived in India, she'd be sacred."

Sincerely,
Martin Fridson
New York, New York

---

inconceivable conceptions

The exploration of olive sizes—medium is small; jumbo is fairly big; colossal is large— has led us to the nomenclature of tornadoes.

Tornadoes come in seven sizes and are classified by the Fujita-Pearson scale. Professor T. Theodore Fujita of the University of Chicago, who has done for scaling big storms what Richter has done for earthquakes, judges tornadoes by wind speed, path length, and width.

"Very weak" is the first size, with winds up to 72 miles per hour; snaps off TV antennas. Then "weak," up to 112 mph, overturning trailers. Next come "strong" tornadoes, which tear roofs off houses and blow autos off highways with winds up to 157 mph. "Severe" is the next category, up to 206 mph winds, uprooting trees and blowing down walls, followed by "devastating," up to 260 mph—this compares to "mammoth" in olive sizes—and then "incredible," up to 318 mph winds, carrying houses considerable distances. The final classification is named "inconceivable."

Since 1916, we have had 24,930 tornadoes, of which about 20,000 were in the first three categories, up to "strong." Only 127 tornadoes were "incredible," and we have yet to be afflicted with a single "inconceivable."

"I do not have a sophisticated command of the English language," says Professor Fujita modestly, "and the words I picked for tornadoes were words that seemed right."

Why was "incredible" selected? "Because very few people have seen an

F-5 tornado. For those who have witnessed such a tornado, the event is incredible. Incredible is not impossible, though it is sometimes difficult to believe."

And "inconceivable"? "We have had no report yet on an F-6. Nuclear power plants are required by law to protect against an F-6 tornado. The statistical probability of an F-6's occurring is once every ten million years—and that's in tornado country. I think of it as inconceivable."

Dear Mr. Safire:

I noticed the misuse of a semicolon in the following sentence: " 'Very weak' *is the first size, with winds up to 72 miles per hour; snaps off TV antennas." I'm sure you know that a semicolon is used to connect two complete sentences. The sentence following the semicolon needs a subject as well as a predicate. Thus, a corrected version could read: " 'Very weak' is the first size, with winds up to 72 miles per hour; these winds snap off TV antennas."*

As a college teacher of English to nonnative speakers (and writers), I have noticed that students hate to end sentences with periods; the finality of making the decision to end a sentence seems too much for them. Once the comma and semicolon are taught, students are quick to use these devices as a means of avoiding that decision, the result being the dreaded and omnipresent run-on.

Sincerely,
Susan Dicker
The English Language Center
LaGuardia Community College
New York, New York

---

indecent invasion

"Do you happen to know," inquires Leonard Boasberg of the editorial board of *The Philadelphia Inquirer*, "why politicians and editorial writers who use the word 'aggression' these days feel so compelled to clothe it with the adjective 'naked'?"

Good point; no reason exists for charges of nudity to be leveled at invaders in every instance. "This is an example of disheveled aggression," one might say of an incursion into Cambodia, or "Soviet tanks rolled into Afghanistan today in what diplomats called a case of fairly spiffy aggression."

When words get so close together that they seem lonely by themselves (what's "opposed" without "diametrically"?), it's time to split.

Another example of rampant journalese has been submitted by Robert De Mella of New York, whose teeth are set on edge whenever a television newscaster begins to lay his voice over films of protests with "In a scene reminiscent of the sixties ..." Mr. De Mella observes that "the 1960's were a miserable time for me, since my mother never permitted me to travel outside my neighborhood, to midtown Manhattan, or even to Central Park, for fear that my path would cross with an antiwar demonstration that would turn into a violent clash with the police with me in the middle of a melee. May the children of future generations never have to suffer from such a travel restriction."

Amen. And in a scene reminiscent of the eighties, Gilbert Cranberg, editor of the editorial page of the *Des Moines Register and Tribune*, writes: " 'Analyst' has all but replaced 'observer' as the source of information and knowledge. How did it happen and why?"

The word "observer"—from the term "Western observers"—meant, "I'm quoting myself here." Whenever a foreign editor saw a piece of copy that began "Western observers believe ...," he would take this as a signal that the reporter was staring at a blank wall and interviewing his thumb. In time, readers caught on; the word was torpedoed and sunk by my colleague in columny Russell Baker, who named his column after the invisible source.

"Analysis" (from the Greek "to loosen up") had a more activist sound than mere observation. Just as psychoanalysts loosened up patients, news analysts loosened up the strictures of news coverage, freeing news recipients from the confines of fact. Anyone who begins his answer with "I think" may be fairly cited, or "sourced," as an analyst. (I think, therefore I am an analyst.)

Finally, journalese has taken a flashing sign out of old radio studios and turned its message into an affirmation (what's "affirmation" without "ringing"?) of First Amendment rights, defiance of the insolence of office, and refusal to be pushed around: The locution "stand by," as in "*Newsweek* stands by its story," must now be the first phrase taught in journalism school.

What does it mean? Perhaps "The story, despite denials, is accurate," or "Get lost—I don't have to account to you or anybody," or "The story is well researched, and it may or may not be right, but we're sticking up for our right to print what we did, and our lawyer says we don't have to retract." The locution "standing by a story" is meant to be supportive, as the analysts say, but it is gaining a quality similar to "I shall not turn my back on Alger Hiss." If what is intended is "The story is true, and the denial is a lie," a new formulation is needed—perhaps a defiant "Sez you," which is action-packed but not actionable.

"In a scene reminiscent of the thirties, Aggression—clad only in a G-string—today told analysts she would stand by her story. ..."

Dear Mr. Safire:

Since you are a defender of the English word, I am amazed to find the sentence "Anyone who begins his answer with 'I think' may be fairly cited, or 'sourced,' *as an analyst." "*Sourced*" indeed! I happily source you as the originator of a new verb, presumably "to source," of which "sourced" is presumably the past passive participle. But I am a bit confused. My* Webster *gives the verb "source" as obsolete and calls it intransitive. Has Queen Marie Antoinette been correctly sourced for "Let 'em eat cake?" My-my. I suggest that what is source for the goose is source for the gander.*

Yours sincerely,
Winthrop Sargeant
Salisbury, Connecticut

---

indeed!, *see* wimp mush, indeed!

---

infamy

December 7 is "a day which will live in infamy." How come "infamy"? Franklin Roosevelt drafted that Pearl Harbor speech himself, without the help of speechwriters Samuel Rosenman or Robert Sherwood. The first draft's first sentence read: "Yesterday, December 7, 1941, a date which will live in world history, the United States was simultaneously and deliberately attacked by naval and air forces of the Empire of Japan."

In the second draft, FDR crossed out "world history" and substituted the word that made the speech especially memorable: "infamy." He also changed the too specific "simultaneously" to the more dramatic "suddenly."

This shows what a President with a flair for words can do to rouse and rally the people. It is a practice that some of us hope will be reinstituted.

---

in the loop, *see* ding!

---

is when

" 'Downhills,' " I explained recently, "is when dice are loaded to bring out a low, or down, number, and 'uphills' is when the dice are loaded to come out high."

Snake eyes and boxcars: I was right about the old slang, wrong in my syntax. J. B. Kritzer of West Orange, New Jersey, writes: "The complement clause following a copula must agree with the subject as to case; that is, it should be nominative, and each of your 'when' clauses is adverbial."

I think he means that "when" cannot be used to join a noun to a clause unless the idea of time is involved. It's a mistake to say, "Unemployment is when people are out of work"; it's right to say, "Midnight is when the wolves howl."

"Is when," used in a definition the wrong way, is childlike. A mature writer would write, " 'Downhills' refers to dice which are loaded. . . ." It's more a matter of style than grammar, and I'm not a child anymore. "A solecism is when you make a mistake in English" is the sort of thing a kid would say. A very smart kid.

Dear Bill:

A mature writer would not *write: " 'Downhills' refers to dice which are loaded. . . ." He or she would write: " 'Downhills' refers to dice that are loaded. . . ."*

Have you (too) given up on that/which?

Cordial regards,
Guy Henle
Executive Editor
Consumer Reports
Mount Vernon, New York

Dear Sir:

Mr. Kritzer . . . is only partly right in demanding agreement as to case between subject and predicate when joined by "is."

We need to recognize two intents in "is": a strong (definitive) or a weak (attributive) intent. Thus the "strong": Morning is the interval of time beginning at midnight and ending at noon. Thus the "weak": "Morning's at seven."

Mr. Kritzer's elegant stricture applies only to the strong case.

Yours truly,
T. E. Phipps
Urbana, Illinois

Dear Mr. Saphire,

The witches got to your final paragraph and made you write: " 'Downhills' which are loaded. . . ." Since the clause is essential to the meaning of the sentence, it calls for a "that."

A clause takes "that" if it carries clout,
But the which's clause you can do without.
(Maybe: witch's claws?)

If the clause is virtually in apposition, it takes a "which." And perhaps it's easier to remember from the "which" side:

If the clause can fit between two commas,
Use "which" and sleep in clean pajamas.

Cheers,
Arthur Kneerim
Stonington, Connecticut

Dear Mr. Safire:

Although I do not gamble, I'd like to take a chance and add something to the uphill-downhill matter. Both kinds of dice are what you say they are, but they are not what you say they are the way you say they are. Downhills are dice that are loaded to bring out a low number; uphills are dice that are loaded to bring out a high number. Or better yet, downhills are (refers to) dice loaded to bring out a low number, etc.

Followed by "which," uphills and downhills are simply dice. Followed by "that," they are what you say they are.

"Which" and "that" are an abused pair here in America. I fear we fought for our freedom from England for nothing.

Sincerely,
Sam Finnell
Linden, New Jersey

Dear Mr. Safire:

Once more into the breach.

My motive, believe me, is not to belabor the "is when" issue but rather to try to resolve what, to me, is a challenging academic point.

Since copulas can only link, or connect, parallel structures, the clause following the copula must be a noun clause used as a complement to the noun clause preceding the copula; therefore, "is when" can never be structurally acceptable, style aside. "Midnight is when the wolves howl . . ." is identical grammatically to "Unemployment is when people are out of work . . ." and is, consequently, equally unacceptable. "Unemployment is a period when . . ." and "Midnight is that hour when . . ." would solve the problem nicely.

Sincerely,
J. B. Kritzer
West Orange, New Jersey

Dear Mr. Safire:

You've done it again! In the final paragraph of your piece, you make the amazing claim " 'Is when,' used in a definition the wrong way, is childlike."

Please check the definition of "childlike." Most dictionaries go to great pains to point out that "childlike" carries the connotation of "innocent, trusting, possessing the favorable qualities of a child." The appropriate word for the meaning that I think you were trying to convey is "childish."

Sincerely,
Paul A. Berchielli
Rocky Hill, Connecticut

P.S.: Your mistake is becoming a common one.

P.P.S.: Why do I have this queasy feeling that I have just fallen into some kind of trap?

---

it was me, *see* me Jane

-ive, *see* ives have it

---

ives have it

The first itch that signaled a rash of usage came with the popularity of "supportive." In the late 1960's this adjectival form of the noun and verb "support" was seized by psychiatrists, with whom it soon became an obsession: The near opposite of the ever-popular "hostile" became "supportive," which sounded firmer than "friendly." Today "supportive" is used by language trendies to denote any kind of behavior that does not include a gratuitous kick in the teeth.

The next symptom appeared with the change in meaning of "assertive." Most dictionaries defined the word to mean "confident in spite of lack of proof," but I recall a clear whiff of pejoration—"assertive" meant "uppity, pushy," and was directed at people who insolently demanded their rights. Today the word's coloration has changed, and I find myself using "assertive" to mean "praiseworthy and forthright." In a piece attributing that quality to Rosalynn Carter, Nancy Reagan, and Keke Anderson, I used "assertive" too often—proof that the word's changed emphasis had sunk in like a harpoon.

The third symptom—supportive of the early diagnosis and assertive to the point of narrowed-lapel grabbing—came with the announcement of the failed rescue mission in Iran. The word almost universally used by newsmen to describe the mission was "abortive." An alert reader noticed. "I expect correct usage from the reporters and commentators of our electronic media," complained Daniel Ekstein of New City, New York. "About half of the above reported on our 'abortive' attempt to rescue the hostages. My plans for extended listening were aborted."

Of course—the raid was not an "abortive" mission; it was an "aborted" mission. The suffix *ive* implies "continuing" or "permanent"—we all know how hard it is to shake loose from supportive friends—and to attribute continuation to a specific abortion is an absurdity. "Abortive efforts" should be used only when the emphasis is on a series of past failures. An "abortive mission" is one whose abrupt and early termination was planned all along, a charge that not even conspiracy theorists are prepared to make. "Abortive" was used widely because it rhymed with "supportive," not because the speakers wanted to suggest a continuous process of aborting.

What we have here is an outbreak of *ives.* About 2,000 words end in *ive,* four-fifths of them *tive,* and more are being minted every day. For an explanation of this phenomenon, I turned to my favorite suffix man, Sol Steinmetz, editor of the new and valuable *Second Barnhart Dictionary of New English.*

"Unlike the synonymous adjective ending *ing,*" opined this lexicographer, "the suffix *ive* implies a permanent or habitual quality (compare coercive/coercing, suppressive/suppressing, procreative/procreating, etc.), which makes it very attractive (not attracting) to writers who wish to sound definitive or conclusive."

The careful reader will note that Mr. Steinmetz studded his explanation with *ives.* "The suffix *ive* is one of the most productive formatives in English, especially in technical language. ... You can add it to innumerable nouns just by replacing *ion* with *ive.*" Why the outbreak? "The influence of particular *ive* words that have seeped into common usage from the social sciences," he suggests. "Words like 'alternative' (as in alternative press, life-style), 'assertive' (now used in approbative rather than pejorative sense), 'permissive,' 'addictive,' 'evaluative' ..."

"Executive privilege" confirms the identification of an *ives* outbreak. When "executive" was used mainly as a noun, as in "chief executive," the word behaved itself; however, with the onset of the *ives* epidemic, trendies made an executive decision to latch on to "executive jet," "executive summary" (for big shots too busy to read details), "executive lunch," and the latest—"executive-length socks."

Speakers who scorn form prefer "substantive" to the stylish "of substance." In derogating the departed Secretary of State Vance, President Carter called Mr. Muskie "a more evocative spokesman." People afflicted with *ives* have been known to add unnecessary syllables to the root word (or root causative). Doctors used to talk about "preventive medicine"; recently—*ta-dah!*—an extra *ta* has appeared in that *ive,* and the word has stretched itself out to "preventative."

Dr. John S. Marr, assistant commissioner for preventable diseases at New York City's Department of Health, condemns this added *ta* as "another example of adding extra fat to a common word, making it sound more important." He has a cure: "Whenever someone uses 'preventative,' I counter with 'preventatative.' " (An ounce of preventive beats a pound of preventatative.)

Who was the first to latch on to the commercial potential in *ives*? Estée Lauder is one of those cosmetics houses attuned to the revolution in makeup motivation: Today's woman seeks assurance that taking care of her skin is really part of taking care of her health. Needed: a medical "feeling" to advertising copy. The most effective word—"prescription"—is too close to what a doctor prescribes, so the copywriter came up with the *ive* solution: "Lauder Prescriptives is the first broad-spectrum leap in skin care in a decade. Talk to the Prescriptives expert."

If you need confidence before making that broad-spectrum leap, talk to your supportives expert. He may suggest a preventative preemptive strike.

Dear Mr. Safire:

If the medical profession has been using the word "preventative" instead of "preventive," it is because the distinction between adjectives and nouns has become blurred.

I will give you a vitamin C capsule as a hoped-for preventative against the common cold. I will be practicing what I conceive to be preventive medicine.

Yours sincerely,
John L. Meyer II, M.D.
Woodstock, Connecticut

Dear Mr. Safire:

Your recent discussion of whether our recent mission to Iran was aborted or abortive reminded me of what surprised me most about that usage: There was a time when that word wasn't used in polite society at all.

Yours,
Stephanie de Pue
Brooklyn Heights, New York

Dear Mr. Safire:

My copy of Webster's New International Dictionary of the English Language, *second edition, gives the following definition for the word "abortive":*

> *3. Coming to naught; failing in its effect; miscarrying; fruitless; unsuccessful; as, an abortive enterprise.*

"Fruitless" and "unsuccessful" do seem to be appropriate descriptions of the mission to rescue the hostages in Teheran.

Nor is this usage neology. The date on the title page of my Webster's *is 1947.*

Sincerely yours,
Richard P. Hunt
NBC News
New York, New York

Dear Mr. Safire:

The substitution of "preventative" for "preventive" goes back at least twenty-seven years. When I was drafted into the army in 1953, that usage had currency among the military. Another common military substitution was "orientate" for "orient," as in training films to orientate the troops in the proper use of rifles.

Sincerely,
Richard Frank
Editor
National Journal
Washington, D.C.

Dear Mr. Safire:

I disagree with your disapproval of "preventative." You—and you are not alone—seem to believe that "preventative" is a pointless, and recent, stretching of "preventive."

Not so, even if Theodore M. Bernstein, in The Careful Writer, *did say, "Most authorities agree that the form* preventive *is preferable."*

To be objective, I think that all you objectors are missing the point. "Preventative" and "preventive" are two different words, and their difference, which is of long standing, serves a purpose. "Preventive" is an adjective; "preventative" is a noun. Thus, "preventive medicine" is the study and practice of the averting of disease. A "preventative" is a procedure or agent that averts disease, such as a vaccine—or, presumably, a procedure or agent that averts anything else, such as the erosion of our language.

Best wishes,
Albert Kreindler
The Bronx, New York

---

jackleg, *see* getting down

---

kangaroos and clothespins

"A couple of kangaroo tickets will lead to a big clothespin vote."

That sage, if obscure, observation was made to me by a liberal friend who was disappointed in the choice before him in the presidential campaign. It illustrates the richness of our political vocabulary.

A "kangaroo ticket" is one that is stronger in the second spot than in the first. A kangaroo—a leaping marsupial— is known for its powerful rump. A "rump convention" in 1888 was called a "kangaroo convention," and in 1932 supporters of John Nance Garner thought so highly of their man, and so little of Franklin Roosevelt, that they called the FDR-Garner team a "kangaroo ticket."

Since then, whenever a ticket's hindquarters are considered stronger than its forequarters, the "kangaroo ticket" phrase comes bounding out. In this case, my liberal friend thought Walter Mondale was more appealing than Jimmy Carter, and George Bush more appealing than Ronald Reagan.

A "clothespin vote" is nowhere to be found in the political dictionaries, including my own. To a generation equipped with electric dryers, it is necessary to explain first that a clothespin is a wooden peg or clamp which is used to fasten clothes on a line. In cartoons early in the century, a clothespin was affixed to a person's nose to illustrate his desire to dissociate himself from his surroundings. It was a form of holding your nose.

Thus, a "clothespin vote" is one made by a voter with an extreme lack of enthusiasm. It follows, as my liberal friend said, that a couple of kangaroo tickets may lead to a big clothespin vote.

Kissingerese, *see* nonstarter

see nonstarter

language lib

The counterreaction is upon us. For nearly two decades, ever since *Webster's Third International Dictionary* refused to put a "substandard" label on all forms of "ain't," language lovers have been up in alarums.

This antisloppiness brigade—which should dub itself "the prolanguage lobby"—has inveighed against the lowering of standard English and flayed the cliché users and jargoneers abusing our tongue. English teachers organized; television's Edwin Newman sold millions of books excoriating the hopeless "hopefullys"; theater critic John Simon became the paragon of prescriptivists; and even in this space, better-than-common usage and "correct English" found a friend.

The tide appeared to be turning; as Americans yearned for the old standards and values, both the politics of language and the language of politics became more conservative. As a literate public became happily aroused, permissivism became a dirty word. "Anything goes" no longer went.

Now the good-grammar set's honeymoon is over. In a counterattack reminiscent of Rundstedt's lunge in the winter of 1944, the linguistic permissivists have appeared with their no-standards standards flying. Two books lead the way:

In *American Tongue and Cheek: A Populist Guide to Our Language,* Jim Quinn, a poet and food columnist, embraces the kind of language that would have taken over if downtroddenism had triumphed. "All language is poetry," he argues, and no rules should exist. "The slang of the poor, the new technical terms and jargon of the professionals, the cant of journalism, the simplistic language notions of pop grammarians—all keep language from going stale."

With obvious zest (and incongruently, for him, in precise prose), Quinn shows how the greatest writers made what some of us call mistakes in English: Shakespeare wrote "between you and I" in *The Merchant of Venice,* and Dickens wrote "nobody will miss her *like* I do" in a letter, much as the like-a-cigarette-should copywriter suggested. Who do these pop grammarians think they are, Quinn demands, to put their artificial rules ahead of the usage of great writers—as well as the common use of most other people? (I well remember Pops Grammarian, the great Armenian jazz trumpeter.)

Populist Quinn says he is in favor of "true conservatives," by which he means "people who still say 'icebox.' ... A conservative almost never corrects others, however. For example, your aunt who still says 'icebox' does not have a sign on her door that says, 'The word fridge must not be used in this house. Violators will be humiliated.' " Quinn asserts that he can "never bring myself to say 'film' for 'movie.' "

Despite this engaging proclivity for the old-fashioned, this antipop grammarian—or populist antigrammarian—flays the "Yahoo Right," who "publish interminable death of English despairs and private lists of language peeves. Professional busybodies and righters of imaginary wrongs, they are the Sunday visitors of language, dropping in weekly on the local poor to make sure that everything is up to their own idea of Standard...."

That shoe fits me. Mr. Quinn cultivates the garden of controversy with great glee: He is deliberately and delightfully outrageous, and as refreshing as a swift kick in the teeth. May his diatribe increase.

The heavy artillery of the permissivist counterattack is Dwight Bolinger, author of *Language: The Loaded Weapon.* The triggerman of this slim but explosive volume is described on the cover as "formerly professor of Romance languages and literatures at Harvard University, where he is now emeritus professor." (That seems to mean he teaches a course in emeritus. But I shouldn't snipe at blurb writers: On the flap copy of my own book on language, the word "pretension"—of all words—is misspelled "pretention," and too many fellow nitpickers have called my attension to it.)

"In language there are no licensed practitioners," writes Professor Bolinger, "but the woods are full of midwives, herbalists, colonic irrigationists, bonesetters and general-purpose witch doctors, some abysmally ignorant, others with a rich fund of practical knowledge—whom we shall lump together and call *shamans.*"

Most of these language shamans (from the Sanskrit word for "ascetic"), says Bolinger, "are as uninformed about linguistic structure as their herbal counterparts are about anatomy and physiology." These seeming experts search for the particular errors—inept choice of words, arch genteelisms, marshmallow pomposities, dangling clauses—and try to offer social salvation by providing a list of do's and don't's, as if language were a matter of etiquette. In so doing, argues the scientific linguist with the indisputable credentials, the shamans (or pop grammarians) miss the Big Picture of language change and development.

Take the misplaced "only," a frequent target of incantations and incense burning in this space. "He only died a week ago" is wrong, say I; it should be "He died only a week ago." But Professor Bolinger argues that this overlooks intonation: " 'He only died a *week* ago' leaves no doubt that only goes primarily with week," he points out. "The language is more subtle even than that—by giving freedom of movement to only, it enables the word to do double duty . . . the sentence *I only want orange juice* not only limits the choice to orange juice but tones down the demand—'this is the extent of my want.' . . ."

Bolinger's trouble is that he knows too much. I do not pretend to be in his linguistic league, but if a cat can look at a king, a colonic irrigationist can look at a brain surgeon. It seems to me that in waltzing around with the nuances, Professor Bolinger is losing sight of the trouble caused by a confusing order of words. Note that he writes, "The language is more subtle even than that," which is correct, and not, "The language is even more subtle than that," which is what most of us would have mistakenly written. He excuses error but does not fall into it, and his avoidance of solecism shouts out that correctness is alive and well and important.

"The editor who threatens his reporters with extinction if they insist on writing transpire for happen," writes the professor, ". . . is doing what he is paid to do. The harm comes in promoting local preferences into a universal code of ethics." Calling standard English a "local preference" is what bugs grammarians about linguists, and Professor Bolinger—an admirable fellow seeking to build a bridge between shamans and scientific linguists—is sensitive enough to realize that the linguists run a certain risk in insisting that "He doesn't know any better" ain't no better than "He don't know no better."

"The linguist, as far as the shaman-educator is concerned," admits Bolinger, "is a person for whom 'anything goes,' who has influenced the makers of dictionaries to adopt their policy of 'open admissions' and coaxed the Government, with his pretense of being scientific, into spending millions on revisions in language-arts teaching that have led to lower and lower rates of literacy." The professor thinks such an impression is all wrong, but he states the case against the permissivist with a force that old Pops Grammarian would envy.

There you have the opening salvo against us reactionaries of pop grammar—a poet and a professor, the first seeking a confrontation and the second a synthesis—and I hope their work is spread-eagled over television talk shows. Each will be offered this space on a week when I take a vacation (or "go on holiday," or "take off"). For too long, we in the offended-at-bad-usage crowd have had the field to ourselves. Read the Quinn and Bolinger books; both authors write well. We would do well to write the way they write—but not to write the way they tell us it's alright to write.

Dear Bill:

I was very glad to see your review of Bolinger's recent book (Bolinger is an incredible resource who has been underutilized outside of the linguistic profession) and also to read that he will do a column for you during your vacation. I think, though, that when you speak of Quinn and Bolinger both as "permissivists," you are obscuring a distinction comparable to that between a pantheist and an atheist. Bolinger doesn't see beauty and divinity in everything that has vowels and suffixes the way that Quinn does; his position isn't that "anything goes" but that it is irresponsible to make judgments about expressions and constructions unless one has a solid understanding of how they function, what the alternatives to them are, and what the implications are of the value system on which one bases one's prescriptions. Bolinger's attitude towards prescriptive grammarians is in fact quite parallel to Jane Jacobs' attitude towards city planners (in her Death and Life of Great American Cities *and* The Economy of Cities*); in both cases, the author regards the enterprise as worthwhile but is appalled at the general myopia and narcissism of its practitioners.*

With best wishes,
Jim McCawley
Department of Linguistics
University of Chicago
Chicago, Illinois

Dear Mr. Safire:

You make the mistake of deriving the word "shaman" from the Sanskrit term for "an ascetic." In fact, "shaman" comes from the language of the Tungus, an aboriginal reindeer-herding people of Siberia. It refers to "witch-doctors," healers, and diviners whose special powers arise from their contacts with spirits. Similar practitioners are found in many other societies, and anthropologists have extended the Tungus word to include them. Similar borrowings from native languages include "totem" (from Ojibwa, an Algonquian language of the Great Lakes region) and "taboo" (from Polynesian). Back in the 1920's, a few linguists argued that the Tungus word could itself be a borrowing from Sanskrit "sramana"; this suggestion has not been widely accepted.

SHAMAN YOU! Do a little more research in the future.

Sincerely yours,
Stuart J. Fiedel
Assistant Professor, Anthropology
SUNY at Purchase

let justice be done

When the two top executives at the First National Bank of Chicago became locked in a power struggle not long ago, the board of directors threw both men out. A former colleague was quoted in *The New York Times* as crowing: "I don't know of anybody who better deserves this kind of just dessert."

Professor Cynthia Dessen of the University of North Carolina at Chapel Hill, who teaches a course on word formation, circles that spelling and writes: "It is time to do a piece on deserts vs. dessert vs. desert.... Confusion reigns in the public mind."

When you toss your assault rifle in the air and head for the hills, you "desert," and the verb is pronounced "di-ZERT." When you commit this act in a sandy spot a long way from an oasis, you are in a "desert," a noun pronounced "DEZ-ert." What you eat at the end of a meal is a "dessert," a noun pronounced "di-ZURT," nearly the same as the aforementioned verb.

Now here comes the tricky bit: When you get your comeuppance—as when a deserting soldier eats too much dessert in the desert and gets sick—you get your just "desert." That is pronounced "di-ZERT," exactly the same as the verb for "quit" and nearly the same as the noun for "fruit and cheese after a pleasant repast."

Why one *s*? In French, the verb *desservir* means "to clear the table"—the opposite of *servir,* "to set the table" or "to serve a meal." From that verb with the double *s* comes "dessert," the course that is served after the table is cleared.

A different French verb, with one *s*—*déserter,* "to withdraw"—is the root of the English verb "to desert." And a third, quite different verb with one *s*—the ancient *deservir,* "to deserve"—is the root of "desert," the noun for "deserved reward or punishment."

Thus, the deserter in the desert who became nauseated after eating dessert got his just desert.

---

listen up, *see* upmanship

---

list to this

"List"—a friendly word, as in "shopping list"—has been acquiring a pejorative connotation.

The word started out as the German term for "edge" or "border," soon became associated with a long, narrow slip of paper, and finally took on the meaning of a series of items written on such a slip.

However, the Mafia grabbed the word by the throat and used it in "hit list"—an enumeration of those marked for "hits," or murders—based on an obscene phrase with which it rhymed.

Politics took up "hit list" as a useful phrase to mean any group of officeholders destined to be replaced by the faithful after an election. "... a so-called 'hit list' of incumbent U.S. Ambassadors in sensitive places (notably Central America) was leaked," wroth-waxed a *Washington Star* editorial. "The compilation and circulation of this prejudicial list was [*sic*] an unbelievable exercise in cheap vindictiveness."

At the same time, columnist Henry Brandon was extending the pejoration of "list" in a piece about methods used to discourage the Russians from invading Poland: "... on the theory that deterrence might be weakened if they were presented with a Western threat list."

The setting down of a list now implies a threat: "I've got a little list" has had ominous overtones ever since Gilbert and Sullivan used that phrase in *The Mikado*. An "enemies list"—John Dean's term for what Charles Colson called "an opponents list"—sent a chill through the body politic.

About the only lists left that anyone would want to be on are "the Queen's honors list" and the "short list" of candidates for appointment. For those who wish to avoid listing toward lists, a neutral term is available—"inventory"—and an honorable connotation is given a set of names with "roll."

An itemization of subjects can be called a "checklist," which is not as sinister as most other lists and sells under list price. The same list can be called an "agenda," but that sounds vaguely liberal; agendas are on the list this year.

Dear Mr. Safire:

In your discussion of the word "list," you say the Mafia used the word in the expression "hit list . . . based on an obscene phrase with which it rhymed."

Don't you mean "scatological," rather than "obscene"?

True, "obscene" can mean (according to Webster's Third New International Dictionary*) disgusting to the senses, filthy, grotesque, grossly repugnant to what are generally accepted notions of propriety, etc., and I suppose a reference to ordure, as in the phrase with which "hit list" rhymes, could be considered disgusting, filthy, grossly repugnant, etc.; however, the phrase is more scatological than obscene.*

Webster's second *preferred definition of "obscene" gives the more popular understanding of that word, as abhorrent to morality or virtue, stressing, or reveling in, the lewd or lustful, and inviting or designed to incite lust, depravity, or indecency, and in its definition of "scatological" (of or pertaining to the study of excrement) quotes as an example "the [scatological] rather than the sexual element prevailed." Implicit in this example, I think, is the proposition that had the sexual rather than the scatological element prevailed, the author might have said "the obscene rather than the scatological element prevailed."*

Very truly yours,
Francis G. Weller
New Orleans, Louisiana

Dear Mr. Safire:

Your discussion brings to mind that "list" is nowadays neglected by pre-election speakers in favor of "litany," as in "a litany of reform, complaints, proposals, etc."

Cordially,
Joseph F. Gelband
New York, New York

Mr. Safire—

I fear you will miss not having been on the Dean's List—

Best,
Gene Raskin
New York, New York

---

living in synonymy

Synonymy is the delicious business of splitting verbal hairs. In the world of irritability, what's the difference between "peevish," "snappish," and "waspish"? Plenty: "Peevish" brings to mind a cranky child making petty complaints; one who is "snappish" is more adult, making nasty comments or asking cutting questions, and "waspish" implies the ability to sting someone who does not deserve to be hurt. (The word is not intended to be an ethnic slur of white Anglo-Saxon Protestants, though it is now sometimes taken that way.)

If this sort of sorting out of meanings leaves you out of sorts—testy, petulant, huffy, or fretful—synonymy is not for you. But if you delight in making the fine distinctions, join the fun at the Justice Department over the word "discussion."

When asked, "Did you . . . ever talk to the President [on the Billy Carter case]?" Attorney General Benjamin Civiletti replied, "No." Soon after President Carter recalled a talk between them on this subject, the attorney general explained that it had been "an informal, brief exchange." He later told the Senate: "I drew the distinction between a substantive discussion about the conduct of an investigation and the brief conversation I had. . . ."

In the meantime, Billy Carter was asked if he had any discussions with his brother about Libya, and replied, "It wasn't a discussion; it was just a talk."

What's the difference between a "conversation," a "talk," "discussion," and an "exchange"? Throw in one more: In testimony, the attorney general said about a conversation between two aides: "They had a dialogue about it."

The common denominator in these terms is the idea of more than one person speaking. To differentiate, think about purpose or intensity: A "conversation" is neutral, low-key, two or more people chewing the fat, shooting the breeze, or passing the time of day; it sometimes develops into "an intelligent conversation." A "talk" is no longer aimless or meandering; thanks to "I'll have a little talk with him," the primary meaning of the noun "talk" is now a lecture or an admonition. (Billy Carter's "just a talk" is acceptable as dialect, of course, but is not in the mainstream of meaning.)

Add a pinch of earnestness by each participant and you have a "discussion." More seriousness is implied by this word than mere conversation: In a discussion, sober-sided consideration is given a subject, often paving the way for a decision. A discussion's intensity is well short of an "argument," and not as far-reaching as a "dispute."

An "exchange" connotes an exchange of fire, a short and fierce give-and-take: *Webster's Third* defines it as "a usually brief and often heated, acrid, or witty dialogue." Mr. Civiletti did not intend to suggest his conversation with the President was either caustic or cause for thigh-slapping, but his use of "exchange" to connote brevity was correct.

Finally, "dialogue" is a word that used to conjure a picture of characters in a play. In 1952 Adlai Stevenson called for "a national dialogue," and the term has since become a worn-out vogue word used to add pretension to a discussion. When modified by "meaningful," dialogue becomes meaningless.

The embattled (not yet besieged) attorney general, recognizing the attention to synonymy given his words, answered a question from Senator Richard Lugar of Indiana in this inclusive way: "No, I haven't had a discussion, a conversation, or an exchange about that."

That flash of humor showed he was not even touchy, when others would have been testy, cross, nettled, splenetic, or even choleric.

Dear Mr. Safire:

This letter (written on a postcard) is an admonishment concerning your column "Living in Synonymy." I, the admonisher, admonish you with the admonition to look (in the dictionary) before you leap (into the sea of synonymous synonyms). The "talk" you refer to in your article is better termed "admonishment"; the "admonition" is the core of the talk, or admonishment. If the admonishment consisted of the admonition only, it is highly unlikely to be an effective talk—to wit, this letter.

Bob Lehr
New York, New York

"... slur of"?
Surely this should be slur on, *Mr. Safire?!?*

Very truly yours,
Sylvia R. Freedland
Elkins Park, Pennsylvania

Dear Mr. Safire,

That dialogue-discussion-exchange business has some interesting equivalents in Spanish. For example, when two or more Spaniards are talking to each other at the same time and in increasingly louder tones, with the result that nobody is really paying attention to the others, it's called a diálogo de sordos—*"a dialogue of the deaf." It's extremely common here and, as you say, an excellent political term.*

Discutir *does not mean "to discuss," but almost always means "to argue about something," and a* discusión *is an argument. When two Spaniards are "discussing," with shouts and even insults, observers sometimes cynically call it a* cambio de impresiones, *an "exchange of impressions." When push comes to shove, it's a* contraste de pareceres, *a "contrast of points of view."*

With best regards,
William B. Lyon
Madrid, Spain

---

loyal apposition

The New York Times refuses to bow to "bogus titling." Says *The Times Manual of Style and Usage:* "Only genuine titles—not mere descriptions, whether lowercase or capitalized—should be affixed to names. Do not, for example, write *harpsichordist Joan Manley.* ... But a phrase in apposition, preceded by *the,* is acceptable: *the sociologist Margaret Manley.*"

To that dictum, I say, "Yes, but." Certainly we should avoid what Wallace Carroll, former editor of the Winston-Salem *Journal and Sentinel,* called "Morkrumbo," the language of the Morkrum printer, which chattered, "Former North Carolina State University's head basketball coach Everett Case today declared ..." And good writers wince at "Consumer Advocate Ralph Nader" (as if he were elected to that post) or "Fugitive Financier Robert Vesco" (I prefer "Robert Vesco, the renegade richie ...").

But. The titling style popularized by *Time* magazine—"cinemoppet Shirley Temple," "adman Ed Meyer," "pundit Walter Lippmann"—can be short, sweet, and graceful, provided the identification remains a single word. A one-word description before a name will gain acceptance: "Linebacker Monte Coleman" sounds better, to my ear, than the stilted "Monte Coleman, the linebacker." So says columnist Safire, the language maven.

Dear Mr. Safire,

The discussion in your column of phrases like "harpsichordist Joan Manley" has resulted in a postponement of my reading the rest of today's Times *while I ponder that momentous issue (first things first, after all).*

My feeling is that the common noun in those expressions has a very different function from true titles (as in "Captain John Smith"*): The title is used out of deference to the person referred to (you'd be being impolite to him if you omitted the title), whereas the common noun serves to inform readers who may well lack the information that the noun carries. (And there's a difference between "linebacker Monte Coleman" and "Monte Coleman, the linebacker": The one provides information for people who don't know who Monte Coleman is;* the latter provides information for people who may know two Monte Colemans but don't know which one is being referred to). *The frequency with which such expressions turn up in* Time *may reflect the breadth of* Time*'s circulation: The more people it reaches, the more likely that some of them don't know who Walter Lippmann is and thus the more likely that some of them would need the minimal introduction to Lippmann that is provided by the phrase "pundit Walter Lippmann." (If I ever have a copy of* Time *and a couple of hours and nothing better to do with my time and* Time, *I might try counting the occurrences of these phrases: I conjecture that the "common noun + proper name" combination would be extremely common as a first mention of the person but fairly uncommon in subsequent references to him; titles, on the other hand, are retained in later references to the person, e.g., you would refer back to Captain Smith [with obligatory omission of the first name] but not to linebacker Coleman).*

The example of "Morkrumbo" that you quote sounds horrible for an extraneous reason—namely, the genitive ending in something that follows "former": "Former North Carolina State University's *head basketball coach Everett Case. . . ." "Former" can only modify a noun (even a highly complex compound noun) but cannot modify what is technically a* noun phrase *such as a genitive + noun combination. Without the* 's, *what follows "former" ("North Carolina State University head basketball coach") would be a compound noun, and thus, "former" would be in the "adjective + noun" structure that it demands. Actually, the quotation as you give it suggests an alternative interpretation—namely, that in which "former" modifies "North Carolina State University" (i.e., Everett Case is currently head basketball coach at an institution that used to be North Carolina State University but now has a new name).*

*By the way, was it you or the typesetter that was responsible for the capitalization in "*Consumer Advocate *Ralph Nader" and "*Fugitive Financier *Robert Vesco"? Here the typography and not the syntax is responsible for the suggestion that the modifier is a title.*

With best wishes,
James D. McCawley
Department of Linguistics
University of Chicago
Chicago, Illinois

Dear Mr. Safire:

I heartily share your scorn at The Times*'s aversion to "bogus titling." Why not point out, too, how illogical and silly some of the paper's alternatives sound?*

"Joan Manley, the harpsichordist," suggests that she's either the only harpsichordist in the world (false) or the only one illustrious enough to be worth mentioning (grossly unfair to the others). "Joan Manley, a harpsichordist," on the other hand, would imply that she's a virtually unknown member of an undistinguished multitude (grossly unfair to her). "Harpsichordist Joan Manley" avoids both pitfalls. It identifies her for those who don't recognize her name without any taint of either sycophancy or disparagement.

Stubborn loyalty to the "phrase in apposition" can produce some ludicrous results: "Herman Zilch, the clothing manufacturer," "Joe Zilch, the pickpocket," "Sabrina Zilch, the secretary," etc.

Sincerely,
Susan M. Seidman
East Hampton, New York

man the pumps!

"Are all women's shoes 'pumps,'" asks N.S. Leibowitz of New York, "or only certain types? (I mean certain types of shoes, not certain types of women.)"

A pump is a low shoe without a fastening; it grips the foot at the toe and heel, and the wearer does not have to fiddle with a buckle. Originally a pump was a shoe worn by a dancer, acrobat, duelist, or anybody with a need for a light foot covering that could be put on or taken off without the use of the hands.

That's the easy part; now the mystery. For a time, linguists thought the word might be rooted in the German *Pumpstiefel* and *Pumphosen,* stockings so named because of their tubular, pipelike legs, but that theory has gone down the tube. Others have suggested a relation to "pomp" or "show," but no proof has been offered to connect pump and circumstance.

"It may have been an echoic word," speculates the *Oxford English Dictionary,* straining, "suggested by the dull flapping sound made by slippers as distinct from the stomp of heavy shoes." I do not go for that; to my ears, the sound of slippers is "clop," and I have a nice pair of clops to go with my bathrobe.

"Pump," spelled *poumpe, pompe,* and *pumpe,* is traced to 1555: "Their shoes are not fastened on with Lachettes, but Lyke a poumpe close about the foote." That's four centuries in fashion use, and nobody's been able to figure out the origin. If anybody has the answer, step on it.

Dear Sir:

From personal experience (residence in London for four years in the early 1970's), I can tell you that the kind of shoe that American (and Canadian) women call a "pump" is called a "court shoe" in England. I never encountered any shoe salesman or saleswoman in any London store (from the Harrods level on down) who knew what I meant when I asked for a pump. I soon learned to use the English term and was rewarded by being shown the style I desired. My English lady friends were similarly ignorant of the American term, although possibly they have become familiar with it by now. (I suspect *that "pump" in England refers traditionally only to the slip-on shoe that is worn with formal attire by men.)*

Sincerely,
Heather L. Taylor
Chicago, Illinois

---

mattress-ese: never say soft

When gang wars erupt, members of the mob are said to "go to the mattresses"—to hole up in abandoned lofts, with mattresses on the floor. But whether the mattresses are used in a gangland hideout or a woman's boudoir, this question arises: What adjective can be used to describe the most important quality of a mattress?

"Most people use the word 'firm,' " confides Roy Unger, vice-president of Sealy Posturepedic mattresses, "but 'firm' means different things to different people. There's a lack of vocabulary to describe the idea of firmness."

What about a word like "soft"?

"We shy away from 'soft,' " says the Sealy man. "A person who says he wants a soft mattress wants it to feel soft, but at the same time wants firm support. We made a decision here—there are no gradations of firmness. All our mattresses have deep-down support. The difference is in the comfort level—meaning the levels of upholstery and the ingredients in the quilt and the cover."

What about a word like "hard"?

"Some people like a taut surface, so we offer a choice in comfort levels—'Extra Firm Comfort,' and 'Gently Firm Comfort.' Both are firm, but one is more firm."

Another manufacturer, Stearns & Foster, advertises this range: "Firm! Deluxe extra firm! Super firm! Ultra firm!"

Yet another mattress company, Simmons U.S.A., bounces away from the word "firm." Its Beautyrest models are named Exquisite, Elite, Back Care, and Super. Only one model admits the forbidden word: Super comes both "extra firm" and "luxury firm." The latter is—I almost said "softer"—less firm.

What would be closest to sleeping on a marble floor?

"Back Care is our firmest model," says Leonard Gaby, vice president for merchandising at Simmons. "The difference in firmness is achieved by the gauge of wire in the coils, and we use the heaviest gauge in the Back Care model. We use the most luxurious cover on the Exquisite model."

Are tastes in mattresses tending toward hard or soft?

"Usually the customer is looking for firmness," says Mr. Gaby, "with a growing trend toward comfort."

Since "hard" is a hard word, and "soft" is for sissies, what's a poor sleep-set manufacturer (formerly bed maker) to do? "Solid" is misleading, and "unyielding" won't sell. That leaves only the pliant "firm," with adjectives like "super" and "ultra" denoting degrees of hardness, and "comfort" used as a euphemism for the dreaded "soft." And, as diarist Samuel Pepys used to say, so to bed.

Dear Sir:

Re your article on bedding, I must be superfirm with you. The former name for a sleep-set manufacturer was "mattress-maker," pronounced MAT-RISS MA-KER. A bed maker—a person who makes the bed—is a chambermaid et al.

Having gotten this off my aching back, I can now rest in comfort.

Sid Cohen
Amagansett, New York

mediquack: listening to what the doctor says

"The tern buffed up the gomer, who had the dwindles and figured he would have a bounceback," said a doctor to a nurse, "but the player flatlined from fascinoma, and we all hit the fluids and electrolytes."

In the inside lingo of the medical profession, a "tern" is an intern; "to buff up" means to prepare a patient for discharge ("The Sultan of Frogmore needs that bed; buff this guy up and send him home."); a "gomer" is a patient (often called a "player") who is whining and otherwise undesirable. The term is said to be an acronym for "Get out of my emergency room," but may originate in "gomeral," Scottish dialect for "simpleton," influenced by the television hillbilly Gomer Pyle.

Paul Horvits, a *Times* colleague who has a friend in medical school, passed along many of these terms. He adds that "the dwindles" is medical jargon for advancing years leading to death from old age; "a bounceback" is a recidivist patient, or one who keeps coming back to the hospital; "to flatline" is to expire, a verb taken from the lack of activity on the scope measuring vital signs; "fascinoma" is any interesting disease; and "fluids and electrolytes" is the beer, wine, and other booze that interns and nurses head for after too many players are "boxed," or lost.

Other students of hospital language have noticed how doctors have become addicted to initialese and arcane symbols. In *The New England Journal of Medicine,* Dr. Nicholas Christy chastised interns who say "Zero Delta" when asked about patients' progress; such talk scares patients, who do not know the symbol means merely "no change." He added that "oids" has become a word in itself: "What are you giving this lady?" "Oids." This is meditalk for "steroids," which in turn is a shortened version of corticosteroids. Patients have been known to turn "gomeroid."

In response to Dr. Christy's article, Dr. Jay Wish of the Tufts-New England Medical Center injected his criticism of the familiar "PERRLA" jotted on so many patient forms ("pupils equal, round, reactive to light and accommodation"), along with the ever-popular "WDWN in NAD" ("well developed, well nourished, in no acute distress"). He objects to the verbification of initials, as in "the patient was TTAed" (underwent transtracheal aspiration). He cites other unnecessary verbifying—"The patient was broncked" (underwent bronchoscopy), "was cathed" (catheterization)—and Dr. Wish inveighs against "the patient tubed" for "the patient went down the tube."

Other initialese that patients should know to keep up with the mystery of medical treatment is "QR," which stands for "quiet room," the latest euphemism in psychiatric wards for the place with the padding on the walls; "OR," for "operating room"; "CC," not for cubic centimeter but for "chief complaint"; and "ROS" for "review of symptoms." The patient who sees "SOB" on his chart should not take umbrage, as it is usually intended to mean "short of breath." (Not to be confused with SOOB, for "sit out of bed.") Sometimes the initialese is a source of comfort: A patient with "chronic obstructive lung disease" sees only "COLD" on his chart. Informal abbreviations include "LOL in NAD" ("little old lady in no apparent distress") and "ROR" ("relationship on rocks").

A classic work in the literature of medical lingo was done by Philip Kolin in *American Speech* magazine. He reported a surge in pompous titling: An orderly (or trainee) is now a "nursing tech"; clerks are now part of the "unit services staff"; anybody who works in the kitchen or delivers the meals is a member of the "dietary staff"; the hospital chaplain punches your card in the "pastoral care office." The famed "scrub nurse" is now an "OR nurse," as if scrubbing in the operating room—or "pit"—were demeaning; the "dirty nurse" of yesteryear has changed her name to "floor" or "staff nurse."

When nurses apply a manual oxygen mask, they are said to "bag a patient"; when they perform external cardiac massage, they "pump a patient"; when they apply electroshock therapy, they "zap a patient."

Although such argot enlivens hospital discourse, many doctors deaden it with pretentious words. Lois DeBakey produced a list in the *Archives of Surgery,* criticizing physicians who say "cholelithiasis" instead of "gallstones," "edentulous" rather than "toothless," "pyrexia" for "fever," and "hermatochezia" for "bloody stools."

If the breezy approach by people in medicine to the serious business of life and death leaves you "gorked"—stupefied, as if by an anesthetic—a little forgiveness is in order. Language is sometimes used to lessen the terrors of reality, and macabre humor need not mean insensitivity. A doctor would not put "dying" on a chart, lest the patient see it or lest the real word depress the next chart reader. Instead, he initials "MFC," a sadly sassy signal that means "measure for coffin."

"Terns" grow up into "jars" and "sars"—junior assistant residents and senior assistant residents—and too often look down on the "LMD." That's a "local M.D."—a doctor in private practice not affiliated with a teaching hospital, Barbara Pinson explained in *Philadelphia* magazine. In self-defense, these local physicians call themselves "real doctors," compared to the "theoretical doctors" who never made a house call, specialists who—upon hearing hoofbeats—think of zebras rather than horses.

"A surgeon is a 'blade,'" I am informed by Dr. Jeff Kaufman of the department of surgery at Massachusetts General. "A radiologist is a 'shadow gazer'; a nuclear-medicine specialist is an 'unclear medicine person'; an internist is a 'flea' (because they hover about the bed, talking, like fleas on a dog) or 'mope' (medical officer par excellence), and an oral surgeon is a 'fanger.' "

This article is likely to open a red pipe of mail. (A "red pipe" is an artery; a "blue pipe," a vein.) That's because journalists are notoriously inaccurate in reporting causes of death. When you see a story that reads, "He died of heart failure," remember the immortal admonition of city editor Stanley Walker: "Everybody dies of heart failure." And when you see the seemingly more careful "He died of apparent heart failure," remember that nobody ever died of "apparent" anything.

Dear Mr. Safire,

Further jargon may be of interest to you. A patient that expires (how come they never die?) is "transferred to the ECU" (eternal care unit) or "to the $n^{th}+1$ *floor"* (n *being the top floor of the hospital). Patients in coma are "loxed out" perhaps referring to the flaccidity of a piece of lox, while complicated patients where many things are wrong, or many things have gone wrong during hospitalization (as the progressive deterioration of the English language in this letter) are referred to as "horrendiomas," as in "horrendous."*

Sincerely yours,
Jerold B. Spitz, M.D.
Hartford, Connecticut

Dear Mr. Safire:

Other confusions occur in medicine: "aural," having to do with the ears, and "oral," having to do with the mouth; "auscultation," referring to hearing, usually with a stethoscope, and "osculation," referring, as you very well know, to kissing. This last confusion occurs only in young medical secretaries; their elders knowing very well the difference between listening and kissing.

Cordially,
Shepard G. Aronson, M.D.
New York, New York

Dear Mr. Safire,

Other bits of jargon for your files: "turf," verb; to remove from one jurisdiction to another, as "We turfed him to the meddies." Use for patients; not just undesirable patients, as to the overworked house officer any *patient is undesirable. The more patients you can get rid of, the better. This is called "diuresing the service." There is also a jocular meaning attached to the term "service revolver"—it's what you wish you could use on the patients who stubbornly refuse to be buffed.*

Speaking of euphemisms for death: "box," verb. "She boxed just after pup rounds." "Pup rounds"? The end-of-day numbers trading (informing the others who're covering your patients overnight what the most recent lab values are, and identifying actual or potential problems to keep an eye on) that helps pick up the pieces. And of course, you know about the "DNR" designation—

"do not resuscitate," for those patients whose total-body failure means that God is trying to tell you something.

Dr. Kaufman mentioned some of the terms that are current on the surgical services at MGH ("Man's Greatest Hospital"), but the medical boys have their own way of differentiating "flea" from "flea," referring to renal specialists as "nephrons," pulmonary men as "pulmons," and even radiologists as "radons"—perhaps the vaguely Greek ending adds a little class. You mentioned that the termination -oid *gets heavy play. It sure does. Anything can be made into an adjective and be made to sound weighty and imposing if you attach* -oid. *But I think Dr. Kaufman has the wrong etiology for "flea"—I've always been given to understand that it's because they're obsessed with performing laboratory tests for obscure and improbable disorders at the very bottom of the differential diagnosis list, and most of the weird studies involve drawing another tube of blood.*

One word that pleases and amuses me is the verb "twit," intensified by adding "out," and with companion adjective "twitty." Derivation? Maybe "twitch." It refers to the state of nervousness (hyperventilation optional) present in some private physicians when they're worried that the house staff isn't tending their patients properly. This is more noticeable among surgeons, and understandably so, since an enthusiastic intern with a knife—"scalpel" to the laity—should inspire dread in anyone.

And what about the words that are current only in medicine? I refer you to "gurry" (check it yourself!), which has, besides its use in whaling, the meaning of the grumous matter so often encountered inside intra-abdominal unpleasantness—abscesses, cysts, centrally necrotic tumor, and so forth. I never heard it till I came here. Whaling and medicine—strange combination.

Last, perhaps you can help trace the derivation of a word I haven't been able to locate in the dictionaries I have at hand. It's "gurney," and it means those wheeled stretchers used to transport patients from one area of the hospital to another. "Where's my hit [admission]?" "Out on the gurney outside the trauma room." I think I've heard it used outside the hospital to mean a similar device, but I may have misremembered "gantry."

Al Knisely
Fourth-year student, Harvard
Roxbury, Massachusetts

Dear Mr. Safire,

"To stroke out" means "to have a CVA" (cerebro-vascular accident), as opposed to "CVA tenderness" (pain in the area of the costovertebral angle where the kidneys are located). This is most often caused by a "UTI" (urinary tract infection), while a "URI" (upper respiratory infection) usually results from the common cold.

All "terns" hope to "turf" (transfer their "player" to another service) their patient to the "GU" (genitourinary) service when he needs a "TURP" (transurethral resection of the prostate) or "TURB" (transurethral resection of the bladder).

"WNL" is the abbreviation of "within normal limits," though I'm told that it often signifies "we never looked, we never listened."

Sincerely,
David Levin, M.D.
The Bronx, New York

Dear Mr. Safire:

Your column provoked me to add to your medical thesaurus. Physicians, especially the younger of us, feel pressed for time and impelled to the laconic. Thus, we hear that a person "arrested," an economy of words compared to "was stricken with cardiac arrest."

Euphemisms also mitigate the macabre, but more for practitioners than for patients. We have been counseled that bold, image-evoking verbs command the attention of listener and reader. And to avoid becoming trite, we must continually be inventive. The other day I learned that a patient had "demised."

It is a perilous course. Brevity, levity, and audacity may stultify communication, not only between physician and patient but also among physicians. Even now conversations require a nimble and enlightened mind. Hence, although I have come to recognize that when a patient "seizes," he is having a seizure, I was recently startled to hear that a man had "com'd." It took me a few minutes to comprehend that coma has supervened.

Sincerely,
James C. Sisson, M.D.
Ann Arbor, Michigan

Dear Mr. Safire:

Several inaccuracies:

1. *"To buff" (as you noted in your previous column, there is no need to up the verb) means to make a patient look better than he actually is in order that a consultant will take him on his service.*
2. *The noun "gomer" comes from the Hebrew root* G-M-R *which means "to finish." "Gomer" is the present tense of that verb, and a patient who is a gomer is not whining or otherwise undesirable. He is in the process of finishing his existence on the face of this earth. The term started in New York City, where many Jewish house staff officers sprinkled the medical language with words from Hebrew and Yiddish. Obviously WASP interns had to find other explanations for the term, and hence the acronym was invented for "get out of my emergency room."*
3. *The "dwindles" implies a patient is dwindling in front of your eyes despite your efforts and is about to expire.*

4. *A "bounceback" is a recidivist, as you noted, but also a patient on whom you gave up and who then, for some unknown reason, started to do better, much to your surprise.*
5. *"ROS" stands for "review of systems," not "review of symptoms." The review of symptoms should be done under CC.*
6. *The "pit" is the ER, emergency room, not the "OR," operating room.*
7. *"Real doctors" refer to themselves as R.D.'s.*

Good words to you,
Adam Naaman, M.D.
Clifton Springs, New York

Dear Mr. Safire:

The definition you provided for "bag a patient" is not the most common usage. "Bag a patient" comes from the use of a portable hand-operated resuscitator trade named Ambu-bag. Its purpose is to provide oxygen under emergency circumstances before the transport of the patient from the site of cardiac episode or other trauma affecting breathing until the arrival of more sophisticated electrically driven resuscitation apparatus.

The medical fraternity and health care professionals in general are a prolific source of jargon, euphemisms, and alphabetization of their special language. One newer example, which I find amusing, is the diagnosis offered by neurologists caring for patients with elusive (illusory) pain—of "GMG." The initials refer to the Yiddish phrase gurnisht mit gurnisht *("nothing with nothing"). Orthopedists treating patients with lower back pain occasionally use the same label.*

Very truly yours,
Donald Meyers
Whitestone, New York

Dear Mr. Safire:

Although I am sure you will be inundated with abbreviations and acronyms you did not include in your recent column on medical jargon, may I presume to add two more to your list? The first is the infamous "FLK," for "funny-looking kid." This notation I understand is no longer used, but was once routinely entered onto patients' charts as a catchall description of a child with no quickly diagnosable ailment save that something was obviously peculiar. (The aesthetic or unaesthetic appearance of a patient is often part of some diagnoses.)

The second abbreviation has its origin, according to a friend of mine who is a pediatrics resident, at Oakland Children's Hospital, whence it has been transported to Boston: "BTH&H"—for "boogying toward health and happiness," used to signify improvement that precedes discharge from the pediatrics ward.

May I add that you might find it interesting to investigate the euphemisms (and dysphemisms) for hospital morgues—e.g., "Ward X" or, at the Massachusetts General Hospital, "Allen Street." Such circumlocutions seem to harden medical personnel in facing the deaths of their patients, as much as they seem to mystify the laymen.

Geoffrey R. Stern
Boston, Massachusetts

You missed only the "ivy pole." One undergoes an operation which has left one a wee groggy, but not much worse for the experience, and one hates to call a nurse for such a petty errand, and one decides to get out of bed and cross the room to the WC. Sitting up is no problem, and slipping into the slippers is no problem, but putting the weight on the floor rapidly develops into a rather panicky feeling about how to remain erect. One sways, and one grabs at whatever is near—and there it is: the ivy pole. It has three casters and seems quite reliable as a steadier and a walker.

I had heard of the ivy pole but thought it might be akin to a maypole around which maidens danced with ribands of braided ivy. The nurse stormed in from the hall and said, "Why didn't you call? Where do you think you are going with your intravenous rack?" She whisked away and returned with a square tubular frame telling that that was a proper walker. So I picked it up and carried it to the bathroom. She screamed for the orderly who showed me how cripples go to the bathroom. So much for the IV rack.

Paul H. Stone
Yonkers, New York

Dear Mr. Safire:

I would like to propose another explanation for the origin of the term "gomer." In the past, I am told, it was customary for hospital patients actually to see and talk to their doctors daily. Then it was also not unusual to keep a patient in the hospital for a period of recovery, giving him time not only to gain consciousness but also to get sick and tired of being in bed. When the doctor went on his daily rounds, the patient whined, "Can I go home today, Doc?" After a few days of this, the particularly persistent patient was perhaps referred to as the "go-home-er." Hence "gomer."

Sincerely,
Perry Chapman
Alexandria, Virginia

Dear Mr. Safire:

I am currently a hospital administrator and have not (yet) heard "gomer" used in the manner you described, but I did hear the term while serving in the air force in Southeast Asia in 1969. There the term "gomer" meant a North Vietnamese or Vietcong soldier and supposedly was the acronym of "guy on motorable enemy route."

The term was used by forward air controllers and recce pilots, as in "There are six gomers on route nine charlie at delta thirty-seven." I also heard the term used by U.S. Army troops to refer to NVA or VC soldiers. While the NVA and VC troops were undesirable depending on one's viewpoint, they most certainly were not simpletons.

Sincerely yours,
James M. Pierce
Middletown, New York

---

meet up, *see* upmanship

---

me Jane

"Why do I protect the source," I wondered aloud in a political column, "when it was me?"

A great many readers felt called upon to protect the source of our communication—namely, the English language, which traditionally calls for a subjective pronoun (I, we, he, she, they, who) whenever the word is joined to the subject by a linking verb. Thus, by all that used to be correct in grammar, I should have written "when it was I." Similarly, the old correctness called for the subjective "That is he," not the objective "That is him."

But in this case, the old correctness has become the new error of pedantry. Nobody picks a suspect out of a lineup with a shouted "That's he!" In the real world, "That is him" or "That is her" is the preferred form. It's time we stopped differentiating between spoken and written English on such pronouns: I don't like the idea of claiming "It is I" is right for writing and "It is me" is acceptable for speaking. The colloquial form has taken over.

The subjective form (I, they) should be used only when the word looks and sounds like the subject. But when it looks like the object (as in "It's them"), use the objective (me, them). If anybody demands to know who told you to do this horrible deed, tell them it was me.

Dear Mr. Safire:

As to the "it's me" discussion, I am sure you have heard the story of the two Harvard students in their room when a knock comes at the door.

"Who's there?" asked one of the students.

"It's me," came the reply.

One student looked at the other student and said: "It can't be anybody we know."

Regards,
John H. O'Brien
Ann Arbor, Michigan

Dear Mr. Safire:

I can attest to suffocating effects of insistence on "proper" usage in this particular case. We were happily awaiting the appearance of the actual troupe of Monty Python, in person, at the Hollywood Bowl some weeks back. I really couldn't believe that the whole lot would actually be there. The houselights dimmed, the stage lights went on, and there, by God, they were. As we applauded and screamed our welcome, I shouted in disbelief, "It's them! It's them!" A lady next to me leaned over and said, "It's they,*" with no exclamation. It didn't ruin the evening for me, but it must have made it an unpleasant occasion for her to be among the unwashed and grammatically grubby. This, mind you, at a presentation of a group who have simultaneously elevated and rubbished the English language, to my great delight.*

Frank Buxton
Los Angeles, California

Dear Mr. Safire:

I was horrified, disillusioned, and just downright angry to discover that you feel "it is I" is so pedantic that you advocate its abolishment to the trash heaps of yesteryear.

I really don't think that one should shrug one's shoulders and sink to a lower level simply because it seems that "everyone says so" or "everyone thinks that."

Granted, in the excitement of a police lineup one would probably gasp, "That's him," but when writing a column for The Times *there should be more correct grammar used. If you feel it is "an error in pedantry," I cannot help feeling you must continually associate with poorly educated people, so that you feel uncomfortable with what previously you felt at ease with.*

You might be amazed at the number of very young people who will, on the telephone, say, "This is she speaking." If people like you, who profess to tell the ignorant public what is correct, cannot maintain standards, how can we expect the English language to be upheld or even to be taken seriously as a subject that does *have rules for correct usage? If common usage makes the rules of grammar, in certain cities true English would not be correct at all. And we do the uneducated no favor by pretending that their colloquialisms are correct, if they find them to be a hindrance when they try to find a good job.*

It truly is no terrible difficulty to learn that "it is I" is correct, if it is taught and insisted upon, just as 2 x 2 = 4 is taught and insisted upon.

In certain circles it is considered eccentric, probably even "fascist," to believe that certain standards should be maintained. Certainly dressing for dinner in the jungle is eccentric, to say the least. But when a language as magnificent as English is allowed to deteriorate simply because people are too lazy, ignorant, stubborn, perverse, et al., to take care when they use it, it is really very sad. Particularly when it is so easy to be correct. It costs nothing; it doesn't hurt; one doesn't need a special appointment; it's not illegal; it requires no special stamina or endurance—except the strength of will to use the correct form. And a little encouragement and guidance from those who are in a position to do so.

Throwing up your hands and saying it is stuffy to use the nominative where required and the objective where required are failing to live up to your own potential. Next thing, you'll be saying "between you and I" and "he gave it to she and I"! Heaven forfend!

If you want something to discourse on, how about the use of "real" when one means "really," as in "It's real pretty"? Or "like" when one should say "as if," as in "I feel like I go on and on, but shall end here"?

Very truly yours,
Virginia Burke
Farmington, Connecticut

Dear Mr. Safire:

I wince at your defense of "it was me" as the belated acceptance into formal English of a colloquial objective where a nominative is logically required.

I scorn people who can bring themselves to say or write, "It was I." They have fourth-grade erudition instead of Sprachgefühl.

Anyway, your argument is wrong, because like all our fourth-grade teachers, you confuse case with form. What is the case of puellae, *or even the number? The* case *is where the word* falls, *not what it looks like.*

"Me" is a perfectly good nominative form—a disjunctive *nominative, as in "it was me." Rule: Before the verb, use the conjunctive form. After the verb, use the disjunctive.*

A hoary joke is about a shop with a sign in the window saying, "Ici on parle français."

Customer: Qui est-ce qui parle français ici?

Clerk: Je.

Ask me again anytime you need guidance.

Winifred Scott
New York, New York

Dear Mr. Safire:

Remember Shelley's statement in "Ode to the West Wind"? "Be thou me, impetuous one!" he wrote. Or Hyman Kaplan's response, after he knocked at a door. To "Who is it?" he said, "It's Kaplan!" thereby destroying another of Mr. Parkhill's lessons.

Your best precedent is Winston Churchill. In the year of the Fulton speech, Churchill was on his way back to Britain, announcing his intention, now that he was voted out of office, of writing a history of World War II. As a tribute to the great man, the Soundscriber Corporation (in Connecticut) gave him a dictating machine (tape, I believe) to help in his future project. It was a machine that was fabricated after *working hours, the workers giving their time gratis and the company contributing the materials.*

In gratitude, Churchill recorded a short (for him) thank-you speech which was played over the plant PA system. To everyone's amazement, he began, "Hello, everybody at Soundscriber. This is me, Winston Churchill." The solecism was echoed all over the country, duly reported, I'm sure, in The Times. The Times *did not turn to Theodore Bernstein in this case; it surveyed the English department chairmen of the Ivy League and other prestigious universities. The result? Practically everyone agreed that Churchill was basically right and that "This is I" was puristically Pecksniffian. As one of them put it, "It's men like Churchill who* make *the language!" So if it's good enough from Churchill, it's good enough from Safire, I guess.*

Sincerely yours,
J. C. Bernstein
Glen Ridge, New Jersey

Dear Mr. Safire:

If you are still queasy about "It's me," buck up. It's the Queen's English.

I remember perfectly clearly from the news some years back a news story about Queen Elizabeth in a carriage in some kind of procession. I think she was stopped long enough in the street to hear one little girl tell another, "Garn I tell you, it's Margaret."

She leaned—leant?—out in her nice way and said to them, "No, it's me." And if it was her, who's to argue?

Sincerely,
William Howells
Kittery Point, Maine

Dear Mr. Safire:

I agree with your conclusion about "it was me," but your reason is not persuasive. It is neither necessary nor desirable to differentiate between spoken and written English.

Marshall McLuhan explained it all somewhere. He said that following the invention of the printing press, word order replaced inflection (inflection is the notion of fixed subjective and objective case forms) as the basis for the form of pronouns. As proof he gave something like these two sentences: "I was given a book" and "A book was given me." The two sentences are of course identical except for the word order, yet nobody would question that both the "I" and the "me" are correct. Yet both are indirect objects so that the "I," like the "me," is in the objective case.

The point is that "I" is correct when used at or near the beginning of a sentence and "me" when used at or near the end. But either of them might be in the nominative case or the objective case depending on the use.

Your position should be not only that the "me" in "it was me" sounds right (because it is at the end) but also that it is in the nominative case because it is so used.

Sincerely yours,
Nathan Grossman
Valley Stream, New York

---

mentor, *see* perils of the fast track

---

menumania

"I am looking at the room-service menu supplied by this hotel," writes one of my colleagues. "I may have my choice of chilled juices, two farm-fresh eggs, golden-rich pancakes, or a crisp golden waffle, not to mention fragrant, fresh-brewed coffee."

The hard sell of menu writers is distasteful to this hard-boiled reporter. "Was the onion soup ever created that wasn't 'French Onion Soup'? Was there ever a gazpacho that wasn't 'Andaluz,' whatever that means? Was a salad ever constructed of anything except 'fresh garden greens'? And what's a 'rasher' of bacon?"

A "rasher" is akin to "raze," or scraping—a piece of pork scraped from the pig, as if by a razor—now taken to mean a serving of several strips of bacon. As for the rest of the menu minuet, consider this tidbit contributed by Eleanor Billmyer, which she calls "cannibalism in Albany, New York": cream of vegetarian soup.

William Safire

metaphors askew

This dossier was opened when Dianne Feinstein, mayor of San Francisco, complained that inequity in criminal sentencing was "a very hard blow to swallow." It grew when Senator Lowell Weicker of Connecticut, speaking about the spirit of the American people, said, "It's vital to find out whether that spirit remains bright or whether we accept a little tarnish to keep the boat from rocking."

From journalism came the *Journal of Commerce* headline that the "Slowdown Is Accelerating," and *The Washington Post*'s editorial concern about whether—in the Iranian revolution—"at this advanced stage... the United States can fine tune the end game."

A subdivision of the file was set up to accommodate "metafives"—metaphors not so much mixed as mistaken. Mark Moseley, the underpaid place-kicker for the Washington Redskins, said, "They know I've been playing for peanuts for a long time. Now they're going to have to play the fiddle." Only if he had said what he meant—"pay the fiddler"—would he have successfully mixed a metaphor.

Similarly, Lowell Flanders, president of the United Nations Staff Association, was quoted on the front page of *The New York Times* as saying, "The career system is going down the pike." Writes Solomon Kunis of Bellerose, New York: "The phrase Mr. Flanders intended to use (and probably did) was 'down the pipe'... derived from the irretrievable condition of material which has been flushed down a drain. 'Down the pike,' on the other hand, is related to 'down the road a piece,' and refers to a situation which one anticipates will occur further along, or sometime in the future."

Another example of a metafive was supplied by Congressman Anthony Beilenson of California, who reports that a witness came before his committee to say, "We're embarking up a different tree."

These skewed metaphors are not to be confused with the mixed variety. A perfect example of metaphor mixture—almost fusion—was provided by Hazel Rollins, administrator of the Economic Regulatory Administration, who told a Senate energy subcommittee that she had a big job and a small staff, and "there is no quick lunch here." Writes Guy Carruthers of San Francisco: "Apparently what Administrator Rollins meant to say was that 'there is no free fix,' but she backed away from that because of its narcotics connotation." With quick fixes, there can be no free lunch.

Metaphor lovers also collect word pictures in series: neither skewed nor mixed, but strung out like lights in a tunnel with no light at the end. Donald Adams, Republican party chairman in Illinois, reviewed the post-

New Hampshire primary scene and crowded his gallery with three sports metaphors in succession: "It's a yo-yo situation. We've had the second inning of a 38-inning ball game. Reagan did very well, but it's still a horse race."

The gentlest yet most effective way to put down a writer who mangles, mixes, or strings out his images is to draw a little cartoon of what he has written. Mrs. F. H. Nicoll of Princeton, New Jersey, sent me a drawing of a long needle, out of which a branch was growing incongruously; at the end of the branch was an apple—a person was tasting the apple, making a face, and saying, "Yech!" She enclosed a clipping from a column of mine in which I chastised a Department of Justice official for being one who "reluctantly authorized the probe that is now bearing bitter fruit." Wrote Mrs. Nicoll: "This is the nearest I can get to a probe bearing bitter fruit."

Dear Mr. Safire:

I was surprised and delighted to see my comments on the mixed metaphor in your column. My wife was equally pleased, and she expressed her appreciation in the poem I am enclosing.

ALL IS NOT LOST
by Rena Garter Kunis

Solomon Kunis of Bellerose, En Wye,
Noted for wielding a wit that is wry,
Noticed one Sunday, while reading the Times,
Several dire philological crimes.

Solomon Kunis of Bellerose, En Wye,
Uttered a most philological cry,
Then took up his weapon, more potent than swords,
To emend Safire's glitch in some well-chosen words.

Solomon Kunis of Bellerose, En Wye,
Put down his pen with a bellyfelt sigh,
"What is this world coming to," moans he in terror,
"When the Times *and Bill Safire can make such an error?"*

Some Sundays elapsed, and no word could he find,
And Solomon Kunis to fate was resigned,
When on March 23, in some words wise and solemn,
At last he was quoted in Bill Safire's column.

"There's hope for our language, and too, for our youth,
"When Safire still stands for correctness and truth.
"Henceforth on his work I will keep a sharp eye,"
Vowed Solomon Kunis of Bellerose, En Wye.

And errors there were, which he duly corrected.
Each column by Safire he fully dissected.
And a brilliant guest column appeared by and by,
By Solomon Kunis of Bellerose, En Wye.

Sincerely,
Sol Kunis
New York, New York

Dear Mr. Safire:

A young civilian man was bitterly complaining about the poor railroad service during World War II. I took the liberty of reminding him that railroads were woefully short of manpower because of losses to the military, that new equipment was unobtainable, that materials to repair old equipment and roadbeds were difficult to come by while at the same time demands for passenger and freight service had skyrocketed.

He thought about it for a while and then responded with this jewel:

"I guess the railroads do have a headache on their hands."

Sincerely,
Dan E. McGugin, Jr.
Nashville, Tennessee

Dear Mr. Safire:

A young man, eager to impress his young lady but finding both body and spirit dampening as they stood in the rain trying to hail a cab, grumbled, "I can't understand why there're no cabs. They're usually thick as thieves around here!"

Sincerely,
Emily Perl Kingsley
Chappaqua, New York

Dear Mr. Safire,

When I was an AP correspondent in Berlin in 1939, I was sitting in the Pam Pam Café in Schwäbische Strasse listening to a radio rabble-rouser given by Dr. Josef Goebbels in his creamy, Rhineland-accented voice.

*He unloaded my all-time winner: "The tooth of time will not let grass grow over this wound!" (*Der Zahn der Zeit wird nicht Grass über diese Wunde wachsen lassen!*).*

My father reared me on the parliamentary gem attributed to (by the Oxford Dictionary of Quotations*) Sir Boyle Roche (1743-1807): "Mr. Speaker, I smell a rat; I see him forming in the air and darkening the sky; but I'll nip him in the bud."*

Keep up your watch on the ramparts. An army of illiterates is abroad in our land.

Sincerely,
Angus MacLean Thuermer
Middleburg, Virginia

Dear Mr. Safire,

With respect to "skewed metaphors," isn't "metafives" an unnecessarily arch (punning) way of describing a mistake that already has a name when it concerns words? Sheridan's Mrs. Malaprop (in The Rivals*) has the affliction of skewing words ("malapropisms"). Your "skewed metaphors" are better termed "malaphors."*

Juergen Schulz
Providence, Rhode Island

Dear Mr. Safire:

Your article on "Metaphors Askew" prompted me to look for my own collection of such things.

"You'll wind up spinning your wheels and go off the deep end." (This one seems particularly suited to the cartoon treatment suggested by one of your correspondents.)

At the opening of the St. Lawrence Seaway: "This will put the heart of America on the doorstep of Europe." (Grisly thought.)

"You're treading on thin ground." (I've heard this countless times.)

"They're doing a land mine business." (Business is booming, I guess.)

"Don't look a gift horse in the eye." (I think everyone has heard that one. A symptom of urbanization.)

And, finally, in self-defense, I made up a few. My favorite is: "You can't make an omelet without opening up a can of worms."

Very truly yours,
David P. Hawkins
New York, New York

---

millennium, *see* come the millennium

---

missing persons

Nothing personal, of course, but "persons" has just taken a kick in the head.

For a time, "persons" seemed hell-bent to replace "people." Voguish announcers intoned that "thousands of persons" attended an event. At the same time, under the baleful glare of feminists, "person" was used to replace "man" in many job titles—spokesperson, chairperson, etc. Both "man" in its inclusive form as "mankind" and "people" with its collectivist aura went into decline.

It's ending. *The Associated Press Stylebook and Libel Manual* says of hyphenpersons: "Do not use coined words such as *chairperson* or *spokesperson* in regular text. Instead, use chairman or spokesman if referring to a man or the office in general. Use chairwoman or spokeswoman if referring to a woman. Or, if applicable, use a neutral word such as *leader* or *representative*."

Hats off to you, stylish usageperson! Even better, the AP entry on people/persons takes an unequivocal stand on a confusing pair of words: "The word *people* is preferred to *persons* in all plural uses. For example: *Thousands of people attended the fair. Some rich people pay few taxes. There were 17 people in the room.*"

All plural uses? *The New York Times Manual of Style and Usage* still suggests "persons" for quite precise or small numbers—397 persons, as if to show you counted them individually, or two persons, as if to suggest that a couple doesn't amount to "people." Judging from the general delight shown around *The Times*'s newsroom at the AP decision, I imagine *Times* style will come around to "people for all plural uses."

What is the root difference between "persons" and "people"?

"People" comes from the Latin *populus,* meaning "a people," as in "a nation"; "persons" comes from the Latin *persona,* meaning "masks."

Miss Nomer

Great, expensive objects sometimes get named by mistake. The story is told of the decision by the Cunard Line in the early 1930's to name its first

Queen after Queen Elizabeth I. In imparting this good news to King George V, Cunard's chief said, "We intend to name this vessel after one of England's greatest queens." Before the shipowner could finish, His Majesty said, "Her Majesty will be delighted." The Cunard man gulped, smiled, and the vessel was christened the *Queen Mary.*

A similar episode, possibly apocryphal, is called to mind by the current controversy about the "Stealth" bomber. Republicans have charged that the Pentagon leaked top secret information about this radar-evading weapon for political purposes.

In 1964, old defense hands recall, Lyndon Johnson was anxious about candidate Barry Goldwater's charges of defense weakness, so he leaked a story about a speedy, high-flying replacement for the U-2 reconnaissance aircraft. The supersecret plane had been called the RS-71, for "Reconnaissance, Strategic." (The military likes the noun-comma-adjective construction: I recall a sign reading GARBAGE, EDIBLE.)

However, goes the story, which is grimly denied by Lockheed, the President got the letters mixed up and called it the "SR-71." With supersonic alacrity, the Air Force turned the mistake into reality: If that's what the President called it, that's what its name was.

Which is why, even today—though the *Queen Mary* is long gone—the plane up there taking pictures of the Kremlin license plates is the SR-71.

Dear Mr. Safire:

Cunard ships were always designated with names ending in ia (Mauretania, Lusitania, Carpathia, *etc.). Thus, when the Cunard chief said he wanted to name the ship after one of England's greatest queens, he was obviously referring to Queen Victoria. King George must have really surprised the Cunard man when he said, "Her Majesty will be delighted," referring to Queen Mary.*

Very truly yours,
Carl T. Murzin
Great Neck, New York

Dear Bill,

For what it's worth, my recollection of the RS/SR-71 story jibes with yours; however, to call Johnson's handling of the plane's existence a "leak" rather stretches any definition I've ever heard of that term.

More like the Johnstown flood. He had the Pentagon fly two planeloads of reporters—everyone who wasn't out of town at the time, as I was only occasionally covering either the White House or defense then—to Edwards AFB to see the SR-71. It made some low passes over the field at top speed, something which impressed most of us, not least with the guts of the air force test pilots.

Regards,
Gordon Eliot White
Washington Correspondent
Deseret News
Washington, D.C.

Sir:

Anent your allusion to the military predilection for the noun-comma-adjective format, I recall seeing in a British Quartermasters' Corps catalogue, circa 1944, the following entry:

"Pot, chamber, handles (without), rubber, officers (lunatic) for the use of."

Yours faithfully,
David N. Leff
Pleasantville, New York

Dear Mr. Safire:

On the liking of the military noun-comma-adjective construction, I swear to you that in Bombay in 1942, I heard a beggar on the street say, "Allah, for the love of, alms."

My companion sniffed. "Must be Supply Corps."

Sincerely,
F. G. Gooding Jr.
Virginia Beach, Virginia

---

mod modifiers

A few weeks ago I passed the desk of my colleague Richard Lyons, who said two words: "Assault rifle." Why, I wondered, was the Soviet assault rifle—the Kalashnikov AK-47—on his mind? Was the United States Army's M-16—widely referred to as an assault rifle—somehow inadequate?

Last week, passing his desk, I heard him mutter two other words: "Battle tank." A picture of our XM-1 battle tank had been on the front page, and comparisons had been made with the Soviet battle tank. What connection did "battle tank" have with "assault rifle"?

This morning I paused beside his desk for my two-word weekly fix and was given a nonmilitary usage: "Parking garage."

Of course. What other kind of garage is there than a parking garage? The word "garage" comes from the French *garer,* "to guard, preserve, protect," which is why we pay that whopping daily rental for parking. The "parking" in "parking garage" is as redundant as the "pie" in "pizza pie." Similarly, one may ask: What other kind of rifle is there except an assault rifle? Do we issue special, backward-pointing rifles for retreats?

And what kind of tank is there other than a battle tank? Were all previously owned tanks produced for mock skirmishes? Is the Pentagon trying to differentiate between a regular tank and a think tank?

Mod modifiers—those nouns-turned-adjectives, like "farm" eggs, "garden" salad, "decorator" colors, and "designer" sportswear, that give panache but no added meaning to a noun—probably came into vogue with "attack bomber," which put all other bombers on the defensive. The Air Force dropped "attack bomber"—we now have fighter-bombers and strategic bombers—but the yen for mouth-filling modifiers spread elsewhere in the armed forces.

Because the Russians were calling Mr. Kalashnikov's invention an "assault" rifle, we started doing the same (though most riflemen continue to say "my weapon").

The origin of "battle" tank is more Orwellian. We stopped producing a "heavy" tank, carrying a 120-millimeter gun, in the fifties; our most powerful tank then became a medium tank. But what army wants to call its big gun a medium gun? By the mid-sixties, during a controversy about building a bigger tank, the "main battle tank" phrase was bandied about. Our XM-1 now qualifies as what used to be called "heavy," but in an age that celebrates trimness, "heavy" is a state to be avoided; hence we call it—informally, but widely—a "battle" tank.

Another version of the origin of "battle" tank has a historical rationale, which you can believe if you like:

Battlefields, when they were very large, used to be divided into sections: The main battle area was the primary action area, and other sections were "forward of main" and "corps rear area." The biggest tanks were used in the main battle area and came to be called, in NATO terminology, "main battle tanks."

Sorry; the shells from the battle tanks do not reach across Credibility Gap. We have dispensed with sensible descriptions like "light," "medium," and "heavy" only to fill the void felt by the armed services ever since battleships disappeared.

We can name a specific weapon for anybody or anything, but in naming classifications of weapons, we are all better off with descriptions that describe. Battle tanks belong in parking garages.

Dear Mr. Safire:

The term "assault rifle" I believe has a more dramatic origin and a more precise meaning than you are aware of. Toward the end of the Second World War the Germans, copying the Russians, began to build infantry divisions around the cheaply made but highly effective machine pistol and automatic rifle and their variations, which were uniformly light, automatic, shoulder-fired weapons carried by a line infantryman. These divisions, called Volksgrenadier divisions, were about two-thirds the size of the normal German infantry division. They included a number of so-called assault battalions whose men were armed with the rapidly firing weapons described. Their mission was to storm enemy positions and through rapid and close-in firing to overwhelm the defenders. These divisions were used extensively against the Americans in the Battle of the Bulge. At the time the American infantry was armed mainly with the standard M-1 rifle, which no one to my knowledge ever termed "an assault rifle," and with cumbersome BARs (Browning automatic rifles). Subsequent to the Second World War, of course, the American infantry also adopted the light automatic weapons more suitable for closing with the enemy, as the military put it.

Sincerely,
Joseph C. Doherty
Washington, D.C.

Dear Mr. Safire:

In the early part of this century, which I remember quite well, an automobile owner stored his car in his barn, shed, stable, or other building, except in the cities where houses were not fitted with outbuildings. The owner of a car went down (always down, never over, out, or up) to the garage for gasoline, repairs, free air, and accessories.

Then stores specializing in petroleum products were built, identified as filling stations. The garages continued to sell gasoline. Then some filling stations added tires, accessories, and minor repairs, and became service stations.

The metropolitan garages began dropping their repair services but kept on with gasoline. This continued until after World War II. The new buildings were not provided with tanks for gasoline for fire-safety and insurance reasons but provided parking space. Commercial parking buildings were put up, again without gasoline or repairs. To simplify life for the cruising motorist expecting to find gasoline at a garage, such garages advertised their limitations and called themselves, yep, you guessed it. At the other end of the spectrum, particularly along First and Eleventh avenues, you can find "full-service" garages.

The MG sports car got its title from Morris Garages. Does that sound like storage?

Re the "battle" tank: Do you suppose that is to avoid confusion with toilet tanks, gasoline tanks, and t'anks for ever't'ing?

Sincerely, I guess
John Edwin Peitz
Salem, New York

Dear Mr. Safire:

This time I must protest. If we didn't precede them with what you call mod modifiers, how could we tell your examples from deer rifles, water tanks, or cootie garages?

And while we're on the subject, doesn't the modifier "battle" add meaning to the noun "fatigue"? Or "tank" to "top"? Or "garage" to "mechanic"?

Parkyakarkis and beginagain, Finnegan.

Yours truly,
Miriam Hurewitz
New York, New York

Dear Bill Safire:

Re Mod Modifiers—

"He speaks five different *languages."*

Cordially,
Steve Labunski
New York, New York

Dear Mr. Safire:

You state that the first word in the term "assault rifle" is redundant. In fact, it is a useful adjective, defining a particular type of weapon. Assault rifles use smaller or weaker cartridges than those used in infantry rifles a generation ago. As a result, the rifles themselves are lighter and can be fired like a machine gun with some pretense of accuracy. They have the drawbacks of being accurate within a much shorter range (no more than 500 yards, as opposed to over 1,000 yards for the M-1 or M-14) and firing bullets which are more likely to be deflected by branches or other obstacles. Both the weapon and the term seem to have come from Germany during World War II. (These two types of weapons are distinguished from the submachine gun, which fires pistol ammunition.)

The situation has been complicated by the fact that both the United States and the Soviet Union now use assault rifles as their standard infantry weapon and have abandoned "rifles" except for special purposes such as sniping. All other states have not yet followed this trend, however, so there are still a lot of "rifles" in service as opposed to "assault rifles." No one seems to have come up with another term for the weapons firing the larger cartridges.

Your comment that assault troops may require different weapons from defenders, although made in jest, may in fact account for the term. At least in military theory, where this sort of thing always looks quite plausible, defenders have nothing better to do than to fire from cover at troops advancing over terrain whose ranges have been precisely measured in advance; they thus need a rifle which is accurate at long ranges, while the weight of the weapon and its ammunition is of little consequence. Assault troops, on the other hand, are running considerable distances, making aimed fire impossible in any case; they need light weapons (since they have to carry them) which can make an impressive noise by firing automatically.

Sincerely yours,
Roy E. Licklider
Highland Park, New Jersey

Dear Sir:

The Russians shouldn't get the credit for developing the term "assault rifle"; it actually belongs to the Germans.

*In 1942 the Germans introduced on a limited basis a weapon capable of selective (full- or semiautomatic) fire which fired a so-called intermediate size cartridge, or one smaller than the normal German rifle cartridge of the period. This weapon was found to be particularly useful on the eastern front, where great firepower was required, and was found to fill a niche between the relatively low-powered submachine gun and the relatively high-powered rifle cartridge then in use. The weapon went under various designations during its period of manufacture, starting out designated as a machine carbine and then designated a submachine gun. (*Maschinenkarabiner; Maschinenpistole.*) In 1944-45 the weapon was redesignated as a* Sturmgewehr, *the literal translation of which is "assault rifle." The development of the intermediate cartridge and the selective fire weapon set the pattern for postwar developments such as the AK-47.*

Regards,
Craig W. C. Brown
Museum Director
First Corps of Cadets Museum
Boston, Massachusetts

Good Sir:

Decco colors are keyed, coded, and catalogued into harmonic groups by the Decorators' Establishment, so that you may buy, for your Green Room, at any drive-in shopping center, a rug, towel, or antimacassar which, if not matching, is at least harmonizing sans malséance.

"Artist's" colors have a classic nomenclature, although the various manufacturers produce nearly identical definitive names of their own. Commercial manufacturers employ their own poets. Scientific colors employ math and geometric diagrams which render the art very simple.

Respectfully,
Paul H. Stone
Yonkers, New York

Dear Mr. Safire:

It would be nice if there were balance in the breakdowns of rifle and tank types. If there were indeed light, medium, and heavy tanks, as there once were.

If there were sniper, general duty, and assault rifles. If there were a West Bay to match the East Bay in the San Francisco area. And a South Hollywood to balance North Hollywood in Los Angeles. Because these balancing names don't exist doesn't mean the distinctions drawn by the adjectives that are *used are not worth making.*

Yours truly,
Michael McCarthy
San Lorenzo, California

Dear Mr. Safire:

The Germans may also bear the burden of giving us "battle tank" since the German for "tank," Panzerkampfwagen, *has the word "battle" smack in its center. A phrase I find even funnier than "battle tank" is "armored fighting vehicles," AFV to the trade, which strongly implies that there are some armored machines which are pacifist.*

Yours truly,
Lenny Rubenstein
New York, New York

Dear Mr. Safire:

Today's armies use, in addition to assault rifles, recoilless rifles, semi-automatic rifles, and automatic rifles (only some of which may be assault rifles).

It's wonderful every Sunday to see you fighting the good fight, but in the future, please—choose the right weapon.

Sincerely,
Bruce E. Goldman
Fairfield, Connecticut

Dear Bill,

Some copy desk men I know (and you do, too) pride themselves on being able to edit all unnecessary words out of a story, and in so doing, they manage to edit all the "love" out of a story. That's what you do when you change "garden salad" to "salad" and "farm eggs" to "eggs."

Not only that (in these instances). You are making meanings unclear. I frequently have a cottage cheese and pineapple salad. That is not a garden salad.

I have been to farms where chickens lay eggs. I also have been to "egg factories" which are fifty feet off a four-lane highway and could never be called farms.

As for "garage," that word standing alone could mean (1) the place where I take my car for an oil change and tuneup, (2) the building on my property where I put my car overnight, also the children's bikes and the power mower, or (3) a commercial establishment which charges me two dollars a day for parking my car when I go to work.

If one word is expendable in "parking garage," it is the word "garage." "Parking" is the word we want. I know there are parking "lots" and parking "garages," but you can see for yourself what it is when you drive up.

I once worked with a crackerjack copy editor in Boston who claimed he could improve any sentence with judicious editing—with one exception: "Jesus wept" (John 11:35).

George R. Plagenz
Religion Editor
The Cleveland Press
Cleveland, Ohio

Dear Mr. Safire:

No. "Parking garage" is not a redundancy. By chance I had a copy of The Great Gatsby *handy when I read your piece on the subject. That book contains an early (I suppose) fictional depiction of an automobile repair shop—* "Repairs. *George B. Wilson.* Cars bought and sold— " *(Portable Library edition, p. 22)—labeled a "garage" ("the third [of the shops] was a garage") and manifestly not intended for parking. As still used in the common phrase "My car's in the garage" etc., the word "garage," standing alone, retains Fitzgerald's meaning as a repair shop or service station. A "parking garage" is a distinct, and latterly devised, institution, not a redundancy.*

Sincerely,
Henry D. Fetter
New York, New York

Dear Mr. Safire:

I follow your column with great interest. It may well be that in terms of "ultimate" etymology garer *and* garder *have a common origin. But in contemporary usage* garer *does not mean "to guard, preserve, protect" (which is what* garder *means), but simply "to park." This would have made your criticism of "parking garage" that much more meaningful.*

Very cordially,
Danielle Salti
New Brunswick, New Jersey

Dear Mr. Safire:

When I drive into New York from my home in Amagansett, I leave my car at the Hippodrome, a "parking" garage. When my car is in need of repairs, I take it to Tucker's Garage, in Amagansett, which, in the words of the American Heritage Dictionary, *is "A commercial establishment where cars are repaired and serviced."*

Sincerely,
Berton Roueché
The New Yorker
New York, New York

Dear Mr. Safire:

Granted that the "pie" is redundant in "pizza pie," but surely an "assault rifle" differentiates from a "hunting rifle," a "battle tank" from a "petrol tank," and a "parking garage" from the type that does repairs (in the U.K. at least).

Sincerely,
Peter C. Gillies
Rye, New York

Dear Mr. Safire:

"What kind of tank is there other than a battle tank?"

Toilet tank,
Gasoline tank, and
Jersey "tank."

I enclose some ads for women's summer "tank tops"—abbreviated simply as "tanks." The term derives from those gray jersey "tank suits" we had to wear in the school swimming pool years ago. They were of hideous cut and incredible shapelessness.

Tanks!
Janice M. Jensen
Syracuse, New York

Dear Mr. Safire:

Your admirable qualifications as a philologist unfortunately do not qualify you to write on military matters. You speak of the Soviet AK-47 assault rifle and of rifles in general. . . . By definition, an assault rifle is a medium-caliber, compact rifle used, as the name implies, in assaults—for instance, breaking down doors and things like this, which needs a maneuverable rifle but of a strong caliber. There are other types of rifles and military weapons. There is the "battle rifle," which is a full-caliber, such as the 30.06- or .308-caliber, used when the target might be barricaded and a larger caliber is needed. There is the "submachine gun," which is a smaller pistol caliber used for closer ranges where higher velocity is not needed. And there is, of course, the "automatic rifle" which is also a heavy caliber with a heavy barrel used to fire for continuous periods of time.

Some of these rifles are classified as assault rifles by people who don't know, but contrary to the statement in your column, there are many other types of rifles besides the assault rifle. Also, you state that the Soviets started to call Mr. Kalishnikov's invention an "assault rifle" and that we started doing the same. Well, standard Soviet military practice is to refer to the Soviet AK-47 and its look-alike predecessor, the AKM, as a "submachine gun." They seem to prefer this term, although, by definition, the AK-47 is not a submachine gun. Also, the word "assault rifle" and the assault rifle itself are not Soviet inventions. The first gun regarded as a true assault rifle was the Sturmgewehr *44, which was designed by the Germans toward the end of World War II. It was a medium-caliber, fully automatic rifle of compact dimensions. It bears a striking resemblance to the AK-47.*

Sincerely,
David B. Thomas
Raleigh, North Carolina

molar mashers and sob sisters

Ethnic slurs draw harsh rejoinders, but occupational derogations—especially colorful or imaginative ones—no longer get people's danders up. Lawyers may threaten action at "shyster," and some doctors grow choleric at "quack," but most auto mechanics do not race their engines at "grease monkey," nor would most dancers kick about "hoofer."

The world of medicine is rife with occu-slurs: from chiropractors who are called "bone crushers" to doctors and pharmacists who wish patients would dispense with "pill pusher" and "pill peddler" to surgeons who answer to "sawbones." The most common mild derogation—often spoken with affection—is "shrink" for psychiatrist, from the witch doctor's practice of shrinking heads. Dentists have been known to gnash their teeth at "molar masher," but that field is poor in occu-slurs—nothing dentured, nothing gained.

Businessmen hang lively monikers on each other's specialties. A "bean counter" is, as aspiring bookkeepers know, an accountant; a "headhunter," etymological cousin to the jungle shrink, is an executive recruiter; a "bit fiddler," or "bit tweaker," is a computer programmer more entranced by the machine than its product.

In advertising for aid on this valuable linguistic project, I erred in calling a bureaucrat a "paper pusher." "You mixed a slur," writes Winsor Lott of Guilderland, New York. "The proper way to slur a bureaucrat is to call him or her a 'paper shuffler,' not a 'paper pusher,' which is just another name for a 'thumbsucker.' "

"Thumbsucker" is the new term for "pundit"—from the Hindu for "learned person"—which *Time* magazine popularized to mean "long-headed commentator"; surely such "media biggies" are a more deliberative breed of pencil pushers. At least these terms are not as pejorative as "numbers cruncher," applied to a researcher, financial analyst, or pollster who bends a statistic to fit a favored theory, or who puts too much faith in figures.

Some of the zip has gone out of the airline industry as the sexless "flight attendant" has replaced the breezy "stew," and "your captain speaking" has taken over from "sky jockey" (are all captains named Speaking?). Only "hangar rat" remains to add color to those who hang around aircraft.

Some of the best designations hang in there—"roughnecks" still work the oil rigs and "sandhogs" dig the tunnels—but farmers, or agribusinessmen, no longer hear "sodbuster" or "clodhopper." Layers of railroad track are hardly ever called "gandy dancers."

In politics, a hanger-on who likes to be called a "key aide" is usually referred to as a "gofer" (because he'll go fer coffee). Diplomats are still called "cookie pushers" because of their frequent attendance at teas and cocktail parties. A pol willing to "work the fence" is occasionally dubbed "flesh presser," which is not to be confused with "flesh peddler," the slur for theatrical agent.

The worst thing you can call a television announcer is a "rip and reader," and you may get the terminal frizzies if you are caught referring to a coiffeuse as a "hair bender." But call a person a "spook" and you will receive no scary looks—the designation is accepted by ghostwriters as well as by members of the beleaguered intelligence community.

Some professions are more sensitive than others: Volunteer firemen shrug off "winkies," but public relations people flare up at "flack," often preferring the new "public-policy adviser."

I have a list of pejorative job descriptions from Peter Taub of the Gannett Rochester newspapers, running from "sob sister," for gossip columnist, to "hashslinger," for short-order cook, and concluding with "stringer," defined as "part-time newspaper correspondent." Mr. Taub, in his self-identification, illustrates the love-hate feeling of members of a group both unified and derogated by an occupational slur: "*Times* stringer in Rochester."

Dear Mr. Safire:

Regarding "pundit": This is a Hindi *word (actually, a Sanskrit word used in Hindi). "Hindu" designates religion; there is no language by this name.*

This very common confusion may be caused by the obsolete term "Hindustani" ("Language of the land of the Hindus"), used to refer to the colloquial form of what is now called "Hindi."

Sincerely yours,
Richard Salomon
Visiting Assistant Professor of Sanskrit
University of Minnesota
Minneapolis, Minnesota

Dear Mr. Safire,

Regarding your article on "Molar Mashers": A "roughneck" works on a drilling *rig, not on an* oil *rig. I'm sure you can see the sense in this. After all, what would you do if natural gas, instead of oil, came out of the ground? Throw it away? Or call the rig a "gas rig"? Basically, a roughneck's job is to drill a hole in the ground, not to find oil. If oil (or gas) comes out of the hole, I'm sure that the oil company and the owner are happy, but I doubt that the roughneck cares too much: He's being paid an hourly wage (quite low for the danger involved) and never sees a single royalty.*

Sincerely,
Marlin Risinger
Onetime Roughneck
Arlington, Virginia

Dear Mr. Safire:

A gandy dancer may be a tracklayer but, if so, only by extension. They were track examiners, *checking ties, bolts, track, and roadbed for necessary repairs, thus ensuring train safety. The name stems from the peculiar gait enforced by the spacing of the ties on one who tries to run along them. It does look like a kind of dance and—here I speculate—possibly like a gander's waddle?*

Sincerely,
Rima M. Segal
Rochester, New York

Dear Mr. Safire:

Unless you are ready for angry reprisal, verbal or physical, don't call an American black, male or female, a spook. This word is opprobrious, not so pejorative as nigger, jig, spade, and shine but still disparaging.

Albert Van Riper
The Bronx, New York

---

morkrumbo, ***see*** **loyal apposition**

---

mothering, *see* writering

multplug, *see* plug not ugly

natural, *see* getting down

nature boy

Watch out for a newly popular way of stringing out adjectives. Whenever you hear, "The moves were nonbelligerent in nature" or "My attempt was peaceful in character," ask yourself: Why "in nature"? Why "in character"?

The speaker may be trying to say "essentially," which is itself a tricky adverb often used to insinuate "no matter what else it seems to be." Or he may just be rounding out his modifier with an intellectual-sounding fillip. But "nature" and "character" are powerful words and should be used only when the speaker's remarks are sincere in quality.

While you're on guard, apply a peeled eye to other "dribble-off" constructions. Douglas Chapman 3d of Chapel Hill, North Carolina, protests the proliferation of "emergency situation" (an emergency is a situation), "precautionary measure" (a precaution is a measure), and "thunderstorm activity" (inactive thunderstorms are rare).

Fight dribbling off. Avoid verbiage.

Dear Mr. Safire:

My favorite TV weather forecaster activityism ("thunderstorm activity," "precipitation activity," "snow activity") came a few nights ago when Tim Welch, weatherman at WRGB-TV, Channel 6, Schenectady, New York, looked earnestly into the camera and said, "Well, a lot of activity fell from the sky today." Nice.

Yours sincerely,
Richard Lipez
Lanesboro, Massachusetts

neatness counts

The mood of next spring's fashion is one of gilt-edged innocence. Decadence has had its day. No more tie-dyed T-shirts and faded jeans, no more studied sloppiness, no more aching by the newly rich to look like the *nouveau pauvre.*

The word that sums up the rage of the fashion world is "preppie," from "prep school," denoting those institutions organized in pre-Scott Fitzgerald times to prepare the children of the elite for higher education. Suddenly neatness counts, the buttons are down, the sweaters and skirts are back, and grownups—lusting, as always, after the fashions of their children—are pretending that prep school days are here again. *Women's Wear Daily,* which coined "midiskirt" in the sixties, insists it did not coin the adjective "preppie," but certainly has done much to make it the trigger word in fashion terminology this year. With thanks to Eleanor Lambert, a fashion czarina who never went to prep school, here are the clichés you need to drape around your tongue this year:

"Swingy": A garment cut to swirl around the figure as the wearer moves. The big-band word is the title of a musical produced by Stuart Ostrow on its way to Broadway. "To swing out" is a phrase traced in its current fashion sense to 1851: Hall's *College Words* defined it then as "to appear in something new." ("Swingy" is spelled with a *y,* in contrast with "preppie," most often spelled with an *ie*—the latter is intended to be feminine.)

"Innocent dress": A Victorian or Edwardian outline, usually in sheer white cotton with lace insertions and a ribbon sash, suggesting the time of junior proms and debutante cotillions. Worn with a Fifth Amendment corsage.

"Veranda dress": Slightly jazzier than the innocent dress, harking back to an era when courting took place on outside porches, and "spooning" and "sparking" were the terms for today's "making out." ("Making out," which used to mean "going all the way," now most often means merely "necking and petting," also called "smoochin' and fussin'.")

"Handkerchief hemline": The bottom of this skirt dips in points, like an upside-down man's handkerchief. This contrasts with a "trumpet flare," close-fitting at the hip and flaring out at the hem, looking like Satchmo's horn, and the "tulip skirt," also called the "bubble skirt," which is full from the waist to the knee, where it tucks up into a narrow hem and restricts the stride.

Above the waist, sweaters are knitted with "intarsia patterns," which mix colors to look like tapestry. "Tank tops" are in—a sleeveless bodice cut like a bathing suit designed by Mack Sennett—and this sexy outfit is sometimes called a "camisole," which *New York Times* fashion reporter Bernardine Morris calls "a strapless top with straps on."

"Asymmetric," describing a garment cut to emphasize diagonal lines and an off-center effect, is a word associated with designer Halston, who describes his style as "clean." He tells me that the conservative, back-to-prep-school fashion reflects political and economic trends: "As the word of the seventies was 'quality,' the word of the eighties is 'value.'" Looking beyond preppiness, he foresees a return to extravagance at night.

But today's woman has taken her cue from the slogan of the Boy Scouts: "Be preppie" speaks to an era three generations back, to a stage in life a rich teenager experienced before setting out for the Ivy League. Innocence may be our plea, but a certain feminine hardiness undergirds the preppie fashion, recalling those stern-faced pioneer women who set out across this continent in covered buttons.

Dear Mr. Safire:

I am the founder and sole owner of The Custom Shop Shirtmakers, forty-four stores coast to coast. I have been collecting sartorial clichés since I started my business forty-two years ago.

SHIRT

Stuffed shirt—pompous person.
Keep your shirt on—be calm.
Give the shirt off one's back—generosity.
Shirttail—editorial column in a newspaper, or shirttail kin.
Boiled shirt—dress shirt, with heavily starched bosom.
Fried shirt—person lacking in human warmth.
Shirt up—for myself, to my advantage.

CUFF

On the cuff—credit (Quote: A little mouse came in one night with a party of six. It was not a spending party, strictly cufferoo).

Shooting the cuff—When a man puts on a long-sleeved shirt, his jacket eats up the sleeves, and to get the cuffs out and showing again, he quickly has to jerk the hands outward. This is called "shooting the cuff," a term that originated in Louisiana.

BUTTONS

Button—to accomplish a task.
Button down—to peg someone.
On the button—exactly right.
Button chopper—a laundry or proprietor of a laundry.

COLLAR

Collar—arrest.

To collar a nod—to sleep.

SLEEVE

Up one's sleeve—a secret.

To wear one's heart upon one's sleeve—love.

Even though I am a shirtmaker, actually le Roi des Chemises, *there is still room in my heart for other items of men's apparel. For example, to expand this sartorial subject even further, there are vested interests . . . by the seat of your pants . . . suit yourself . . . belt you one . . . an old shoe . . . the cut of his jib . . . too big for his breeches . . . hat's off . . . keeping it under your hat, etc., etc.*

Keep smiling.
Mortimer Levitt
New York, New York

Note from W.S.: My correspondents usually give me unshirted hell.

Dear Mr. Safire:

Contrary to your statement . . . today's woman has not taken her cue from the slogan of the Boy Scouts: "Be preppie."

"Be preppie" is not the slogan of the Boy Scouts of America. "Be prepared" is not the slogan either. The slogan is: "Do a good turn daily." A slogan has to do with an aim or purpose of a group. The ideal outcome of a Scout's training is to "do a good turn daily."

"Be prepared" is the motto *of the Boy Scouts of America. Our motto (like any motto) serves as a rule of conduct and should not be confused with our slogan, which represents the product of our work. In other words, a Scout should be prepared to do a good turn daily, but being prepared is not a good turn in itself.*

"Be preppie," as you know deep in your heart, has nothing at all to do with the Boy Scouts of America. Despite the recent introduction of the Oscar de la Renta-designed Scout uniforms, Scouting has nothing to do with preppiness, camisoles, intarsia patterns, tank tops, handkerchief hemlines, trumpet flares, or veranda dresses.

Please don't insult our efforts to make a worthwhile contribution to our society by thoughtlessly linking the Boy Scouts of America with such frivolity. Such a cheap shot is far beneath your talents.

Yours in Scouting,
Edward King
Scoutmaster, Troop 1
Honesdale, Pennsylvania

nerd, *see* words for nerds

New York-ese

People have been standing on line to ask, "How do I tawk like a Noo Yawkuh?" These seekers of a sense of belonging think that pronunciation is the key, and expect to be accepted as soon as they learn that "vanilla" is "vanella," or that "super" is "soupa," or that no letter exists between *q* and *s*.

That's a soupaficial approach. In recent years, *r* has been making a comeback. But to pass for a longtime resident, you have to live in the city syntax. You must stand "on" line—not, as other Americans say, "in" line. (You get "on" line if you join it at the end, but you are permitted to say, "Get in line," if you are one of a bunch of kids lining up, or "lining gup.")

When others "go to work," New Yorkers "go to business." When others "play the piano," New Yorkers "play piano"—same eighty-eight keys, but no "the." The rube may ask for change "for" a dollar, but the New Yorker will give him change "of" a dollar. An out-of-towner may think he has bumped into a New Yorker, but the native knows he has been "bunked into." (The phonetic substitution of *k* for *p* is common: "To bunk into" is rooted neither in buncombe nor in bunker psychology.)

The New York verb "to have" is irregular. Outsiders with a ball and glove like to "play catch," while New Yorkers invite each other to "have a catch." However, when other hostesses "have a dinner," the New Yorker will "hold a dinner." The west-of-the-Hudson crowd will "have a haircut," but the hirsute Manhattanite "takes" a haircut (a formation that led New York émigrés who became Hollywood magnates to "take a meeting").

The preposition "to" is disposable. "We went down the shore," says a New Yorker, where another native will invite him to "come over my house." Within contractions, the letter *d* is deemed unnecessary: "He dint come over my house when we went down the shore." Although nonnatives turn "I'm going to" into the slurred "Ommina," the New Yorker prefers a Bert Lahrian "ongana."

Two nouns with a New York flavor stem from New Amsterdam: A "sliding pond" is a metal slide in a playground, and has nothing to do with a body of water. The "pond" may be from "slide upon," but is more likely from the Dutch *baan*, or "track." A "stoop," from the Dutch word for "step," is a description of the porch and front steps on which Brooklynites sit and schmooze or against which they play stoopball. No other word for front steps is the exact same.

"Exactly the same" is the way most Americans would describe absolute identicality; "the exact same" is New York-ese. "To nudge" is a familiar American jab-in-the-ribs verb, but "noodge," or pest, is a New York verb and noun; non-New Yorkers also say "nag."

In New York-ese, politeness is important: "Thank you" becomes "I really appreciate"; "Yes" is "No objection"; "You're welcome" is often curiously expressed in the locution "No problem."

New Yorkers say "the Bronx"; visitors, and letter writers, often say only "Bronx" (the apocryphal question by a carpetbagging politician: "Where *are* the Bronx?").

The shibboleth that separates natives from visitors beyond all doubt is the name of the place: To an out-of-towner, New York City is New York City. No New Yorker ever says that: The Big Apple is either New York or "the city." Beware anyone who says, "I come from New York City"—he does not come from New York.

My favorite New Yorkism was supplied by Burton Epstein of the city. "On a crowded IRT ride uptown after work, the disembodied voice of the subway conductor admonished passengers: 'Please lean off the doors.' Everybody knew what he meant, and in a moment, the train departed.... It calls to mind one of the early American flags and the admonishment there—'Don't tread on me.' Somehow, 'tread off me' doesn't quite fill the bill."

It's a soupa dialect. If you don't like it, don't be a noodge. Lean off. No problem.

Dear Mr. Safire:

You have just exonerated my husband—a Brooklyn-born boy who has what I consider some strange ways of speaking. We've had a number of discussions about "bunked into." I see red when he uses this, but I realized that other people from out "there" also used it, so I've had to accept it as another interesting but irritating excursion from what is considered acceptable.

Now, what about "short shift"? He insists that this is the only proper way of saying "short shrift." It has the proper flavor, he says, and is what everyone used when he was growing up.

Other usages I've discovered since coming to New York are the way people who've grown up in apartments say they're going out: "I'm going down." Or, how about going over to see a relative: "I'm going to my mother Sunday." Not to my mother's or to my mother's house—sometimes they'll say "by my mother." Is this from Yiddish, or what (another New York way of saying something)?

Sally Kilby
New York, New York

Dear Mr. Safire:

As a child in New England I was urged to "hurry up." Only on moving to

Brooklyn (which, incidentally, we thought qualified us as residents of "the city"—a claim we now find reserved for Manhattanites) did I learn from our daughters' teachers to "listen up."

Lee Stookey
Brooklyn, New York

My dear Mr. Safire,

I would not dispute your asseverations with one exception. I have never heard any native New Yorker use the word "shore" when referring to the seaside. In my fairly wide experience, we leave that word to the New Jerseyites (ians?) and Pennsylvanians and employ "beach" instead.

Sincerely,
Joan Shay Vinci
New York, New York

Dear Mr. Safire,

If you had ever been one of a group of youngsters who lined up to take in turn a running start toward a few moments of bliss as a skateless wonder sliding over a ten-foot stretch of frozen puddle, you would grieve indeed to see the term "sliding pond" given a grammarian's funeral as being nothing but a metal playground slide in a playground or a Dutch waterless anomaly. In Brooklyn, in winter, on our way to school we slid over all the sliding ponds we were lucky enough to find in our course. What they lacked in ease of passage at first was soon polished away by the many happy feet that skidded their length.

For another note on "New York-ese," it seems strange now to recall: When we took the subway from Brooklyn to Manhattan, we said that we were going to New York.

Sincerely yours,
Gertrude Friedberg
New York, New York

Dear Mr. Safire:

Perhaps because of masculine gender, you have omitted the definitive shibboleth: "potsy." Nowhere else in the world, I believe, do little girls play potsy—they all play a weak, namby-pamby imitation called hopscotch. Try that on your would-be New Yorkers.

Yours very truly,
Estelle M. Steinberg
West Orange, New Jersey

Dear William Safire,

I think you have got the wrong idear about the r *returning to the speech of the city. Long ago it was exported to northern New Jersey, where it is in much too heavy use for you to expect its early return.*

For example, your Washington Heights housewife can do very well without an r *in speaking a phrase like "My husband's a lawyeh." But her sister, who lives no more than five miles to the west in Fort Lee, desperately needs that* r. *Because in her northern New Jersey dialect, the same phrase is: "My husband's a laryer." She calls her little daughter Ritar, instead of Rita, as you in the city would. And when she reads nursery rhymes to her, one of them comes out sounding like "Bar, bar, black sheep. . . ."*

They need so many r*'s in Bergen and Passaic counties here in New Jersey that they have had to steal them from parts of the state farther south. This accounts for place names like Poith Amboy and Joisey City.*

So if your ear tells you that you are hearing more r*'s in the speech of the city, then you probably have been listening to some New Jersey commuters.*

Sincehly,
Larry Churchill
Bernardsville, New Jersey

Dear Mr. Safire:

*You might have explained the story behind "*the *Bronx"—namely, Johannes Bronck, a Danish émigré, was the first person to settle (1639) in the area beyond the Harlem River. When people living on Manhattan Island would visit him or the area, they told friends that they were going "to the Bronck's," meaning "to the Bronck's farm." Eventually the* ck*'s became an* x *(à la "thanx" from "thanks" and "sox" from "socks")—hence "the Bronx."*

Sincerely,
L. Edw. Lucaire
New York, New York

Dear Mr. Safire:

In "New York-ese," you say that "the r *is making a comeback." I'd like to point out that it's a lot more complicated than that. The* r *was never gone from New York, just misplaced. Ask a New Yorker if he's seen the new Woody Allen movie, and he'll reply, "Yes, I sore it."*

The roving New York r *is often missing where it should be present and present where it should be missing. It's an enigma to anyone except a New Yorker. A friend of mine at school (the University of Pennsylvania) from Blue Bell, Pennsylvania, was very amused when his roommate from Queens said, "I sore an intaview." Singer Billy Joel, however, wouldn't find anything odd about this way of speaking. In one song he croons, "I don't want clevah convasation," while in another he sings us the story of "Brender and Eddie."*

Personally, I think the idear of the roving r *is anotha thing that makes "New York-ese" so interesting.*

Sincerely,
Susan Chumsky
Baldwin, New York

Dear Mr. Safire:

You correctly point out that New Yorkers "get on line" instead of "in line" except for kids lining up. But you leave the subject hanging, like a forlorn participle, with no explanation. The reason for the usage is that if a line already exists when one approaches, one gets into it like into a preexisting room elsewhere, but in New York the line is more accurately seen to be, actually or in imagination, painted on the ground. That is, a line is one-dimensional to a New Yorker, and though one can get on it, it really cannot be entered. On the other hand, if the line does not yet exist, the teacher asks the children to "get in (the form or shape of a) line." The usage is simple, logical, and, to foreigners from west of the Hudson, unfamiliar.

New Yorkers "go to business" rather than to work because, to a higher degree than elsewhere, New York is occupied with business rather than factory jobs. Others play the piano, grammatically implying a particular piano. New Yorkers are more versatile and can play any piano at all. After all, one doesn't swim the water.

Sincerely yours,
Herbert Malamud
Westbury, New York

Dear Mr. Safire:

You are right, the Dutch houden een feest, diner *etc. ("hold a feast, dinner"). The "slide pond," which is called a* glijbaan, *should really be a "glide pond." You're right again.*

But a stoep *("stoop") is more than a step. It's a flight of steps leading up to a platform in front of the door. The stoops in front of brownstones in Brooklyn and the city are identical in structure to the* stoepen *in front of eighteenth- and nineteenth-century houses in the Netherlands.* Op de stoep zitten, *"to sit on the stoop," is an art practiced on both sides of the Atlantic. By the way, a step in a flight is called a* trede, *a doorstep is called a* drempel, *and a step (stride), a* stap.

Sincerely,
H. Van Wouw Koeleman
Dauphin, Pennsylvania

Dear Mr. Safire,

It is true that r *has been making a comeback in New York-ese. However, the rise of this 26th letter seems quite arbitrary. I discovered this fact with the help of a friend who proudly pronounces her "Yewston" origins.*

R *is frequently audible in the case of words ending with* a. *For example, walk into any corner establishment which dispenses a simple delight, and you will hear "Gimme a slica pizzer anna soder." Other favorites might be expressed as follows: "I sore huh drawring pikshuhs of birds in the pawk."*

Sincerely,
Laurie R. Abramson
New York, New York

Dear Mr. Safire:

In listing "noodge" as a New York word I wonder whether you are aware of its origin.

The Yiddish (borrowed from the Slavic) nudnik, *"a bore, a pesterer," possibly one who utters* nu, nu-nu, *or any variation and intonation, led to the verb* nudger, *"to bore, to pester." There is also the adjective* nudre, *which, by extension, even implies boredom to the point of nausea. From these, you see, there is a short way indeed to the (Yinglish) word "noodge," which, incidentally, could never be considered a part of a good Yiddish speaker's vocabulary.*

Emma B. Zahler
Little Neck, New York

Dear Mr. Safire:

Of course, "noodge" is none other than нудник *(*nudnyik*) which comes from the Russian verb* нудить *(*nudyit*), "to annoy."*

Matthew E. Zaret
Ann Arbor, Michigan

Dear Mr. Safire:

My father was trying to place a phone call one day to his native Fordham section of the Bronx and enlisted the help of an operator in finding a phone number. My father offered the street address of the party to the operator as "Beaumont Avenue" (pronounced "bow-mont"). The operator denied the existence of any "Bow-mont" Avenue despite my father's protestations. Finally, she saw the light and exclaimed, "Oh, you must mean Beaumont*" (which she pronounced "byoo-mont"). "And you," my father answered, "must be from the neighborhood." Sure enough, she was a Fordham native herself.*

Sincerely,
Matilde Parente
San Francisco, California

Dear Mr. Safire:

One phrase that you omitted is "making the light."

In a high-pressure city where speed is of the essence, "making the light"—or crossing the street before the traffic signal changes—is imperative. Only a New Yorker understands it, though. When I chanced to use the phrase in Philadelphia, a companion thought I had bizarre sexual proclivities.

Sincerely,
Carol Lippert Gray
Newton, New Jersey

Dear Sir:

In your "New York-ese" you have made a glaring error. You say, "He dint come over my house when we went down the shore."

OK except for one detail. New Yorkers never never never *say they are gunna go down the shore. New Yorkers are gunna go duh da beach. People from New Jersey or Connecticut go to the shore—not New Yorkers—we gutta da beach.*

No problem,
Davis C. Levitt
Wantagh, New York

Dear Bill:

Charlie Kuralt and I have had a running argument for some fifteen years about the way he says New Yorkers mispronounce certain words and phrases, notably food and landmarks. At lunch the other day I ordered "APPLE pie" for dessert, to distinguish it, as we New Yorkers do, from "PEACH pie" or "CHERRY pie." My Tarheel friend ordered "apple PIE," to ensure he didn't get "appleSAUCE." He dines on "ham SANDWICH"; I select a "HAM sandwich."

Should an out-of-towner ask us to tell him where the New York Knicks play roundball, I would direct him to "Madison SQUARE Garden." He would send the visitor to "Madison Square GARDEN."

Best . . .
Philip Scheffler
Senior Producer
60 Minutes
New York, New York

Dear Bill Safire:

Tainted perhaps by growing up in Cleveland, Ohio, and despite the heroic "lenths" I have gone in some forty-five years of Gotham sojourn and subway riding, I have been unable to arrive at that delectable station—the glottal stop—where I am told informal seminars are held to teach that splendid phonetic utterance which distinguishes so many of my beloved native New Yorkers.

Harry C. Levin
New York, New York

Dear Mr. Safire:

I have located the hiding place of the missing r *in the name of the second month as pronounced by many in and around New York, including Walter Cronkite (Feb-you-airy)!*

That r *has inserted itself between the second* e *and the* t *in the word "sherbet."*

When I first heard it this summer, I thought someone was replying in the affirmative to a question from someone named Bert, as in "Sure, Bert."

But no Bert was to be seen anywhere.

I think your public should be advised that when speaking of their favorite fruit-flavored ice, they should think of a bookie being asked whether a wager should be placed. "Sure, bet."

Very truly yours,
Paul A. Rubinstein
New York, New York

Dear Mr. Safire:

I would like to submit an expression which I believe is in common usage throughout the United States with the exception of the New York City metropolitan area. The expression is "to sleep in," meaning "to sleep late or oversleep."

A native New Yorker, I had never heard this expression until my mid-twenties on a trip to Pittsburgh. Since then I have heard it in the Midwest, the South, the Far West, and even New York State. When used in New York City it is invariably spoken by a nonnative.

The intriguing thing about this is that rather than being an expression which originated in and whose usage is generally limited to a geographic region, this one seems to be excluded from a specific geographic area.

Yours truly,
Stephen J. Lehman
Brooklyn, New York

Note from W.S.: New Yorkers "crash."

nifty

"I was shocked," writes Linda Rawson of New York, "to see the word 'nifty' appearing in *The Wall Street Journal* recently. . . . Where did this word come from and why is it so popular? Perhaps you could also suggest an alternative word." (She meant to write "alternate word" or "alternative.")

The use in *The Wall Street Journal* was: "The Republicans said it seemed like a nifty way to upstage the President."

In that context, the word means "clever, adroit," with an overtone of harmless trickiness. The word is always used in an admiring sense: as "graceful" or "slick," as in "a nifty move," or "stylish, natty," as in "a nifty jacket" worn by the down-stuffed Sleeveless Generation.

According to Bret Harte in 1868, "nifty" was derived from "magnificent." His use: "Smart, you bet your life 'twas that! Nifty! Short for magnificat." His friend Mark Twain picked it up as well, in *Innocents at Home* in 1882: "He was always nifty himself, and so you bet his funeral ain't going to be no slouch."

After a century in active use, the word is deftly slipping out of the slang category and beginning to insinuate itself adroitly in the "informal" range. In its meaning of "excellent" or "very good," I consider it slang; in its other meaning of "smart, stylish," it is still slang and slightly outmoded; in its third meaning of "clever"—nimble in a shifty way—the word has a unique place in the language and has earned its "informal" rating.

Like the adjective "ace," "nifty" has a feel of deliberate raciness or jazziness and is used by people who pitch campiness. You will find no precise alternative, until niftiness reaches the state of being "peachy keen."

Dear Bill:

Just a quick footnote to your recent item about "nifty." I wasn't aware that the word had actually crept into the Journal *in print, but it's long been a favorite in conversation among old* Journal *hands—and that is due almost entirely to its frequent use by someone who is now one of your competitors in the word-columning business. When Mike Gartner (now* Des Moines Register*) was our front-page editor, that was one of his favorite words to describe a really well-done front-page feature—much the way "sweet" was used in an earlier time ("That's a sweet story" or "a sweet piece of writing"). "Nifty" was practically Mike's highest praise, and it truly combined for him all the meanings you assigned it: "Excellent," "stylish," "clever."*

Best,
Alan
[Alan Otten]
European Bureau Chief
The Wall Street Journal
London, England

Dear Mr. Safire:

I disagreed with the connotation you attributed to "nifty." I have encountered the word a fair amount in the financial press, though I am unfamiliar with the example provided by The Wall Street Journal. *Rather than connote cleverness in an admiring sense, "nifty," as I have seen it used, implies an obvious and contemptible brand of cuteness. Most business people would resent being called "nifty," and a "nifty" solution to a problem is one of flair with little substance. In other words, niftiness* has *reached the state of being "peachy keen."*

Though it is hard to say based on the limited context, the use you cited might well accommodate such an interpretation. There is the element of trickiness you described, but also an element of foolishness, of serious effort being wasted on superficial ends. Perhaps the full context bears me out on the niftiness of "nifty."

Sincerely,
Louis Montesano
New York, New York

alter ego

The only thing more embarrassing than to make a usage mistake in a language column is to correct somebody else's mistake—and to turn out to be wrong.

Linda Rawson was quoted here as "shocked" to see the word "nifty" in *The Wall Street Journal* and suggested that I come up with "an alternative word." With no little patronization, I observed, "She meant to write 'alternate word' or 'alternative.' "

Zap! The assistant page one editor of *The Wall Street Journal,* Mack B. Solomon, springs to her defense: "I think the lady wrote exactly what she meant." He and she are right: "Alternative" as an adjective means "presenting a second thing or proposition for choice," while "alternate" as an adjective means "occurring by turns," as "on alternate days."

Mr. Solomon, whose title might better be Page One Assistant Editor, concludes: "In short, even if Linda Rawson doesn't like our use of 'nifty,' I like her use of 'alternative.' As to 'alternate' and 'alternative,' I think there's a nice (if not nifty) distinction."

none are right

"The word 'none,' " it was patiently explained to me, "is rooted in 'not one,' or 'no one.' Right?"

Right.

"And subjects should be followed by predicates that agree—right?"

Right.

"Then why do you say 'none *are,*' you blithering idiot, when the correct usage is 'none *is*'?"

Wrong. Sometimes you should say "none is," and at other times you should say "none are." The real question is—how many or how much do you mean by "none"?

If you mean "Not one of those blithering idiots ever gets it right," then you can say "none is" or "none ever gets"; if you mean "Not even a few of those blithering idiots," it should be "none are."

Since that requires mind reading on the part of your listener, it makes sense to say "not one" when you mean "not one," and not to fuzz up the atmosphere: Let "none" stand as a collective noun to be construed as plural. "Nobody's perfect" says, "Not one of us is perfect"; if you want to lump in a few other imperfect souls as part of your subject, say, "None of us are perfect."

A collective-noun collector named Stephen Nojeim of Amherst (pronounced without the *h* sound), Massachusetts, sent me a test. Since flunking exams is unbecoming to language columnists, I sent it along to Jacques Barzun, in the house of intellect at Scribner's, where he updates *Modern American Usage.* The upper-case choices within the parentheses are Barzun's.

"A group of college students (was/WERE) discussing the subject of collective nouns the other day. A few of us (was/WERE) under the impression that if the noun encompassed a totality, the singular form should be used. But something I saw while jogging later that day forced me to question that. I saw a pair of dogs that (was/WERE) fighting. Or was it that a couple of dogs (was/WERE) fighting?"

Comments Mr. Barzun: "The verb forms underlined [shown here in upper case] are those that come without second thought to any idiomatic speaker or writer. Some forms are impossible and some demonstrably wrong—e.g., 'A few of us was.' 'Few' is more than one, and the preceding *a* does not make it singular.

"That very example," continues Mr. Barzun, "leads straight to the important point that the letter writer overlooked: Most of his sentences are so framed that the relative pronoun most naturally refers to a plural noun: 'Dogs that were fighting.' When that is true, it would take a mental contortion to make *that* refer to *pair* and say, '*was* fighting.' "

The letter test by Mr. Nojeim continues: "A number of my colleagues (has/HAVE) approached me to determine just what it is I am investigating. I tell them that a variety of methods (has/HAVE) been employed to study stress levels of students trying to learn grammar.... There (IS/are) a bunch more questions I have, but (it/THEY) can wait."

Says Mr. Barzun: "As soon as he adds a plural modifier, doubt is at an end." (When Mr. Nojeim adds "a number of" and "a variety of," he knows clearly he is talking about more than one, and his meaning calls for a plural verb.) "As for a rule on the collective noun," advises Mr. Barzun, "there is only one reliable one: Interpret the noun as you like, but stick to singular or plural after you've made your choice. What is bad is: 'The army was in high spirits but their boots were defective.' "

I would go for a tougher rule: Use "none" to mean quantity ("Let's have none of that") and not to mean "not one." When you mean "nobody," say "nobody"—don't go around singing "None knows the troubles I've seen."

Dear Mr. Safire:

All of Mr. Barzun's arguments are reasonable. Most are irrelevant to your thesis. Many of your readers are doubtless puzzled. Some of your arguments are illogical. Few are pertinent. None is persuasive.

Yours very truly,
Claude Conyers
New York, New York

Dear Sir:

I disagree with Mr. Barzun in the use of "were" in the first sentence of the inquisitorial from Mr. Nojeim.

The word "group" denotes a singular collection and has a plural—namely, "groups." A modifying description of what the group was composed of—namely, students—does not change the singularity of the grouping.

The other subjects ("few," "pairs," "couple") denote multiplicity in this particular usage; therefore, "were" should be correct.

It could be said, if others agree with me, that a group was formed to disagree.

I also disagree with Mr. Barzun on the army description. If armies were to be in high spirits, fine, but a single collective army that was in high spirits is also fine. Each subject in a multiple subject sentence should bear the entire responsibility for the verb referring to it.

Which of the following three sentences is correct?

I was in doubt, but the boots were defective.
I was in doubt, but the boots was defective.
I were in doubt, but the boots were defective.

Very truly yours,
Elliot S. Kohn
East Hills, New York

Dear Mr. Safire:

*In Chicago we have a radio station that calls itself WFMT Fine Arts (*sic*) Broadcasting, a rather pompous outfit that refuses to run recorded commercials, instead insisting on writing its own and reading them live over the radio. About twenty years ago I noticed that about 75 percent of the commercials violated our rule; for example, "Nahigian invites you to inspect their carpets." I wrote to them; no response or effect. About eight years later, after a few years in California, I returned to Chicago,* déjà vu, *so I phoned and spoke to one of the bigwigs at WFMT, a guy who ruins classical music broadcasts with enthusiastic analytical verbosity in much the same way as Gene Shalit ruined theater in his intros to* Mystery Theatre *on PBS and Howard Cosell ravages every sportscast he touches (the only difference being that while our WFMT grammarian interrupts concertos for his analyses, Cosell has never stopped a football game with his). The conversation went:*

BG: The commercial you just read didn't quite fit with your fine arts aspirations; it was ungrammatical.

NP: (Indignant who-do-you-think-you-are-to-presume-you-know-better-than-we response.)

BG: Nahigian invites you to inspect their carpets.

NP: (Response even more indignant—he misses the point.)

BG: "Invites." "Their." Is Nahigian singular or plural? Make up your mind.

NP softens incredulously; he has seen the light; he drenches me with thanks, appreciation, and profuse apologies. We hung up, and I thought, Ah, well, something achieved; certainly not nuclear disarmament, but beggars can't be choosers. For the next day or two I delighted in the announcers' tripping over their words in their attempts to curb their natural ungrammatical inclinations; success was at hand.

Crushing disappointment was to follow, however, for within a few days they lapsed into their old ways. A few years later I tried again by letter to NP, and received a reply from the copy editor in Madison Avenue gobbledygook, explaining the "intimacy" of the singular form, but promising to conform to my rule as much as possible within the intimacy constraints. His problem was that he also had his "image" reasons for the plural *form, so he couldn't go along with me entirely.*

Things only got worse. By now almost all the commercials contain this flaw, with the added fine art of the most ugly of split infinitives. I wrote to NP (one of the manager/owners, by the way) a few weeks ago, since when infinitives have been splitting like atoms.

Well, you can't win 'em all, can you?

Sincerely,
Brian Gluss, Ph.D.
Chicago, Illinois

Mr. Nojeim (is, are) an illiterate wise-ass. "Bunch" (is, are) not an adverb.

Edgar D. Brown Jr.
Schenectady, New York

Dear Mr. Safire,

I recall a note from someone at The Times *a few years ago in response to a chiding letter from me. The Sunday News in Review section, front page, had a box accompanying an article: "Many Agnew rumors—and none of them are true." The reply from the editor of the Week in Review read: " 'None,' as used in the headline, is an adverb, and it can be used in the singular or plural." Live and learn, I always say.*

Now about that singular or plural: How have you been so long able to remain silent on the use of "everyone," "everybody," "someone," "somebody," "a person," et al. with singular verbs and plural pronouns? "Everybody is doing their *thing" always sounds to my old New England ear like "He has egg on their face."*

As you are aware, everybody is doing it these days, including those who should know better. Actually Howard Cosell came closer to good usage a couple of years ago when, reporting from the annual RFK tennis tournament here, he turned "everybody" into a plural—I can't remember the precise quote, but it was something like "Everybody participating here are invited. . . ." That, at least, is a step in the right direction if we're going to continue using the plural pronoun form ("their"). I realize, of course, that we have no appropriate word for "him/her" or "his/her," and all those suggested thus far fall short of acceptability. So let's use the male form unless the female is obviously dictated. Better a little chauvinism than a mess of solecism.

Best regards,
Robert Warren
New York, New York

Dear Mr. Safire,

Anyone who can appeal to Jacques Barzun needs no higher authority. You may, however, find additional comfort in this couplet from Pope, where "none" is an intransigent plural:

'Tis with our judgments as our watches, none
Go just alike, yet each believes his own.
—"Essay on Criticism," 9-10

Best wishes,
Steele Commager
New York, New York

Your justification for flexibility in the treatment of predicates that follow collective nouns was most gratifying. I'm proud to have such distinguished company in my resistance to accept all *such nouns as plurals. It was amusing, however, to note this ad on page 19 of the same* Times Magazine *in which your column "None Are Right" appeared: "Someone close to you is hoping for a Longines. Don't disappoint them."*

Lucia Wernersbach
Bay Shore, New York

Dear Mr. Safire,

In your article "None Are Right" you discuss mainly the question of collective nouns that sound plural when they are followed by plural nouns in prepositional phrases. But the strict construction we all learned in school requires us to ignore prepositional phrases and other modifiers as conscientiously as a jury must ignore all evidence ruled inadmissible. Hence "the Council of Economic Advisers thinks*" and, similarly, "the two-man crew* was *killed." With few exceptions, such as "police," collective nouns are treated as singular and neuter.*

It may be of interest to consider the radical alternative to this usage. In British usage, collective nouns—even standing alone—are commonly treated as plural.

As Balfour declared: "His Majesty's Government view *with favour the establishment in Palestine of a national home for the Jewish people, and will use* their *best endeavours to facilitate the achievement of this object." A few more examples: "The Yard* are *confident of success in the gold bullion robbery case" (from the radio news, in a Peter Sellers film). Or "No doubt the Louvre* were *appalled" (Mr. Steed in* The Avengers*). Or "The Royal Aeronautical Establishment at Farnborough* were *responsible for the development of the aircraft" (Marshal Tedder,* With Prejudice*).*

The treatment of collective nouns depends, in British usage, on whether the context refers to the thoughts, decisions, actions, etc., of the people involved (e.g., "the staff are *convinced that the plan is feasible") or to the purely collective aspect of the group ("the staff* was *reduced by 10 percent because of budget cuts"). Sometimes the choice is not simple. The American Founding Fathers were clearly right in observing (while they were yet British subjects) "that mankind* are *more disposed to suffer, while evils are sufferable, than to right* themselves *by abolishing the forms to which they* are *accustomed." But John Stuart Mill went perhaps too far in writing: "As mankind* improve, *the number of doctrines which are no longer disputed or doubted will be constantly on the increase" (*On Liberty*).*

It is my impression that the plural usage is on the decline in Britain (the main sources of this impression are the Economist *and the BBC World Service), probably as the result of American influence.*

*The conjugation of verbs in Hebrew, as in the Romance languages—as opposed to English—differentiates in all tenses between singular and plural and between masculine and feminine. This would seem the opposite of the kind of flexibility that makes the British plural usage feasible, and indeed, as far as I know, French is even more collectivist than American—*la police, *for example, being treated as feminine singular. Yet biblical and particularly rabbinic Hebrew (as well as talmudic Aramaic) is even more pluralist than British English. For example, "The congregation [feminine singular]* shall judge*" [masculine plural] (Numbers 35:24); "Let the house of Aaron now* say *[m.pl.]" (Psalms 118); and—a particularly extreme case—"O thou that hearest prayer, unto thee* doth *all flesh come" (in the Hebrew, Psalm 65, the verb is masculine plural). Although there are many contrary examples, the very use of the singular was in some cases regarded by the rabbis as requiring explanation, e.g., as suggesting extraordinary unity of thought and feeling.*

"No ordinance may be enacted which most of the public are *unable to bear," says the Talmud, which also has many phrases such as "the whole world* know*" and "a court* who *erred" (masculine plural).*

Curiously enough, modern Israeli Hebrew stands at the opposite end of the spectrum—rigidly collectivist.

Sincerely,
Aaron Siegel
Jerusalem, Israel

nonstarter

In a piece on Kissingerese, I expressed puzzlement at the origin of the word "nonstarter," a locution heard frequently in Foggy Bottom but which has not yet gotten off the ground and into the dictionaries. Though some at the State Department think the word is going nowhere, I thought it had a future and speculated that its root may be in auto racing.

"Close—but no cigar!" writes Robert Claiborne of New York. "The word is English horse-racing jargon, denoting a horse that, having been entered in a race, is withdrawn before the start—what we would call a scratch. He is not left at the post—he never gets to it."

Reached at his stables in West Tisted, Surrey, horse breeder Basil Samuel confirms the usage in English racing and its metaphoric extension into the business world.

But where was the word first used in diplomacy? The Lexicographic Irregulars did themselves proud on that one. Michael Stoil of Arlington, Virginia, found a memo in the British Foreign Office dated February 12, 1918, discussing three possible winners in the competition for power in Russia toward the end of World War I: "The Ukrainian Rada was certainly a bad horse to back," wrote the sports-minded diplomat, "Cossack [the Denikin regime] is almost a nonstarter, but Bolshevik would be the worst of the lot on which to lay our money...."

Adds Dr. Stoil: "The writer was arguing that the Bolsheviks were the least likely of the three regimes to survive. One hopes that he was better at the betting pools than in his foreign-affairs analysis."

Good show. Now, before anyone demands to know the origin of "Close—but no cigar!" let me hasten to say that the expression is not a description of our current policy toward Fidel Castro; rather, it stems from carnival use. As a test of strength, the contestant swung a sledgehammer to drive an arrow up a pole and win the prize of a cigar. When the arrow failed to reach the top and ring the bell, the barker would gleefully commiserate: "Close—but no cigar!" Weaklings too timid to try their strength were nonstarters.

Are weaklings too timid to try their strength nonstarters? I don't think so, if we use "nonstarter" the way you claim British racegoers do.

According to your source, a nonstarter is a horse that, having been entered in a race, is withdrawn before the start. The key, I believe, is "enter."

Have those weaklings you referred to purchased a ticket, thereby entering the cigar chase? If they did make such a purchase and then, for whatever reason, decided not to pit their strength against the sledgehammer, arrow, and bell, they would then be nonstarters. However, if those same weaklings were just standing around, saying, "No way I'm gonna try that," then I don't think "nonstarter" applies.

As racegoers use it, "nonstarter" indicates an initial commitment to participate, though it's a commitment that's eventually broken. If you're just a weakling too timid to test your strength, then you probably wouldn't buy a ticket in the first place. No commitment. No nonstarter.

Very truly yours,
Roger Cohen
Department of Journalism and Urban Communications
Rutgers University
New Brunswick, New Jersey

---

noodge, *see* New York-ese

---

notty problem

"I will miss not being in Congress," said Representative Elizabeth Holtzman, as she prepared to depart Washington. Howard Meyer of Rockville Centre, New York, sent in the clipping with that quotation and this note: "If I had missed not reading this, would I have failed to omit sending it to you?"

Think about that. What will Miss Holtzman be missing—not being in Congress or being in Congress? Of course, it is "being in Congress" that she will miss—"not being in Congress" is what she will have plenty of.

So "miss not being" is wrong, right? Wrong—it is an idiom, so "miss not being" is right. An idiom owes no obeisance to logic and, like beauty, is its own excuse for being. What Miss Holtzman will miss is (all the good times in which she will not participate by virtue of) not being in Congress—with the phrase in parentheses understood.

I'll miss not hearing from Howard Meyer again.

Dear Mr. Safire:

In stating that "I will miss not being in Congress" is an idiom, you seem to have forgotten that mere prevalence of use, even by such highly qualified users as Miss Elizabeth Holtzman, does not automatically turn a solecism into an idiom.

"Miss not being" reminds me of that formerly common disclaimer "I could care less." Both these expressions owe no obeisance to logic, but since they both say exactly the opposite of what the speaker intends, neither of them has any excuse for being.

Cordially,
Albert Kreindler
New York, New York

Dear Mr. Safire:

Feel obliged to question your assertion that "miss not being," as in "I will miss not being in Congress," is an idiom. Seems like just loose talk to me.

According to the American Heritage Dictionary, *an idiom is "a speech form that is peculiar to itself within the usage of a given language." I, for one, am unfamiliar with "miss not being" as legitimate usage to mean, in essence, "miss being." Nor do I know of any bona fide idiom (with the possible exception of an ironic or sarcastic one) which, read literally, says the opposite of what the speaker intends.*

Sincerely,
James G. Starkey
Justice
Supreme Court of the State of New York
Brooklyn, New York

Dear Mr. Safire:

Miss not my not reading further anointment of bass-ackward "idioms."

Sincerely,
Sydney Howe
Potomac, Maryland

---

now, *see* presently

---

now is now

"What's now is now," goes the lyric by Bob Gaudio and Jake Holmes, popularized by Frank Sinatra, "and I'll forget what's happened. . . . "

Time was, locutions comparing present and past practice accentuated the past: "What's past is past." However, the sweet bye and bye is bye-bye, and the emphasis has switched to the present.

When the White House press secretary, Joseph L. Powell, Jr., took exception to some news coverage by ABC-TV's Washington bureau chief, Carl Bernstein, he pointed to precedent; Bernstein is said to have replied, "That was then and now is now." That expression possesses declarative power. A more rigidly parallel construction, "That was then and this is now," is not as effective; to borrow a word from strategic jargon, the asymmetry of Bernstein's sentence gave it added force.

Used to be, finality could best be expressed by a look backward: "What's done is done." But as they say ...

Dear Mr. Safire,

You observe that formerly "locutions comparing present and past practice accentuated the past," that now "emphasis has switched to the present," and that the "sweet bye and bye," meaning the past practice of accentuating the past, is "bye-bye."

You may be right, but what's interesting here is your use of the expression "bye and bye" for something in the past. I understand the expression to suggest neither the past nor the present, but rather the future. *When Polonius summons Hamlet to his mother's chamber, Hamlet replies, "I will come bye and bye," meaning "in a little while; in a few minutes." In a recitative on her aging figure and spreading waistline, Jane, in Gilbert and Sullivan's* Patience, *laments "there will be too much of me in the coming bye and bye." Hence, what's past is past, what's now is now, but what's bye and bye is still to come!*

Yours truly,
Philip B. Linker
Assistant Professor English
Suffolk County Community College
Selden, New York

---

numbers cruncher, *see* molar mashers and sob sisters

---

occupations, *see* molar mashers and sob sisters

---

off his back

The interreaganum is a good time to review some of the language of the 1980 campaign.

When Candidate Reagan charged that President Carter was "badly misinformed," a reader wondered if that was redundant or an unintended double negative: Is to be "badly misinformed" to be informed? Answer: No. The "badly" in that use means "seriously" or "woefully" misinformed in a manner that is bad for the misinformee. (On the other hand, New York senatorial candidate Alfonse D'Amato's denunciation of "spurious lies" was in error: A fake lie could be the truth.)

Governor Reagan's favorite phrase turned out to be "get government off our backs." The origin of this metaphor seems obvious—a burden is often carried on the back—but the earliest dictionary citation of "off my back" is 1880. Twenty years before that, Hotten's *Dictionary of Slang* identified the particular burden: "A man is said to have his monkey up, or the monkey on his back, when he is 'riled,' or out of temper." This locution was later adopted by drug addicts to describe their addiction and especially its withdrawal symptoms.

Without the monkey, the phrase "get off my back" was popularized during World War II. If the President-elect wants to show that he is up-to-date (and to dissociate himself from drug-related lingo), he should begin promising that he will help "get government off our case."

---

ommina, *see* New York-ese

---

one "v"

"Now that the conservatives appear to have taken control of government," writes Roy Furman of New York, "can we find out what happens to the second *v* in the movement toward conservatism?" Why isn't what conservatives believe in called "conservativism"?

Both "conservatism" and "conservativism" have been kicking around since the 1830's to describe the political philosophy of those who want to drag a foot as political life picks up speed. The two words mean the same; "conservatism" has become preferred because it is easier to say. (Then why are doctors perversely changing "preventive" to "preventative"? Because doctors like to say things the hard way.)

"Another point is this," advises Anne Soukhanov of *American Heritage*. "The base is *conservat-*. The adjectival suffix *-ive* means 'having a tendency to; having the nature, character, or quality of.' On the other hand,

-ism is a noun suffix meaning 'a doctrine, theory, or principle.' Thus, the addition of the noun suffix *-ism* to the base *conservat-* is more succinct and is devoid of the extraneous adjectival suffix *-ive.*"

In other words, conservatism saves space.

---

onliest, *see* getting down

---

on line, *see* New York-ese

---

on my case

In "get on my case," I noted the disappearance of "get off my back" and the emergence of "get off my case." The "case," I speculated, came from the welfare caseworker, and I suggested that the expression was rooted in the desire of the welfare recipient to be left alone by the caseworker.

"Where are your citations?" demanded competent etymologists. I was nonplussed, a word meaning "so perplexed as to be unable to go further." Eager to get back on the plussed side, I turned to slang detective Stuart Berg Flexner, who is now at Random House (lexicographers are being traded among publishing houses in a frenzy of bidding equivalent to pro-football quarterbacks).

"The first time I heard 'on my case,'" replied Flexner, staying coolly in the pocket, "was in Los Angeles in 1969 in 'That creep is always on my case,' meaning 'harassing me, waiting for me to make a mistake.' The speaker was an eighteen-year-old in the ghetto who had spent a little juvenile time 'inside' for minor drug/shoplifting....

"My first printed citation," he added, lofting his long bomb, "is 'get off my case,' 1971, in Eugene Landy's *Underground Dictionary.* He defines it as 'leave me alone' and says it is a black term. He was with the Gateways Psychiatric Hospital and working with drug addicts, ghetto youths with problems, etc., when he compiled the book, getting most of his words from his patients."

So my speculation was probably mistaken. From those two citations, available, if skimpy, evidence leads us to believe that the phrase was from black slang referring not to social workers but to parole officers and prison psychiatrists. The "case" seems rooted in law enforcement and prisoner rehabilitation rather than in social welfare.

Now will those persnickety linguists demanding documentation kindly get off whatever it is of mine that they are on?

Dear William Safire:

I remember a Louis Armstrong recording of the late twenties, early thirties, also one by McKinney's Cotton Pickers, of a song called "Black and Blue." The lyrics to the bridge were more or less:

I'm white inside,
But that don't help my case

the refrain being a black man saying: "What did I do, to be so black and blue." It seems to me that the substitution of "case" for "situation," as in "in my case" etc. . . . is so simple as not to require simple antecedents. . . .

José Ferrer
New York, New York

---

on "of"

I dreamed I went to the Lincoln Memorial late one night and the Man climbed down off the big chair, jabbed a huge finger in my chest, and said, "Have you heard those Carter thirty-second television commercials misquoting one of my best lines? I said that America was 'the last best hope of earth.' But he's got me saying, 'The last best hope on earth.' Don't they know the difference? 'On' is ordinary—'of' is what gives that phrase its poetry."

I promised to pass it on to the Carter spot makers exactly as written: "We shall nobly save or meanly lose the last best hope of earth." Then I asked: How come no comma between "last" and "best"?

"Call it poetry," said the Emancipator. "Actually I forgot the comma."

While I had his attention, I asked if he had been aware of the speech made on May 29, 1850—thirteen years before the Gettysburg Address—by Theodore Parker at an antislavery convention in Boston, calling for "a democracy, that is, a government of all the people, by all the people, for all the people. . . ."

"The 'all' broke the rhythm," he muttered, climbing back up into his chair and staring straight ahead.

Dear Mr. Safire:

I was intrigued by your comments on Lincoln's presumed plagiarism of Theodore Parker.

I would suggest to you that both Parker and Lincoln were guilty of plagiarizing [John] Wycliffe! Several months ago, while pursuing a biblical quotation in my Bartlett's Familiar Quotations *(Little, Brown, thirteenth edition), I discovered the following: "This Bible is for the Government of the People, by the People, and for the People." It is attributed to the General Prologue of the Wycliffe translation of the Bible!*

Very truly,
Vernon E. Mikkelson, M.D.
Hayward, California

quoting Lincoln

We have here the first confession from a deliberate quotation cooker.

Avid readers will recall the criticism in this space of a campaign television commercial for President Carter that misquoted a Lincoln phrase, "The last best hope of earth." The poetic "of" was changed on television to "on."

Comes now Harry Miles Muheim, of Silver Spring, Maryland, who writes on his home stationery but who can be tracked down to the Pennsylvania offices of Rafshoon Associates, producers of the Carter TV commercials.

"I changed Lincoln's preposition for three reasons," he writes, all Gaul. "First, I didn't think anybody would notice." (He reckoned without eagle-eared Richard Hanser of Mamaroneck, New York, the same phrase detective who hounded the Library of Congress into tracing "founding fathers" to coinage by Warren G. Harding.)

"Second, I was anxious to keep the viewer's focus on the idea rather than the poetry. Lincoln's line was poetic. Mine was not. Mine said simply this: 'Over a hundred years ago, Abraham Lincoln said that this nation was the last best hope on earth.' In this pedestrian, low-flown observation, the use of the accurate preposition, 'of,' would have caused the TV viewer, who lives in a nonpoetic, high-speed world, to turn to his or her companion and say to him or her:

" 'How come Lincoln didn't say, "on earth," instead of "of earth"? Was he just trying to be classy?'

"As soon as the companion replied, the effectiveness of the spot would have been destroyed. For the remainder of the thirty seconds, they would not be considering whether President Carter was a peacemaker, but whether President Lincoln was pretentious. Gerry Rafshoon, an experienced man in focusing political spots, would have sensed immediately that this was off the mark."

The truthful, if unrepentant, Mr. Muheim concludes: "Third, I did not change the meaning of Lincoln's *idea*—not by a scintilla, a jot, a hair, a smidgen, or even a tittle. And the preservation of underlying ideas is, as your column illustrates in such microscopic detail each week, an important part of writing right."

As Lincoln used to say, "with malice toward hardly any," see "to a tee."

on the square

In simpler times, places had addresses. If you wanted to go to a particular building, you would go to the street that was part of the address and then look around for the number. That's why streets had names or letters that set them apart from other streets.

Forget all that. Plazamania has gripped real estate developers, and only the squares have no squares of their own.

In New York City, try to find Astor Plaza; it's not near Astor Place. Nor is Plaza Lafayette near Lafayette Street. Wall Street Plaza? "When we granted the Wall Street Plaza address," explains Jesse Masyr in the Manhattan borough president's office, "we gave it to the developers, who convinced us that they needed the new address. They were located at 88 Pine Street. The city had closed Pine Street. There was no prestige attached to the address. So we gave them Wall Street Plaza, but you could walk your soles off on Wall Street looking for it, because it is actually located at 88 Pine Street."

In Chicago, plazamania is center-alized. Nobody goes to 111 East Wacker Drive anymore—it's now "Illinois Center 1." Try to find out what street First National Plaza 2 is on—you cannot, because that development uses no street address. "The First National Plaza is a very large, well-known development," says Martin Murphy of Chicago's Department of Planning, "not at all difficult to find." Unless you come from out of town. Sears Tower in Chicago, with 4.5 million feet of office space, has its own ZIP code—60684—which means it does not need any street address at all.

Washington is the heart of plazamania, squareness squared. Across from my office (there's a choice New Yorkism—"across from my office") is International Square. Although the three buildings in the complex are assigned old-fashioned addresses—1850 K Street is one—some tenants list themselves in the telephone book as merely at "International Square." That could be anywhere in the world.

Jack Elford, Washington district sales manager for British Airways, says, "We decided to use International Square as the ticket-office address, and 1850 K Street as the address for our other offices." But what about tourists, the people most likely to visit the ticket office? "We have a telephone; they can call us." Did he mean a customer must call British Airways to find out where the ticket office is? "Most people know where International Square is," Mr. Elford assures us. (I'm not even sure it's across from my office.) "Besides," he confides, "there is no number over the door at the ticket office. The landlord didn't put one there."

That required double-checking with the landlord, Philip Carr of Oliver T. Carr Company, address unknown. "Of course they can have a number," says Mr. Carr, law-abidingly. "Tenants who choose to use International Square as their address should also be using their street address to satisfy postal requirements." Same thing goes for the tenants at Washington's new Metropolitan Square, which used to be 655 Fifteenth Street. Until the boys at the National Metropolitan Bank got stars in their eyes.

Not every American city is so laid-back about the undressing of addressing. "In Los Angeles," says Frank Lombardi of the City Planning Department, "city policy had been to insist on street addresses. Developments are allowed to use a plaza address plus their city address. Broadway Plaza, named for the department store, is four blocks from Broadway on Seventh Street. You have to write to John Jones, Broadway Plaza, 1805 Seventh Street. We insist on that. Same with Times Mirror Square—'First and Spring' is part of the address. Otherwise, you wouldn't be able to find anything." I congratulated Mr. Lombardi on his stand for municipal clarity. "I hope we get some good press from this," he concluded. "We could use it: The weather's been terrible lately."

The resistance to the exploitation of nomenclature by Los Angeles is to be commended. Back to New York: I was writing a fan letter to *Time* magazine—Roger Rosenblatt had brightened its pages with a hilarious essay—and looked in the *Time* masthead for the address. All it said was "Rockefeller Center." That's OK for the mailman—but what if I wanted to go there? How would I know it is located exactly at 1271 Avenue of the Americas—or, even more exactly, just north of Fiftieth on Sixth? I would wander around Rockefeller Center until backward reeled the mind and I would have to seek solace at Hurley's Bar.

Enough with the plazas named for companies which lust for addresses with added prestige, to the confusion of the citizens. Now, about Times Square . . .

Dear Mr. Safire:

"On the Square" really hit home with me because I have been victimized by Plazatosis recently as a result of my job hunting. In fact, The Times *is an accomplice in this obfuscatory practice. A "help wanted" advertisement pinpointed the location of American Express's headquarters as "American Express Plaza," which is tantamount to saying, "I am where I am." Since addresses presumably began at a time when cities became too complicated to*

remember everyone's location, this practice of plazafication is really a reversion to the state of nature. "American Express Plaza" is particularly odious because it carries no clue to its location. At least the folks who brought us "Dag Hammarskjöld Plaza" were coherent enough to place it near the United Nations. Likewise for "Penn Plaza" (near Penn Station) except that 2 Penn Plaza is on Thirty-third Street and 4 Penn Plaza is on Thirty-first Street, also a bit muddled.

One more complaint on a related geographic disaster: Avenue of the Americas. One sure sign of an out-of-towner is anyone with enough leisure time to say "A-ven-ue of the A-mer-i-cas." Whoever foisted that upon New York was obviously too thick to realize that street names have to be catchy and concise, and too cowardly to carry his case to its completion, since most of the subway stations still say "Sixth Avenue." Just one more reason for visitors to be baffled by our subway system. "Sixth Avenue" is recommended both by its brevity and its geometric accuracy, being conveniently placed between Fifth and Seventh avenues.

One bit of credit in this matter must actually go to (of all people) the military. With all the plazas, centers, circles, squares, and triangles, there is only one Pentagon. It is therefore "The Pentagon" and easily located for its uniqueness.

Sincerely,
Alan Blasenstein
Merrick, New York

Dear Mr. Safire:

In Japan the buildings have no numbers, and the streets have no names. If you wish to go somewhere, the hotel porter calls your destination, and there follows fifteen minutes of discussion, ending up with a page of written directions which you give to your cabdriver. It relies heavily on references to well-known buildings, parks, etc. And when you finally arrive, your cab goes forward, backs up, etc., as the driver questions passersby.

Sometimes you just go to the chome *or neighborhood (which fortunately does have a name) and ask at a police booth, of which there are thousands. The police person has books and books and can be seen directing people by pointing this way and that.*

Many business cards have maps printed on the reverse.

Office buildings often have huge numbers on the upper stories. You are referred to, for example, "Tanaka 32." Investigation discloses that Mr. Tanaka is a big real estate developer and this is the thirty-second building he built.

Of course, major hotels and office and government buildings are known by name by everyone, and so cabdrivers have no problem.

When I inquired how buildings could be kept track of for property taxes, I found that in each chome *the municipality numbered each structure* serially, *in the order it was built.*

Mailmen and local deliverymen just get to know where everyone in their little area lives.

Guests going to dinner parties in new locations habitually allow an extra half hour or more for searching.

When I told my wife I'd write a letter to them pointing out how inefficient this all was, she made me promise not to. She said they're overrunning the world commercially as it is. Imagine what they could do if they could find their way around.

Sincerely,
Albert Z. K. Sanders
New York, New York

Dear Mr. Safire:

As students of architecture and other disciplines, we are intrigued by your recent description of Chicago's Sears Tower ("with 4.5 million feet of office space"). We are appalled to find that all mention of such a formidable building was omitted from our curriculum. Although a structure of this dimension would not be a North American parallel to the Great Wall of China, it would nevertheless span from 60684 to 58501 (i.e., Bismarck, North Dakota). We are curious whether the other dimensions are equally impressive.

Oh . . . a thought has just occurred to us. Could you have possibly meant square *feet?*

Never mind.

Janet Dorff
John Hollyday
Joe Feldman
University of Pennsylvania
Philadelphia, Pennsylvania

"o" suffix, *see* taking a whack at wacko

"out" construction, *see* out is in

---

out is in

Although surgery is his speciality, Dr. Albert B. Lowenfels of Thornwood, New York, assisted recently at the birth of a new word.

"How's our patient doing?" he asked the house physician at his hospital.

"Fine until midnight," was the reply, "when suddenly he crumped out. I've been with him all night."

Crumped? Dr. Lowenfels reports that he scratched his head. Then he realized that "crumped" was a spanking new verb derived from "crumpled," and given life by the pervasive "out" construction. That night, his wife asked him what kind of day he'd had.

"Not bad," he told her, and tried out the word. "Until about four-forty, when I crumped out."

"I thought so," she said. "You look it."

As that episode illustrates, the "out" construction is in. "Cancel out" is traceable to 1530 and helped lead the way. Generations ago, "knock out" and "eat out" became popular, but those forms used "out" to designate a specific place or state—to be knocked out of this world or to eat outside the home. Similarly, "to ship out" meant "out to sea," and "to pass out" meant "out of consciousness." Later "to drop out" followed this metaphor: to drop out of the unity of a school, just as thieves "fell out" of the unity of their conspiracy and intellectuals "opted out" of the embrace of society.

In the past decade, however, "out" has taken a new turn. Following the "chicken out" of World War II, it is now a combining form that turns any bit of slang in noun or adjective form into a useful, with-it phrasal verb. Hashheads are "spaced out"; inebriates are "zonked out"; acidheads are "tripped out"; and listeners to loud music are "rocked out."

In the same way, a theatrical producer "turkeys out," a depressive "bums out," an excitable fan "spazzes out" (from "spasm"), a plea bargainer "cops out," a moviegoer "flicks out," a stock market "bottoms out," and—as a Xerox advertisement tells us—a learning system "proves out."

A fast-food freak can both "freak out" and "munch out," though the favorite face-stuffing slang verb of Robert Barnhart of Barnhart Books is "pig out." "I was surprised to find no precedent for 'pig out,' a very picturesque expression," says this lexicographer. "There has been no meaning in the dictionary up to now for the word 'pig' as a verb for 'to gorge.' " (Warning: "To veg out" does not mean "to eat your vegetables." It means "to turn into a vegetable.")

Time magazine's review of the movie *Fatso* was headed "Grossed Out": That played on the earlier meaning of "gross," an adjective meaning "fat," and the current meaning as used by teenagers—"icky" or "yechy," or wholly undesirable.

Although "grossed out" was big last year, it is already on the wane: The new form is "scuzzed out." The "scuz" (rhymes with "fuzz") might come from "disgusted": really with-it slanguists are scuzzed out at the squared-out weirdos who still use "grossed out."

Time out. Sometimes "out" is used to change the meaning of a verb. For example, the verb "to bottom" is a lawyer's way of saying "to base upon," while "bottom out" emphasizes a different meaning—"to go no lower."

"Check it" means to "look twice at something," while "check out" means to "investigate it more thoroughly." When a man in Times Square hands you a leaflet for a massage parlor with the crisp instruction "Check it out!" he suggests another meaning—"to give it a try."

Eric Fader of Bayside, New York, a longtime student of the subject (he's been outing out), offers "cool out," to mean "take it easy" (replacing the old "cool it"), and a variant, "chill out," presumably a command to journalists from judges. "To blimp out" is the result of too much pigging out. Then he came up with this out-and-out surprise: "Out" may be on its way out.

" 'Down' is probably the second most popular compounding word today," reports Mr. Fader. "Some examples are 'smoking down,' 'munching down,' etc. To 'hoop out' is to play basketball, but actually playing is 'hooping down,' not 'out.' "

Thus, the language has lucked out (which means "lucked in," the opposite of "out of luck"). I was about to say this item was running out, which would have caused great groaning among the set that really gets down. The fact is that it is running down.

Dear Sir:

It was over two decades ago, when we, in the nursing department of Nazareth College in Rochester, New York, in the late fifties, used the expression "crumped out" often. When we were tired, we would "crump out," and once in a while our hair dryers or some mechanical apparatus would also "crump out."

Very truly yours,
Valerie Deverell
Weedsport, New York

Dear Mr. Safire:

The verb "crumped" was used at least as early as 1965 in Chapter 6 of The Sterile Cuckoo *by John Nichols. The verb appears in a conversation between Jerry and Pookie, the two main characters in the book.*

"You crumped," she accused.
"I was tired."
"You crumped."
"Okay; I get the idea."
"Crumper!" she giggled.

Perhaps Dr. Lowenfels's use of the phrase "crumped out" is new, but not the use of the verb by itself.

Very truly yours,
Leslie Milton
Short Hills, New Jersey

Dear Mr. Safire:

I'd like to speak out on a slight error in "Out Is In." I'm afraid Mr. Fader is mistaken in his way-out assumption that the expression "cool out" is an update of the previous "cool it."

The term has been in use in the English-speaking Caribbean islands for generations. It does *mean "to take it easy," as Mr. Fader states, but West Indians were "cooling out" in village "cold supper shops," under genip trees, and on their gingerbread-trimmed "galleries" long before we frenetic North Americans nearly flipped out and decided to cool it. Just another case of linguistic "fallout," you might say.*

Sincerely,
Robert J. Grodé
New York, New York

Dear Mr. Safire,

I was burnt up when I did not see any reference to the major topic here—"burnout."

Sincerely,
Pauline Lurie
Bernardsville, New Jersey

Dear Mr. Safire:

Though it may be due to a recent shift in meaning among today's youth, I think you have misinterpreted both the meaning and the etymology of "spaz out." This term was in common use more than twenty years ago when I was a preteen and meant "to be very clumsy or ungainly." If you tripped over your own feet (or someone else's) in the lunchroom and spilled your tray of food on the principal, you "spazzed out." The derivation was from "spastic," not "spasm" (though I realize those two words are cognates), and a person who did this often or was generally ungraceful or awkward, especially in sports, was cruelly called a "spaz" by his schoolmates. This soon degenerated into a general term for someone one did not like, even if he or she was not especially clumsy or uncoordinated. The equivalent today is "nerd" or, simply, "jerk."

Your column on "out" as a combining word reminded me of a similar locution we used in college in the sixties. It seems to have completely disappeared from common usage, but we used it ubiquitously to turn nouns into verbs: the use of "it" as a compounding element. For example, "to flick it" meant "to go to the movies"; "to book it" was "to study"; "to pig it" was our equivalent of today's "to pig out"; "to juke it" was "to dance" (or "to juke," which meant specifically "to do the current dances of the moment"). Frequently "up" was added as an intensifier, as in "to tube it up," or to watch a lot of television. The locution was used indiscriminately to make verb phrases out of any noun, even proper names. If your psych teacher's name was Jones, "to Jones it" meant either "to study for Jones's class" or "to go to it." To go to Buena Vista (the location of the closest girls' school) was "to BV it." It also meant, by implication, that one was dating a girl from that school that weekend.

I admit, it all sounds a little silly now, but it was very hip back then. Then "the bee's knees" and "the cat's pajamas" sound corny today, too.

Twenty-three skidoo!

Richard E. Kramer
New York, New York

Dear Mr. Safire:

One is "grossed out" by one who is "scuzzed out." "Scuzzed out" refers to a state of being or appearance, whereas "grossed out" denotes a reaction to disgusting stimuli. Thus, "scuzzed out" is not used as a replacement for "grossed out"; rather, it is a new form of the adjective "scuzzy."

Sincerely,
Cynthia C. Hogan and Mark M. Katz
Arlington, Virginia

Dear Mr. Safire:

It seems ironic that I, a former student of Dr. Lowenfels, should recognize an old term in the same column in which he has pointed out a new one. I refer to "scuzzed out," a reworked combination from the old "scuzzy," which first befuddled me in 1962 as a recruit at Parris Island.

Added to the welter of military jargon new to me was "scuttlebutt" (originally a "keg of water," then "water fountain," and finally "rumor" or "gossip," 'cause that's what you do around a water fountain or water cooler); "pogy bait" (it actually came to mean "candy"!); "gedunk" (store, or canteen, where you can buy pogy bait); "slopshoot" (bar, the kind where beer is quaffed); and "scuzzy."

The derivation of "scuzzy," used at least as early as the Korean War—er, Police Action—is from "scum" and "fuzzy" (bearded), so you had a good guess. Although it was one of the mildest adjectives directed toward recruits, its most common application was to the unsanitary and unkempt civilian population. Thus spoke, at least, the drill instructors, who were suitable etymologic authorities and whose wisdom it was folly to challenge. And that's no scuttlebutt.

Thomas G. Webber, M.D.
Stamford, Connecticut

Dear Mr. Safire:

Apparently Dr. Albert B. Lowenfels has another specialty besides surgery. The term "crumped out" clearly is derived from the term "crapped out," which Dr. Lowenfels could have learned of only through ill-spent hours gambling as an intern.

Sincerely yours,
Jonathan J. Einhorn
New Haven, Connecticut

Dear Mr. Safire:

It may be that when an excitable fan spazzes out, he or she does so with reference to "spasm." But when a klutz spazzes out, the verb derives from "spasm" by way of the derogatory noun "spastic" (from the adolescent epithet "You spastic!" or, simply, "You spaz!").

As popular expressions go, "gross out" (or the more formal "gross me out") has been a biggie for some time and is often heard in my vicinity, as it is a difficult expression to weed out of one's vocabulary. But if "scuzz out" comes from "disgusted," it does so via the recently vogue adjective "scuzzy," which refers to a physical state of extreme filth and "grossness." The height of scuzziness (or perhaps the depths of scuzziness would be more appropriate) might be reached, for example, by an unshaven young man on a Sunday morning after a late night out gorging and imbibing, followed by a few hours of sleep while still dressed. Now that's *scuzzed out!*

The use of the "out" construction may be on the downswing, but new verbs and adjectives are still being coined. My current favorite is "fuzzed out," which refers to my mental state after too much work and too little sleep. And this past summer, while breakfasting out in Philadelphia, I was invited to "pin out" with a friend. I was afraid to respond until he explained that he intended to pass by a nearby pinball parlor and play video games.

I seem to have run out of pertinent information. I guess I should Z-out (grab a few hours of sleep) so I won't be so fuzzed out.

Check ya out later!
Faith Heisler
Paramus, New Jersey

Dear Mr. Safire:

I was surprised that "crap out" was not included. By coincidence, I had my television on at the time, and a sportscaster was interviewing the woman who finished second in the New York City Marathon who was afraid her legs would crap out on her at one point in the race. (I guess that if her legs had crapped out on her, she would have been crumped out on the curb.)

Yours written out,
Jack Murphy
New Paltz, New York

Dear Mr. Safire:

I don't believe that "out" used with a preceding word has to be derogatory. For example, "zonked out" is more frequently "being intoxicated." Also, "spaced out" can be said to mean to be "baffled" in addition to meaning "high." I find you to use the other "out" particles correctly.

Also, if "down" is the second most popular compounding word, how come you don't list more examples? I think you skipped over some commonly used "downs." For instance, "boogie down" is used to say, "Hey, let's dance!" I haven't heard of many of the examples you used. Here are some of the "downs" my classmates and I came up with: "put down," "throw down," "let down," "run down," "come down," "cool down," "chew down," "buckle down," "low down," "wolf down," and "pig down." I hope these will help you to enlarge your particle vocabulary.

Lastly, personally I don't think "out" is on the way out but just peaking and that "down" is almost down and out. Also, an up-and-coming particle is "up."

Sincerely yours,
Beth Gardner
Great Barrington, Massachusetts

Dear Mr. Safire:

Hashheads (though few THC users, or "stoners" in some circles, like to restrict themselves to hash) are not necessarily "spaced out," although they may become "burned out" after one bowl too many, or "destroyed," "wasted," "dusted," "stoned" (out?), and "feeling no pain"—my favorite. "Space cases," "space cadets," "ether breathers," or merely "cadets" are those who seem a little out of touch with the material world.

"Zonked out" represents a step up from the archaic "tuckered out": "I've had two exams and a ten-page paper due in the past two days, and I haven't slept in three; I'm too zonked out to go to a movie." Note that one is never "zonked out" until after *exams; "crashing" before might be fatal.*

Acidheads are not "tripped out" unless they are tripping, in which case they are said to be "tripping." If acidheads "freak out" too far, they may become "burned" or "zoned out." Rock listeners do not "rock out" even if they go deaf.

"Scuzzed out" is a more general version of "grossed out," the latter of which means "being upset at the way or how much someone else has 'pigged out'" (very important phrase in any student circle, since so much school food inspires less than loyal feelings). Being scuzzed out means being "superlatively nauseated"; a scuzzed-out person may also be someone whom you smell before you see; it seems to derive from the unsayable (at least in high school) nuances of "scum," rather than "disgust."

One last, extremely important phrase here: "veg out," with a soft g *(was this covered in a previous column?), expanded to include anything not immediately productive—that is, watching television, listening to rock and roll, talking, playing electronic games, etc.*

Yours,
Alexander M. Epstein
Carl Tickler
New Haven, Connecticut

Dear Mr. Safire,

It may be interesting to note that gay guys, who also are fond of dangling "out" at the end of everything, have completely altered the older sixties meaning of "trick out." In the early sixties, if a male homosexual "tricked out," it implied that he had a lover guarding the home front who allowed extramarital activities once a week, once a month, whatever the agreement permitted. "Out" is, in this case, distinctly directional since one leaves the house and relationship for a slight duration. Today, however, "tricking out" makes sure that the listener knows that the speaker is the biggest whore on the block, at the baths, in the bars, what have you. "Out" here overemphasizes the amount of tricking done, announcing overindulgence at its top performance.

Intensifier: "crash out" and "flake out," or "to go to sleep," especially after a heavy drug session or intense workout; "pit out," or "to work so hard that the underarms of one's shirt/blouse rot out"; "down out" and "red out," or "to take so many barbiturates as to be incoherent"; "jazz out" (a takeoff of "rock out"), or "to play a great deal of jazz music." "Plumped out," "ripped out," and "puffed out" all refer to the musculature of body builders, though the last is demeaning and indicates that person is in it for only a short time. These last three may be directional since the muscles eventually expand "out to there." And speaking of the directional aspect of "out," one can "muscle out" (of a situation), or quit; "bow out" (of the contest), which is obviously a reedition of "taking a bow" (at the end of a play/performance), or "pulling out"; kids "bug out," older hippies "fall out," and homosexuals "come out"—all meaning to leave someplace, the last being the "closet." And when the mind totally snaps, one "flips" or "wigs out," but before that occurs, he'll possibly "bum out." Youngsters with brand-spanking-new licenses still "peel" and "cut out" every weekend. In some areas they "burn out." In the back seats their girl friends "put out," and if a flashlight is shone upon them, the boy "pulls out"—but quick. Homeward bound, the kids might have a "blowout," and without funds Mr. Big might wish his dear old dad gave him a bigger "handout."

Nouns: Side by side with "blowout" and "handout," we find "grossout," or "something/someone which turns our stomach"; "checkout," or "a corpse"; "stepout" and "walkout," or "a patron who leaves an establishment which allows him to return within a certain established period of time"; "brownout," or prison slang for "unclean anus" (a working over of "grossout"?); "dugout," or "some hipster who's done it all, especially said of a teenage old man (from hip "dig"); "flipout," or "a looney tunes"; and "workout."

In one case, the "out" has been dropped (out) from usage by druggies: "Pass out" has been clipped to "pass," yielding "He passed las'night from too much night life, I guess."

In older bebop slang, "back" strengthened the verb or the action: "He scarfed back" = "He ate a lot" and "I dig you fat back righteous" = "I love you, truly I do." "Back," in this regard, seems to have survived in the mod "laid-back" (taking it easy; most *unconcerned). "Down" is on the upswing primarily because, I believe, of the vigorous—if not altogether fresh—getting downism so prevalent in today's youth movement. Among various elements it even doubles as a verb: "We down on the lounge t'night" = "We are going to rob the lounge [name of an establishment?] tonight" (taken from* Scared Straight! Another Story, *a CBS special televised November 6, 1980) and "We downed the dude!" = "beat the piss out of so-and-so." But "up" is gaining popularity, too. We have "fire up" (to light a cigarette, especially a joint), "lighten up" (to take it easy, especially used as a command "to lay off"), and I can conceivably envision "blimp up" (as an alternative to your "blimp out") taking off in that direction.*

All in all, adverbs and adverbial complements are indispensable as magical props. So much meaning can be changed by just one teensy little word: "First she turned me on; then she turned me down!"

Wiped out,
Bruce Rodgers
Santa Clara, California

Psst! People in these parts use "pork out" for "pig out."

Dear Mr. Safire,

I have recently heard a compound that you didn't mention. The phrase is "to ibble out." Its meaning is roughly "to have your fill of a particular food." For example, people might say that they could eat potato chips forever. In actuality after about thirty or so, they get quite sick of eating any more. Therefore, they have "ibbled out."

Sincerely yours,
Michael Schreibman
Brooklyn, New York

---

out of pocket

"During the past few months," writes Mitzi Filson of New York, "I have heard the phrase 'out of pocket' used to mean 'not available,' 'away.' My guess is that this use is a corruption of 'out of town' or 'out of reach.'

"An earlier, and to me, more descriptive, use of the phrase connoted the expenditure of one's own cash for an item—an unreimbursed business expense. I have also heard a related use to connote being strapped for money. Come to think of it," she concludes, "the derivation of 'being strapped' eludes me. Any thoughts?"

I have been searching for the "unavailable" use of "out of pocket" in print for years. One correspondent, Robert Mack of New York, wrote: "I first encountered the words in wire messages when I was a reporter for UPI in the early fifties. . . . I think reporters may have used it back in the days of filing by telegraph. It is obviously quicker and cheaper to reply to a query with 'He outta pocket' than 'He could not be reached for comment.'"

Lexicographic authorities I consulted had no citations to offer—this meaning is in no dictionary—but the clue that the root may be in journalism sent me to the news desk of the Washington bureau of *The New York Times.* Responses there included "It means 'out of touch,' as in 'I'm going to be out of pocket for a few hours,'" and "It means 'not available for comment,' as in 'He's ducking us, gonna be out of pocket all day.'"

Reaching back into dim history, a wordo can find that the phrase began as "in pocket," meaning to be ahead on a transaction, or profiting thereby; in 1693, a character in a Congreve play, short of funds, said, "Egad, I'm a little out of pocket at present," and in an 1882 novel came the first recorded use suggesting reimbursement: "I am out of pocket for my expenses." The latest mutation—of being out of touch, as if defiantly being in no man's pocket—has been kicking around for nearly a generation and is finally recorded herein.

When either a source or a reporter disappears for a time, he is said to be "out of pocket"; some radar-conscious editors prefer "off the scope."

That solves that; but what of "strapped"? Fred Mish, editorial director of G. & C. Merriam Company, confesses: "Neither our files nor the reference works in our library contain anything—even wild speculation—on the origin of 'strapped.'" He cautiously, not wildly, speculates that one recorded use of the word—to mean "to constrict as if by a strap"—might have been the metaphoric source, especially in view of a similar expression like "belt tightening."

Mr. Mish also points to a citation in the *Oxford English Dictionary* from an 1854 glossary of Northamptonshire dialect: "*Strap* or *Strip*, to draw the last milk from a cow." And in 1881: "*Strap,* to drain the last milk from the udder by a peculiar motion of the thumb and finger. Often metaphorically used for draining anything dry." The Merriam-Webster lexicographer adds: "The step from this to the financial sense of 'strapped' is a very small one."

I am willing to take that step with confidence. If you want further poop on "strapped," Miss Filson, you will find me out of pocket.

Dear Mr. Safire:

Regarding the derivation of "strapped," I think you acquiesced too quickly to the possible English dialect source.

In the absence of evidence, such judgments must be based as you know on probability and common sense. I suggest that "strapped" is more likely to be part of a small semantic cluster that includes "pinched" and "straitened" (both of which are defined synonymously with "strapped" in the appropriate sense in Funk and Wagnalls *and* Webster's Third*) than it is to have come from English* *dialect into American English as late as the early or middle nineteenth century. Mathews's earliest citation is dated 1851, and the British dictionaries tend to ignore the sense; therefore, it seems likely to be an American innovation.*

To speak more generally, the idea of constriction and of friction is connected with both penury and parsimony, themselves not far apart semantically. To list some instances at random, we have "penny pincher," "a close man with a dollar," "money's a bit tight just now," "I'd like to pay you, but things are a little tight this week," and the like. I think that Chaucer's line "For I am shave as nye as any frere" in the complaint to his purse is germane, and the British slang "skint" very likely a part of the same cluster. At least in all these cases the probabilities are auspicious.

Sincerely yours,
Robert L. Chapman
Professor of English
Drew University
Madison, New Jersey

Dear Mr. Safire:

In The Reader's Handbook, *published in 1892, Dr. E. Cobham Brewer refers to:*

> *STRAP (Hugh), a simple, generous, and disinterested adherent of Roderick Random. His generosity and fidelity, however, meet with but a base return from the heartless libertine—T. Smollett,* Roderick Random *(1748)*
>
> *We believe there are few readers who are not disgusted with the miserable reward assigned to Strap in the closing chapter of the novel. Five hundred pounds (scarce the value of the goods he had presented to his master) and the hand of a reclaimed street-walker, even when added to a Highland farm, seem but a poor recompense for his faithful and disinterested attachment—Sir W. Scott*

In his Dictionary of Phrase and Fable, *published by Cassell and Company, Ltd. and distributed by Lippincott in 1902, Dr. Brewer cites the phrase "Strappa'do" in connection with a torture still used in which a torturee is lifted by rope over a beam and then suddenly dropped, causing frequent dislocation of one limb or another. In the same publication "out of pocket" is defined as "To be out of pocket by a transaction is to suffer loss of money thereby. More went out of pocket than came into it."*

Recommending Dr. Brewer's work to you, I remain very truly yours.

John Wilkie Beal
Newburgh, New York

Dear Mr. Safire:

"Strapped" may not be as obscure as you suggested. John Farmer and W. C. Henley in their Dictionary of Slang and its Analogues, *Vol 7 (1904), state that "on strap" had the same meaning as "on tick," i.e., credit. "Strapped" thus meant "having gone to the limit of one's credit." Quite why "on strap" should be the same as "on tick" I am not sure. The latter is obvious, the sums being written on a "ticket." Farmer and Henley state that the phrase originally meant "credit for drink." Could the sums possibly have been written on a leather strap? This seems unlikely. Nevertheless, they cite the usage as "common."*

Yours sincerely,
R. W. M. Frater
The Bronx, New York

Dear Mr. Safire,

I was interested in your etymological derivation of "strapped" for "out of money."

The connection to a German saying is striking. When my mother, during my childhood in Germany, saw somebody milk a cow, she used to say: Stripp, Strapp, Stroll, dann ist der Eimer voll *(literally: "Strip, strap, stroll, the bucket then is full").*

As this nursery rhyme is ancient and clearly not a Neo-High-German Anglicism, it illustrates the deep connections between related languages, in this case the common sense of onomatopoeia between German and English.

Sincerely yours,
Hartmut Grebe
Berkeley, California

Dear Mr. Safire:

Regarding "out of pocket": You quote a Robert Mack of New York as saying, ". . . I was a reporter for UPI in the early fifties. . . ."

If that's true, Mack has the distinction of being a reporter before his time. . . as you well know, in the early fifties there was a United Press (UP) and there was an International News Service (INS). Not until the late fifties (May 24, 1958, to be precise) was there a UPI.

Get on the ball, Safire. You're being taken seriously in some quarters.

Sincerely,
Art McAloon
(UPI 1963-79)
Burbank, California

---

parenting, *see* writering

---

parking garage, *see* mod modifiers

pastries, *see* good night, sweet roll

perils of the fast track

"The Saga of Mary Cunningham," the series was titled—a swift-paced account by Gail Sheehy of the rapid rise of a twenty-nine-year-old woman from executive assistant to vice-president for strategic planning, thanks to her own talent, drive, Harvard Business School training, and the aid of a mentor, the Bendix Corporation's CEO, William Agee. The story of Miss Cunningham's temporary downfall—caused by a reaction to rumors of a romantic liaison with her mentor—was lapped up by newspaper readers across the country.

The episode had linguistic interest as well. Confused proverb aficionados were interested in a comment about Bendix's boss by board member Malcolm Baldrige, who was then chairman of the Scovill Manufacturing Company and is now secretary of commerce: "I think he got so close to the forest on this one that maybe he couldn't see some of the trees." This was inside out. The expression is "He couldn't see the forest for the trees"—that is, the person is too close to the individual trees to gain perspective by seeing the whole forest. (It is possible, however, that Mr. Baldrige's seeming misuse was intentional—that he meant that Mr. Agee had so much perspective that he tripped over a detail.)

According to the series, Miss Cunningham said she was warned by a Bendix board member: "You're being used as the lightning rod to strike at him." In this profoundly confused proverb, "You're being used as a stick to beat him with" has been fused with "You are the rod that attracts the lightning." But a lightning rod is something that is struck, not a stick snatched from the roof to strike anybody with.

Hyperverbification—changing too many nouns to verbs—is also a mark of corporate-jet lingo, and was churned up in the Bendix episode. ("Churned up" means drawn from the bottom; "churned out" means produced rapidly or mindlessly; plain "churned" means mixed or fraudulently made active. Good uses of "up" and "out" to vary the meaning of the root verb.) Mary Cunningham is quoted as saying: "You can always Monday-morning quarterback, but somebody has to trailblaze."

This heavy verbifying could have been avoided with: "You can always be a Monday-morning quarterback, but somebody has to blaze a trail." Thus unverbed, it would become a normally mixed metaphor.

The rocketlike rise of any youthful executive resulted, in the past, in the appellation "boy wonder." Probably because of the decline of "girl," similar achievements by women never cause them to be called "girl wonders." Instead, all upwardly mobile executives are said to be on a "fast track."

"Fast track" was originally a railroad term for a route taken by express freight trains carrying perishable produce to market. This usage was paralleled by another track—a racetrack, where horses traveled quickest if the footing was dry—and horses that ran well in mud were said to do badly on a "fast track."

Which has nothing to do with the fact that Richard Nixon, taking up residence in New York in the mid-1960s, popularized the term in a metaphoric sense: New York City, he explained, was "the fast track." In the seventies the construction industry picked up the term to apply to new ideas in modular and prefabricated houses: "fast-track construction." By 1975, reports Stuart Berg Flexner of Random House, *Business Week* was using the term as it is currently understood in executive-suite patois: "We are looking for fast-track people in the $35,000-$40,000 level." Last year, the same magazine wrote: "Of course, some women managers do leap from job to job with the enthusiasm of a fast-track male." (As a compound adjective, the two words are hyphenated.)

In Miss Cunningham's fast-track saga, the man at the top of the heap at Bendix is called the "CEO." In olden times the boss was called "the president"; by the 1960s many men who ran companies gave that title to impatient fast-trackniks and took the title of chairman. Lest anyone wonder who was running the show, the chairman added that he would retain the post of "chief executive officer," or "CEO"; the pushy hotshot who was threatening to leave if he didn't get the prexy title was then described as "chief operating officer"—or, at some television networks, "this year's president."

Throughout this story, soon to be a minor motion picture, the term "mentor" is tossed about. Today that ancient word means a senior management figure who takes a younger person under his wing, risking rumor and innuendo if the protégée, or mentee, is an attractive woman. The name was chosen by the poet Homer for the man to whom Odysseus entrusted his son, Telemachus, before hitting his own fast—though long—track. The eponymous word "mentor" came to mean "trusted friend and counselor" and was recently adopted in business to mean "career guide and executive nurturer."

But here's the beauty part: In *The Odyssey,* the goddess Athena assumed the disguise of Mentor to act as adviser to young Telemachus. It was all a trick: Across the millenia,* the poet warns us to watch out for mentors. As

Mary Cunningham learned, at the start of her own odyssey to CEO, mentors can be trouble.

°Note from W.S.: For the correct spelling of this word, see "come the millennium."

Dear Mr. Safire:

In "Perils of the Fast Track" you wrote: "Today that ancient word [mentor] means a senior management figure who takes a younger person under his wing, risking rumor and innuendo if the protégée, or mentee, is an attractive woman."

The spelling of protégée, with the double e *at the end, anticipates the "woman." This is the kind of agreement that not even the French would make, since they, like us, read from left to right. "Protégé," being a past particle used as a noun, starts life masculine; it becomes feminine by the addition of the mute* e: *"protégée."*

Or did you neglect to underline "an attractive *woman"?*

Sincerely yours,
Robert E. Kiefer
Evanston, Illinois

Dear Mr. Safire:

You speculated about the reason for there being no usage of the expression "girl wonder" while its parallel, "boy wonder," is common.

The reason is that "boy wonder" has a definite literary allusion—to wit, Batman and Robin the Boy Wonder. When I was in college, more years ago than I care to remember, the term was used with a mixture of respect and derision. One who attached himself to a mentor and aggressively pursued his goals, while at the same time appearing somewhat of a goody-goody, was the ideal boy wonder. There was also a hint of the unscrupulous when the boy wonder dealt with his peers. I believe that over the years the meaning has evolved somewhat, and the unscrupulous connotation [has been] lost.

Paul Burstein
Arlington, Massachusetts

Dear Mr. Safire:

In the construction industry, "fast track" has nothing to do with modular or prefabricated houses. It relates to a method of building ordinary construction projects that saves on the total time it takes to bring a project to completion.

Conventional construction calls for the architectural and engineering drawings to be completed, for the job to be bid, a contract awarded, and the actual construction then begun.

Fast track construction requires that basic decisions about the building be made at the outset of the project . . . and not changed. Then each segment of the work can begin as soon as the drawings relating to that part are complete. This means that the excavations can begin almost at once, the steel framework can be erected before the façade has been designed, and much time can be saved in the process. The fast track method also calls for overlapping of project segments—requiring much cooperation among the different trades and subcontractors.

Fast track construction is a leading cause of gray hair among architects and ulcers among contractors, but it can cut significantly into the time needed to complete a project. In that way it can save much money—in interest payments on the construction loan and in a more rapid production of income for the developer.

Cordially yours,
Andrew Alpern
New York, New York

---

pig out, *see* out is in

---

plug

My pet, Peeve, an information retriever, points out that four lively books about language have insinuated their way into bookstores recently.

One is the *Oxford American Dictionary,* a sassy and helpful addition to any library that already contains one of the solid collegiates. Thanks to at least one of its editors, Stuart Berg Flexner, this concise compendium is strong on new words like "gridlock," and vigorous and original in its treatment of peculiarly American terms like "sashay" ("to walk or move ostentatiously, casually, or diagonally"). Though it eschews etymology, it chews over usage, which most dictionaries refuse to do. For example, under "good": "It is incorrect to say *I feel good* when speaking of one's health. Say *I feel well.*" That's daringly prescriptive, and it makes me feel better. Under "different," the peruser can find a quick guide to "than" and "from" that will make him feel good all over: *"Different than* is sometimes correct, but *different from* is always correct."

If you need more of such this-is-the-way-it-is language direction, try the book by the Prince of Prescriptivism, John Simon. *Paradigms Lost* is the apt title of his collection of essays. (Brother, can you paradigm?) He divides people into "civilized" (himself and maybe his copy editor) and "barbarians" (the rest of us). Although he infuriates many with his gleeful elitism, he strikes a mighty blow for high standards, and makes me feel like some kind of left-winger.

Swinging over into the real world of fresh slang and modern mintages, we find the *Second Barnhart Dictionary of New English.* If you're into rare and intrinsically worthless "collectibles," or plan to equip your souped-up roadster with a "fuzzbuster," or want to hail or denounce the "Sonnenfeldt Doctrine"—this scholarly, no-frills econiche for neologisms makes yumptious reading from here to Bosnywash.

Finally, plaudits (always plural) for John Ciardi's *A Browser's Dictionary,* a delightful poking around in word derivations by a man who approaches the language with a sense of wonderment and good humor. "Plaudits," he tells us, comes from the plea by Roman actors to audiences to respond: "*Plaudite* ["You, applaud"]."

I had never seen the origin of "paregoric," a mild tincture of camphor and opium rubbed on babies' gums to relieve the pain of teething; Ciardi shows how it is rooted in the Greek word for "not engaged in politics." Perfect. I would take issue with him on "pipsqueak," an insignificant runt, which he says comes from a small World War I German shell that squeaked in flight. That's what many good dictionaries say, but the *OED* has a citation from 1910, before the war: "It belongs to one of those measly pipsqueaks." And somewhere in the back of my head, irretrievable even by Peeve, is an even earlier use about "making the pips squeak."

The title of this item—"plug"—is defined by the *Oxford American Dictionary* as "a piece of favorable publicity for a commercial product." If any pipsqueak can come up with the metaphoric base of that term, I'll consider it a collectible.

Dear Mr. Safire:

You mention that the author John Simon would have us all divided into two classes—"civilized" and "barbarous." There seems to be a slight error in parallelism here. Do you mean "civilized" people and hence "barbarian" (no s*) people (or possibly "barbaric" people), or "civilians" (???) and then "barbarians" (with an* s*)?*

Yours truly,
Arnon Siegel
New York, New York

Dear Mr. Safire:

You state, on the authority of John Ciardi, that the word "paregoric" is based on the Greek word for "not engaged in politics." This is not the normal meaning of this Greek word.

If you should check one of the English dictionaries which give etymologies (e.g., American College Dictionary, Oxford Universal Dictionary, *or Skeat's* Concise Etymological Dictionary of the English Language*), you would find* *that the English word comes from the Greek adjective* parēgorikos *which means "addressing," "encouraging," or "soothing" (originally in speech and then extended to other things). Liddell and Scott's* Greek-English Lexicon *confirms this. And "soothing" is, of course, what "paregoric" is supposed to be whether as adjective or noun.*

The meaning printed in your article looks like somebody's playful etymology (which your source has picked up somewhere) based on the meanings or associations of the component parts of the Greek word. Thus, para, *a preposition (also used as a prefix) meaning "beside" or "along," can also mean "contrary to," and* agoreuō, *the verb which is at the root of* parēgorikos, *means "I speak in the* agora,*" the public assembly in Greek democracies like Athens. So it is possible for someone to interpret* parēgorikos *fancifully to mean "contrary to speaking in the* agora,*" hence "not engaged in politics." But I know of no such meanings in the usage of ancient or modern Greek.*

Sincerely,
Samuel Lieberman
Professor
Queens College of Classical Languages
Flushing, New York

Dear Mr. Safire:

Before you endorse the Oxford American Dictionary*'s statement that* "different from *is always correct," I urge you to consider which version of the following sentence you prefer:*

"He took a very different position today (than) (from) he took yesterday."

Yours sincerely,
James D. McCawley
Department of Linguistics
University of Chicago
Chicago, Illinois

Dear Mr. Safire:

In your column you describe the Oxford American Dictionary *as "a sassy and helpful addition to any library that already contains one of the solid collegiates."*

As you know, Merriam has been publishing its Collegiate series of dictionaries since 1898. You may not know that "Collegiate" when applied to dictionaries is a registered trademark of Merriam throughout the world.

The category of dictionaries that includes our Collegiate has been given various labels including college dictionaries, college editions, and desk dictionaries. I hope you will assist us in the protection of our trademark by not using "Collegiate" generically in describing dictionaries.

Very truly yours,
Jim Withgott
Vice-President/Administration
G. & C. Merriam Company
Springfield, Massachusetts

Dear Mr. Safire:

We were all revved up about the Second Barnhart Dictionary of New English *which contains the "fuzzbuster" entry you cited.*

My client, Electrolert, Inc., is the manufacturer of the nation's largest selling radar detector—the Fuzzbuster®. Over one million motorists have equipped their vehicles with Fuzzbusters. As the leader of the pack, it is not surprising that Fuzzbuster continues to make inroads within the radar detector industry as a generic label for all similar devices.

Sparked by the promise of a free plug, we hurried to the library to look up the entry in the Barnhart reference work. We were brought to a screeching halt with the discovery that the entry in question included neither an upper-case spelling nor a reference to Fuzzbuster's brand name standing. It almost appeared as if the lexicographers responsible were determined to drive us around the bend. To demonstrate usage, they had selected a quote from High Times *magazine—a dubious recommendation for the product which also failed to acknowledge or record Fuzzbuster as a brand name. Circumstances such as these are hardly what we would consider "paradise for the dashboard light," to paraphrase a pop tune hit.*

Our only alternative in the clutch, of course, is to refer this matter to Electrolert's attorneys. Trademark laws will undoubtedly drive home the point of the Fuzzbuster with a capital F.

Sincerely,
Janis Burenga
President, The Burenga Public Relations Agency
New York, New York

---

plug not ugly

In my White House years, I was given the code name of Multplug, which is a mechanical device to enable broadcasters to take many "feeds" from a single broadcast source. Thanks to multplugs, a President does not have to face a forest of microphones—one mike feeds all.

The broadcast origin of "multplug" should have given me the clue to the origin of "plug" in its meaning of a favorable mention for a commercial product.

Start with "plug," from the Dutch *plugge,* the word for "stopper," usually a piece of wood wedged into a hole or gap. (The little Dutch boy's thumb was plugged into the dike, and a "shot plug" was the material used to fill the hole made in a wooden ship by a cannonball.)

"You need look no further than the issue of the newspaper containing your query," writes Robert McBride of Pittsburgh, answering an appeal in this space for "plug's" commercial origins, and enclosing a small promotional ad. "In these parts they are 'plugs' or 'pluggers' to fill a hole created by a story running short, or an odd measure created by ads. I venture to speculate that the practice goes back to the earliest newspapers."

Similarly, in early radio, fillers of all sorts—commercials, songs, sermonettes—were "plugged in" to fill time gaps. Ruth Rosenstock of Ann Arbor, Michigan, writes: "I was watching reruns of some of the old black-and-white TV shows, when a forgetful cameraman let the tape run a little too long. There, between segments, was a frame that read, 'Plug Commercial Here,' which seemed to be an instruction to the cameraman to insert the commercial spot. My theory," speculates Miss Rosenstock, "is that 'Plug Commercial Here' was eventually shortened."

Thus, "plug" has had a history of being used as a verb meaning "to insert a commercial or promotional message into a gap in newspaper space or air time." Short hop from verb to noun.

But wait: A wholly different, if fanciful, etymology is passed along by Ira Furman, of the Federal Trade Commission. Tobacco leaves used to be inserted into small holes drilled into trees, so that the tobacco would be sweetened by the sap—hence, a "plug" of tobacco. Pierre Lorillard 3d bound his plugs with a metal marker—"Tin Tag" was its name, and the tobacco company's "plugs" were a form of advertising.

You don't buy that one? Or the one about the free samples given out by melon salesmen? How about this? "Plug" is an old derogation of a tired horse. To go "plugging" was to drag yourself around wearily; in vaudeville and early radio, a "song plugger" was one who hauled his products from producer to disc jockey. The "weary peddler" use of "plug" then merged with the broadcast metaphor of "filling air time" to produce what is now a noun for "favorable editorial mention."

Plugging away at this item, I tripped over the origin of "plug-ugly." In Baltimore just before the Civil War, rowdies would clobber one another in "plug musses," which featured boots with spikes in the toes to plug opponents, much as a gunman "plugs" a victim. The hoodlums were known as "plug-uglies"; along with the weary-horse meaning, this gave "plug" a bad name for a time, until the word was sweetened by its tobacco and favorable-mention usages. For those who wish to dig further—keep plugging.

Dear Mr. Safire,

From The Gangs of New York *by Herbert Asbury (Knopf, 1927-28): ". . . the expressive appellation of the Plug Uglies came from their enormous plug hats, which they stuffed with wool and leather and drew down over their ears to serve as helmets when they went into battle."*

He goes on to say, "The Plug Uglies were for the most part gigantic Irishmen. . . ." The Baltimore claim may be rooted in this: "He was an adept at rough and tumble fighting, and wore heavy boots studded with great hobnails with which he stamped his prostrate and helpless victim."

They were among a number of Irish gangs in the Five Points/Bowery area of Manhattan. They were active beginning in about 1825 and peaked as powers during the Draft Riots in July 1863. Some other gangs were the Roach Guards, the Shirt Tails, the Dead Rabbits, the O'Connell Guards.

C. Thomas O'Connell
South Hadley, Massachusetts

Dear Mr. Safire:

Your writing that my suggestion for the origin of the word "plug" in its meaning as a favorable mention for a commercial product was "fanciful" has hurt my feelings and damaged my professional standing.

I gave instant thought to hiring a lawyer, but fortunately for you I work in an agency loaded with them and avoid talking to any lawyer unless it is absolutely necessary.

As for the subject that sparked my contribution and uncharacteristic perseverance, a logical test of whether "plug" as a free commercial has its origins in broadcasting would seem to be whether it was so used before the 1920's. The first commercial radio station—KDKA, Pittsburgh—began operations in November 1920. Perhaps others will pin the first-use date down for you.

As for my suggestion that "plug" may have had its origins with "plug" (chewing) tobacco, the plugs were not, as you wrote, "bound" with metal tags. The metal tags were not in the vein of a seal on a package exterior, or as on a gas meter, to prevent tampering before the box was opened. Rather, each piece had a commercial message embedded *in it as an anticounterfeiting device. Hence, the commercial message got a* free *ride with every piece of tobacco sold.*

Note that "until 1921 plus tobacco sold as well as cigarettes, and Star was the leading brand." Two points: The practice began in 1870, and as late as 1921 the leading brand carried a free commercial—a "plug" within a plug. Also, . . . the practice was copied widely and was the subject of a court challenge by Lorillard in 1885.

Surely if you are seeking the origin *of the word "plug" as a free commercial message, chewing tobacco was an extremely popular vehicle known for 50 years before modern broadcasting began.*

Sincerely,
Ira J. Furman
Federal Trade Commission
Washington, D.C.

Dear Mr. Safire:

The legend "Plug Commercial Here," appearing on a "paddle" (the euphemism used for in-house written instructions in TV prefeeds), would be an order for an announcer to say something nice about the product before a commercial was rolled ("More in a moment after this word from the makers of the Spiffy Sports Car, the world's most successful rubber-band-powered auto"). Incidentally, the word used around Washington by the broadcast media these days for "multplug" has been shortened simply to "mult," a word whose ancestry is easily understood from your explanation of the longer, original nickname.

Sincerely,
Jim Holton
Vice-President, Radio News
NBC News
Washington, D.C.

---

plural attributive, *see* for attribution

---

pops and sons

"What has become of Mommy and Daddy, and Mom and Dad?" asks Isabelle Bradley, an irate mother from Birdsboro, Pennsylvania. "We are becoming a nation of 'Moms' and 'Pops.' "

I have been wondering for some time why my teenage children have been calling me "Pops," which is the name of an orchestra in Boston. My suspicion is that the addition of an *s* to either Mom or Pop connotes an irreverent affection, or detached intimacy, that enables a young person to address a parent in a manner familial yet cool.

"Mama" and "Papa," the endearments of earlier generations, are becoming rare; they recall immigrant days, or our parents' recollections of their parents. "Ma" is used occasionally, "Pa" rarely. Like "Dad," from "dada," "papa" is rooted in baby talk, and led to an 1838 citation for "pop," meaning "father." Nowadays, "Pop," when capitalized and used as the name for someone who is not your father, refers to a likable geezer or the grizzled night watchman.

The declension of filial address begins with a breezy "Howzit goin', Pops?" to a more respectful "About my allowance, Dad," to a resigned and resentful "Yes, Father." Going back up the scale, it is "Thank you, Mother, I can do it myself" to "Mom—can you come over and baby-sit?" to "Seeya, Moms!"

If you are disconcerted by the addition of *s* to Mom and Pop, try answering by calling your son "Sons" or your daughter "Daughters." If they seem puzzled, tell them it's the new middle-aged lingo.

Dear Bill,

"Pops"—More than forty years ago this was a term of veneration for jazz musicians who were virtuosos and relatively senior—e.g., Sidney "Pops" Bechet, Louis "Pops" Armstrong, and George "Pops" Foster—or some musicians who were merely eminent and senior, such as Paul "Pops" Whiteman. You'll find that the interviewers in Q-and-A articles on Armstrong often addressed him as "Pops."

Soon it became a combined term of affection and a shibboleth (denoting that you were one of the fraternity that appreciated jazz) and had nothing to do with either seniority or virtuosity. It was part of the hipster's vocabulary. In the spring of 1941 a group at Hamilton College, freshmen at that, called each other "Pops." And I can remember some of the musicians with the This Is the Army *band using "Pops" to each other in Hollandia, New Guinea, in 1944 or '45. "Dad" was similarly used without connoting age.*

All the best,
William Ringle
Chief Correspondent,
Gannett Newspapers
McLean, Virginia

Dear Mr. Safire:

My own teenage children have never referred to their parents as "Moms" or "Pops." Jazz trumpeter Louis Armstrong used "Pops" frequently as an affectionate greeting, but to my recollection he never used "Moms." He did however use an occasional "Moma" in greeting females, and of course, there is the black entertainer Moms Mabley. Unlike Mrs. Bradley, I have yet to hear children address their parents in this way, but I have observed a tendency in offspring of all ages to refer to their parents and address them by their first names. I feel sure the parents of these children encourage this.

Cordially,
Warner G. Friedman
Sheffield, Massachusetts

Mr. William Safire:

My roommate at the University of Buffalo calls his mom "Mips." His father is "Pips," and his older sister is referred to as "Sips." I suppose if he had a brother, he would be known as "Bips," but that's only my guess. I'm not sure where these titles come from. My roommate will say only that he picked them up from a friend here in Nickel City.

The other big movement in addressing parents is to call them by their first names, but to me they will always be "Mom and Dad."

Cordially,
Thomas Buchanan
Buffalo, New York

Dear Mr. Safire:

You dealt with the words "mama" and "papa" among others. I thought you might be interested in Carl Jung's interpretation of that. In support of his thesis that infantile thinking and dream thinking are simply a recapitulation of earlier evolutionary stages, he tells of a small girl of three and a half. She had been presented with a baby brother who soon became the object of well-known childish jealousy. One day she said to her mother, "You are two mamas. You are my mama, and your breast is little brother's mama." She had just been observing, with great interest, the act of suckling. Dr. Jung concluded, "It is characteristic of the archaic thinking of the child to call the breast 'Mama.' 'Mamma' is Latin for breast."

If you are interested in this, it can be found in Jung's Symbols of Transformation, *Bollingen Series XX (Princeton University Press).*

Sincerely yours,
Robert W. Estill
Raleigh, North Carolina

---

positive, *see* spokesmanspeak

---

prescriptives, *see* ives have it

---

presently

"In their debate," wrote Sally Urang of *The New York Times*' picture desk, "both Jimmy Carter and Ronald Reagan used 'presently' at least three times apiece—to mean 'at the present time.' As you well know, 'presently' means 'anon,' 'soon,' 'in a little while.' "

In olden times "presently" meant "now"; during the past few hundred years it came to mean "soon"; recently it has begun to mean "now" again. What to do?

Here's what to do—never use the word. If you want to talk about what is going on at present, reject both "currently" and "presently," and instead say "now," "at the moment," "today," or "this week." If you mean "in a moment," say "in a moment," not "momentarily," or if you want to play it safe and not tie yourself down to immediacy, say "soon."

Another word I have shot dead for participating in a time frame-up is "directly." It used to mean "right away"; now, L. T. Anderson of Charleston, West Virginia, points out, " 'I'll do it directly' means 'I'll get to it later, or after a while, or when I have time to do it.' "

How come, in the middle of the Now Generation, we've lost contact with "now"?

Dear William Safire,

After reading your note on "Presently," I realized that I had better write you soon—*in the ancient sense of "immediately"—if I was to get a word in edgewise. You're sure to receive a flood of letters from those in the know, informing you that "soon," "anon," and "by and by," which now mean "in a little while," all originally meant "right away." So what has happened to "presently" only illustrates further the procrastinating tendencies of our language, and these, I suppose, illustrate the procrastinating tendencies of ourselves, the speakers.*

I could say more, but want to mail this forthwith.

Sincerely yours,
Marie Borroff
Professor of English
Yale University
New Haven, Connecticut

Dear Sir:

Now hear this. In South Africa, where English is sometimes spoken, "now" does not mean "now." For reasons which nobody there could explain to me, "now" means "in a moment," as in such often heard sentences as "I'll be with you now" and "The tea will be ready now." At first I thought it was nothing more than an abbreviated form of "just now," and I accepted it as such.

One day, however, I was in a bad mood, and I said, "I don't want my tea now. I want it now*!" The reply I got was: "All right! It'll be ready now now." Now, "now now" means, as I learned later, sooner than "now" which means "in a moment," but not as soon as "right now" which is as close to your definition of "now" as a South African can get, but which is still a slight distance from "at this moment."*

While in South Africa (I was producing a movie entitled Zulu Dawn*), I learned to live with this and other variations of the language. I could even make myself understood; things were done when I wanted them done. By the end of my stay I could even tolerate the accent. But upon my return to California I heard South Africans everywhere. I inquired. The English-speaking population of South Africa is producing a high number of expatriates, people who tell you they are "getting out before it's too late." Unfortunately they are bringing their language with them. Is there any danger of their polluting Los Angeles English? Probably not. At least not now or even now now.*

Yours sincerely,
Nate Kohn
Urbana, Illinois

Dear Mr. Safire:

You ask, "How come, in the middle of the Now Generation, we've lost contact with 'now'?" Well, I'm a writer/editor, and I often choose a synonym for the word, because I know from experience that half the time, typesetters will typo the word into "not," completely skewing the meaning of the sentence. Simple defensive measure. Proofreaders may catch it or they may now . . . er, may not.

Alex Vaughn, Editor
Bureau of Business Practice
Waterford, Connecticut

Dear Mr. Safire:

Not only does the Now Generation refuse to use the word "now," but the Me Generation refuses to use the word "me." I don't notice this problem among my freshman comp students as much as I do among the "beautiful people," especially on the "Coast." Many members of the Perrier set seem to think that "me" is merely an inferior form of "I," to be avoided at all costs. They think that they are being sophisticated when they say: "Would you and Tanya like to play tennis with Camille and I?" Paradoxically, when "I" would be correct, often "myself" is used instead: "Camille and myself are going down to the hot tub."

Doesn't anybody teach cases anymore?

Thine,
Bruce Bawer
Stony Brook, New York

WHAT'S THE GOOD WORD?

Dear Mr. Safire:

You recommend the abandonment of the ambiguous terms "presently" and "currently" in favor of the incisive "now." I feel I must warn you that the consequences of such an action could be the slow degeneration of "now" to mean "soon," "later," or even "never." This would leave us no fallback position since, in a world without "now," everything is remitted. No rascal need scoff here, for there are already signs of erosion.

Despite your expressed distaste for writing about Colombia because of its allegedly difficult spelling, I must use it to illustrate my present fears for the future. In my native city of Bogotá, the question "When will you do it?" will often elicit the reply of ahora, *literally meaning "now," but colloquially understood to mean "soon," "later," or "when I get to it." The refinement to* ahorita *is a typically Colombian diminutive which somewhat shortens the time expected for completion, but may mean "never" if said with the proper emphasis. Even more asynchronous is the frequent answer of* ya, *which literally means "already," but is commonly understood not to call for anticipation with bated breath.*

Lest you smile at the rhetoric of mañana *and presume the linguistic superiority of North Americans, I direct your attention to some corrosive uses of the present to which we have already been exposed in this country. "The Time Is Now," for example, will always be true as an isolated statement of fact, but as a political slogan, its use was ambiguous until election day. When UPI reported Mrs. Reagan's unambiguous use of "now" to indicate when she thought the Carters should vacate the White House, an aide clarified the statement by saying that only future presidents and first ladies were meant. Despite President Ford's exhortations to "Whip Inflation Now," our use of language is as inflated as our currency: What else could account for answering a question like "When do you want it?" with "Yesterday"? What are "Now Accounts," anyway? And doesn't it seem odd that* Apocalypse Now *should take so long to end?*

In short, I submit that it is better to fight the good fight in the jungles of "presently" than on the shores of "now."

Sincerely,
Albert Talero
New York, New York

Dear Mr. Safire:

Well, of course, everyone who delights in language and its correct usage has his own pet peeves about its misuse. One of my particular irritants is to find "since" or "during" followed by a simple past tense, such as in "during the past few hundred years, it came *to mean 'soon' "—in your column.*

Fowler fails me once more, so I cannot give you a scholarly reference. But I know that I was brought up to use "has come" in an instance such as this, which gives the sense of a continuing action over a period of time, as "came" does not. "During" predicates a time span; so does "since." It is such a nice subtlety to have them followed by a tense that confirms their inherent meaning; too bad the usage is lapsing.

Sorrowfully,
Sally Campbell
Cold Spring Harbor, New York

---

presume/assume

Correspondent Henry Stanley, the African explorer of a century ago, was abused here more squarely than roundly for saying, "Dr. Livingstone, I presume?" when I thought he should have said "assume."

I have always used "presume" to mean "to go too far" or to take for granted in an unwarranted way. But I am now informed that "presume" can also be synonymous with "assume," as in "the presumption of innocence." When used in this meaning, "presume" is slightly more emphatic than "assume." (I presume my readers understand this; I assume other people may.)

Robert Machol, who presumes to instruct us in this matter, reads these words in the *International Herald Tribune*; from somewhere in Europe, he passes on this conundrum: "What is the question to which 'Dr. Livingston, I presume' is the answer?" The question: "Dr. Presume, what are your first name and middle initial?"

Dear Mr. Safire,

You refer to Henry Stanley as an "African explorer." English is not my native tongue, but I cannot help but feel that to refer to him as an "explorer of Africa" would be better.

Very truly yours,
Laury Heilpern
West Islip, New York

Dear Mr. Safire,

You write, citing Robert Machol, " 'What is the question to which "Dr. Livingston, I presume" is the answer?' The question: 'Dr. Presume, what are your first name and middle initial?' "

Presumably, the answer to said question would be only "Livingston I." if, as it appears you would have us assume, the person in question were Dr. Livingston Irving Presume.

Rather, the question needed to elicit the desired answer would be something along these lines: "What is the name by which you would like me to introduce you to the august company assembled?" Or, alternatively, "Do you know whose ton of books this is in Dr. Living's room?"—to which a plausible answer would presumably be, "Dr. Living's ton, I presume."

In sincerity,
Avram Israel Reisner
New York, New York

Dear Mr. Safire:

By now you have probably received dozens of letters from lawyers presuming to inform you of the meaning of "presume." For what it's worth, here's Weiss on Presumptions:*

*For one thing, "presume" as a transitive verb means, roughly, "to impose upon" others. It carries an implication that the person doing the presuming is of a lower order than the one presumed upon (*vide *the first sentence of this letter).*

In the sense pertinent to your column, "presume" bears some resemblance to "assume," but they are by no means synonymous. And "presume" certainly does not imply a stronger or more sincerely held belief. On the contrary, a "presumption" is a form of thought control telling us what conclusion to reach if we really don't believe anything or, at least, have some doubt. The presumption of innocence is a good example. No one in his right mind really believes—or "assumes"—that the disreputable character in the dock is innocent; but—since we must begin somewhere, we require the prosecution to present evidence that he is guilty and to bear the risk that the jury won't be persuaded that the evidence excludes every reasonable doubt. In legalese, presumptions are used to fix the burden of proof—they tell us what state of facts must be found if we are not persuaded to the contrary. (I am not dealing here with that grammatical and logical monster the "irrebuttable presumption," which is usually nothing more than a principle of law for which judges don't want to take the blame.)

As for Stanley and Livingstone, if Stanley believed that the gentleman he was addressing was in fact Dr. Livingstone, he should have said "I assume." If Stanley didn't have any idea whom he was addressing but made a practice of giving the benefit of the doubt to every white man he happened to run across in the bush, his use of "presume" was precisely correct. Or perhaps Stanley was graciously conceding that his newspaper-sponsored junket was an imposition on David Livingstone's privacy.

Very truly yours,
Lawrence N. Weiss
New York, New York

**Notice I did not say "to advise you," as many of your other legal correspondents probably did. It might be worthwhile some day to write a column clearly separating the gold of advice from the dross of information. My profession, which should know better, is not entirely without responsibility for the confusion. Advice is something for which I am, or should be, paid handsomely; information is something I sometimes give away gratis.*

Dear Fellow-Times-Columnist,

No doubt you have had plenty of letters pointing out that your Dr. Livingstone question was inadequate. I suggest a question from the telephone company: "Dr. Presume, how do you wish to be listed in our directory?"

Best wishes,
Alan Truscott
Bridge Editor
The New York Times

---

pronomenclature, *see* "bloopies"

---

pronouns, *see* down with "one"

---

pronunciations, *see* shibboleths

---

pumps, *see* man the pumps!

---

puns, *see* a barrel of puns

---

racking, *see* getting down

---

rasher, *see* menumania

---

reference, *see* ding!

---

reinstitute, *see* tenterhooking

reinstitute, *see* tenterhooking

retronyms

A new form of compound word has been created to help old words avoid technological displacement.

Consider the word "guitar." In olden times you could play a Spanish guitar or a Hawaiian guitar, but your instrument was accurately denoted by the single word "guitar."

Along came the electric guitar. No longer could you say, "He plays the guitar," for fear of being immediately asked, "What kind—the electric guitar or the old-fashioned guitar?" Since people do not like to be old-fashioned, especially in the music world, players of "regular," or nonelectric, guitars have come to call their instruments "acoustic guitars."

Similarly, "natural turf" is the phrase now being used by sportscasters to differentiate that old-fashioned field from "artificial turf." Another word for natural turf is "grass"; we can soon expect all signs to read: "Keep off the natural turf."

Frank Mankiewicz, president of National Public Radio, collects these terms and calls them "retronyms"—nouns that have taken an adjective to stay up-to-date and to fend off newer terms.

Other retronyms include "hard-cover book," which was merely a "book" before the soft-cover book came along; "manual transmission," which used to be the "gearshift" before "automatic transmission" became popular; "fresh squeezed orange juice," which we called "orange juice," or "OJ," before the frozen variety, sometimes slyly called "fresh frozen orange juice," grabbed the mass market; and "stage play," which was legitimately called only a "play" until "television play" forced it to take "stage" as a modifier. (A stage play is a "live performance," with the "live" added after the onslaught of "recorded," or even "prerecorded," performances.)

A special category of retronyms is used to defend words from a more general obsolescence: "real cream," for example, is the name of the cow-produced liquid that is not your usual nondairy creamer; "roast coffee," which is neither instant nor freeze-dried; and "natural food," which is not fast and has no preservatives added.

Thank you, Mr. Mankiewicz, but I am still a devotee of private radio.

Dear Mr. Safire:

Thank God for retronyms. Until we read your article, we thought the use of "handwritten manuscripts" in our new brochures was a ghastly mistake that would necessitate reprinting 35,000 brochures.

Now that we know that we are in the vanguard of a new movement in semantics, we can happily retain our present brochures. "Handwritten manuscripts"—formerly known to archivists simply as "manuscripts"—will be the perfect term for hordes of researchers anxious to distinguish between these items and original typewritten materials—now known as "typewritten manuscripts," probably done with the same model Selectric II I'm using now.

Hooray for Mankiewicz!

Sincerely,
Stanton M. Frazar
Director
The Historic New Orleans Collection
New Orleans, Louisiana

Dear Mr. Safire:

As one Syracusan to another I feel constrained to state that you may be a devotee of "broadcast radio," but not of private radio, which, according to the regulations of the Federal Communications Commission, is to be used for business purposes, such as delivery services, taxicabs, etc. Indeed, the FCC has a specific bureau to deal with these matters, called, of all things, the Private Radio Bureau.

With kindest regards, I am,

Sincerely,
Philip R. Hochberg
Washington, D.C.

---

reverend, *see* uncommon prayer

---

rip and reader, *see* molar mashers and sob sisters

---

rule in

Horse racing is the source of all sorts of political clichés: Will John Anderson, the *dark horse, bolt*? Will *front-runner* Reagan prove to be a *shoo-in*? (A shoo-in was a fixed race in which the horse bet upon was shooed in, or helped to win, by the other jockeys in the race.) Who will be the *running mate*, who the *also-ran*, and who will take the *reins* of government?

The sport of kings is also the source of a locution that has become a favorite hedge of candidates: "to rule out." This phrase—originally used to mean "to debar a horse from a race"—was absorbed into the general language as a synonym for "exclude" nearly a century ago. The first citation in the *Oxford English Dictionary* is this 1890 item in the *Spectator* supporting neologisms: "Resolved not to see expressions ruled out of the language merely because they are new."

A candidate who wants to say, "Let's not get into that," or, "I'd prefer to duck that issue," or even, "I'll jump off that bridge when I come to it," but who does not want to appear indecisive or evasive, makes use of the rule-out construction: "I make no commitments along those lines, but [spoken ominously, or broad-mindedly] I don't rule that out." ("Commitment" has replaced the hackneyed "pledge," which replaced the discredited "promise.")

Similarly, newsmen desperate for a lead on a dull day will ask, "Are you ruling out such and such?" If the hapless candidate says, "Hell, I could never do that," the lead becomes "Candidate Forthright today firmly ruled out any consideration of . . ." If the same candidate murmurs, "Do I have to decide that this morning?" the newsman gets his lead the other way: "Candidate Forthright today refused to rule out the possibility of . . ." (When this trap is sprung on a Soviet official, it is called "Russian rule-out.")

Cagey candidates have come up with a defense to rule out roulette: "I'm not ruling it out, but that doesn't mean I'm ruling it in." The odd expression "to rule in" is now current in political usage: Senator Richard Stone, Democrat of Florida, reported that an administration witness before a Foreign Relations subcommittee "ruled out substantial military bases, but ruled in lightly manned, local facilities."

Keep your eye on "rule in"; as the 1890 *Spectator* pointed out, it should not be ruled out of the language merely because it is new.

Dear Mr. Safire:

Anent your article in which "rule in/rule out" (RIRO?) is discussed, I would like to submit this: you note: "originally used to mean 'to debar a horse from a race.' . . ." Taking the phrase literally, I conclude: "to take a rule(r) and draw a line through," as, e.g.,

Seabiscuit
~~*War Admiral*~~
Equipoise
Count Fleet

thus debarring War Admiral from the race.

If such is the case, it seems to me that the origins would predate the sport of horse racing and perhaps go back into the earliest forms of writing when erasing, say, was unheard of. Or perhaps in the earlier forms of accounting and/or bookkeeping when, for whatever reason, the original *entry was needed in order to see* what *it was that was "ruled out." Then, by extension, it was possible to* reconsider *the "ruled-out" item since it was* still visible. *If what I have suggested is correct, or at least accepted, this also precludes that contraphrase (?) "rules in." Or to put it another way—there can be* no such thing *as "ruling in" (see "cagey candidates") or "ruling [it] [back] in." It's an interesting point.*

Stanley L. Howard
Cockeysville, Maryland

---

salutations, *see* dear madams

---

sandbagged, *see* stiffed, sandbagged, and set up

---

schrod, *see* catch of the day

---

scurrilous, *see* cheap shots

---

see the sea change

"Election Brings a Sea Change to U.S. Politics," headlined the *Washington Star.* Throughout punditland, the Reagan landslide and the new majority in the Senate were interpreted not as a change, or even a major change, and certainly not a radical change, but as "a sea change."

Whence this metaphor of the most far-reaching change of all? What phrase coiner came up with a pair of words that means "marked transformation," such as would happen to an object that had spent eons in the corrosive salt water and high pressures of the deep?

Shakespeare, that's who, in *The Tempest*:

> Full fathom five thy father lies;
> Of his bones are coral made:
> Those are pearls that were his eyes:
> Nothing of him that doth fade
> But doth suffer a sea-change
> Into something rich and strange.

Let's face it, that's a big switch. Shakespeare's hyphen has been dropped over the years, and "sea change" is now two words, a compound noun, but the eerie imagery has never been surpassed in the vocabulary of change. It applies perfectly: To many wary bureaucrats in Washington, the incoming Republicans are seen to be "something rich and strange."

Dear Columnist:

Wonder, did you note that the lines you chose to quote from Shakespeare contain what is probably his only grammatical error?

Should have read: "Of his bones is *coral made:"*

Tssk . . .

Arthur Liebers
Remsenburg, New York

Note from W.S.: Shakespeare liked "between you and I," too.

set up, *see* stiffed, sandbagged, and set up

shedding, *see* words for nerds

shibboleths

"Gimme an 'O'!" shouts the Ohio State cheerleader, and the fans roar back with an "O." The name of the state is rousingly spelled out, and the cheer concludes: "O,H,I,O—Ahia!"

"Ahia" is how you pronounce Ohio if you come from that state, according to Charles Stough of the *Dayton Daily News.* He adds that Versailles is pronounced "Ver-SALES" (strange—Kentuckians call their Versailles "Ver-SAWLS"), New Bremen is "New BREE-men," Cadiz is "CAD-dis," and Houston, Ohio, is called "HOW-ston" by the local people. (The last will come as no surprise to New Yorkers, who have been calling Houston Street "HOW-ston" for centuries, and wonder why Texans prefer "HYOO-ston.")

We are talking here of shibboleths, those passwords that signal who is a native and who an outlander. "Shibboleth," the Hebrew word for "stream," was used by the soldiers of Gilead to separate their neighbors from the Ephraimites, who pronounced the *sh* as an *s*; because they couldn't get it right, according to Judges 12:6, 42,000 Ephraimites were slain. In those days, pronunciation meant something.

If an American city is named after a foreign city, chances are it is pronounced differently. In Minnesota, Montevideo is "Montevi-DEE-oh," not "Montevi-DAY-oh." In Idaho, it's "Mos-coh," never "Mos-cow." Sample the *Wienerbrot* in "VY-enna," not Vienna, Georgia, and try the pasta in "MY-lan," which is the way they pronounce Milan in Ahia. In South America, Lima, Peru, may be "LEE-ma, Per-OO," but in Ohio, it's "LY-ma," and in Indiana, it's "PEE-ru." Similarly, say "CAY-ro," not Cairo, Illinois; "New BURR-lin," not New Berlin, Pennsylvania, and "Del-high," New York, not "Del-hee," as in India's New Delhi.

If you're in Quincy, Massachusetts, and don't pronounce it "Kwin-zee," get out of town. Newark, Ohio, is pronounced "Nerk," and Newark, Delaware, is pronounced with two syllables—"NEW-ark"—which residents of Newark, New Jersey, think is hilarious, because they know it should be "Noork." In Oregon (the outsiders say "Ore-gone" and the insiders say "Ory-gun"), my colleague Jack Rosenthal instructs, "the fertile northwest part of the state is organized around not the 'Will-a-METTE Valley,' but the 'Will-AM-ette Valley'—rhymes with 'dammit.' "

Hoosiers, reports Don Wigal ("WHY-gul") from Indianapolis, say "In-yuh-napplus" or simply "Naplus," while tourists insist on six syllables. Scores of readers point to Louisville, Kentucky, which is "Looie-ville" only to outsiders—residents call it "Lou-a-ville" or more often just "Louvul." Nor does anyone meet you in St. Looie, Louis—the pronunciation of that town is Anglicized to "Saint Lewis."

Outsiders get on local nerves with "Frisco" for San Francisco, "Chi" for Chicago ("Chi-CAW-go" if you were born there, "Chi-CAH-go" if you moved in), and local teeth are set on edge by "San Antone" for San Antonio. Curiously, people from Cincinnati, who call their city "Cincinna-tuh," take no umbrage at "Cincy."

The most thunderously mispronounced city names are Miami, New Orleans, and Baltimore. To Miamians, the Tamiami Trail goes through "Miamuh"; tourists call it "Miam-me." The saints go marching in to "Noo-OR-luns" or "Nawlins," while jazzy tourists come marching in to "NOO Or-LEENS." Marylanders live in "Ballimer," while the rest of us are suited to a tee by Bal-ti-more. (Whence "to a tee"?)

Donald E. Schlesinger of New York, a French teacher, has discovered a difference in the sound of clicking dice in Las Vegas, Nevada: "As a frequent visitor to that town, I can vouch for the fact that the universal native pronunciation is 'Los Vaygus, Ne-VAD-da,' whereas outlanders tend to say 'Lahs Vaygus, Ne-VAH-da.' It has always surprised me that they pronounce the 'Las' as if it were the same as 'Los' (Angeles, for example); but I assure you that, particularly on television, they do."

Students of Jeffersoniana travel to Monticello, Virginia, pronounced with a *ch* by visitors and with an *s* by townsfolk; in Monticello, New York, it's the other way around. With determined inconsistency, Iowans call Des Moines "Duh Moyne," but Illinoisans call Des Plaines "Dess Plains." And a person traveling from Lancaster, New York, to Lancaster, Pennsylvania, would go from "Lane-caster" to "Lank-ster."

The correct pronunciation is the local choice. In Great Britain, Cholmondley is "Chum-ley"; to pronounce it the way it looks is the mark of the uninformed. Obeisance to local "ignorance" may distress New York City students who attend the State University at Binghamton, and hear the locals call the street named Beethoven "Bay-THO-van" and Goethe Street called "Go-thee," but—reports Senator Moynihan's aide Timothy Russert—such is life in New York.

These are not mispronunciations, but unexpected pronunciations. They assert group individuality—or, if you like, a benign ethnocentrism. If you come from New Haven, you know it's pronounced "New HAY-ven"; it's fun to spot the outsiders who call it "NEW Haven." Only visitors call Yakima, Washington, "Ya-KEE-ma"—laughing natives "YACK-i-maw." Michiganders who live in "D'troit" will smile at July's Republican conventioneers—looking forward to football's "dee-fense"—calling their town "Dee-troit." There is no "cord" in Concord, nor any "body" in Peabody—those Massachusetts towns are "CONkit" and "PEAB'dy."

The joke sent along most frequently in the mail on shibboleths was "How do you pronounce the name of the capital of Kentucky?" The answer, of course, is neither "Louie-ville" nor "Lou-a-ville"—it's "Frankfort." And people who hold the "fort" in Frankfort are as numerous as the descendants of the Ephraimites.

Dear Mr. Safire:

*Two comments are in order, regarding "On Shibboleths." One is that the proper pronunciation of Montevideo (Minnesota, that is) is "Monna-*video,*" with "video" pronounced exactly the same way that it is pronounced in "videotape" or "Captain Video." You'd be laughed out of Montevideo for calling it "Montevi-dee-oh." (Years of watching weather forecasts in the five-state area are the basis of my correction. I even traveled through there a couple of times.)*

Secondly, why did you omit mention of the pronunciation of the name of the capital of South Dakota? I can imagine the letters you'll be getting from readers from Pierre (pronounced "peer"), demanding equal time.

Sincerely,
Zachary M. Baker
Brooklyn, New York

Dear Mr. Safire:

Concerning your request for regional pronunciations of geographical entities, the New York-ese for Houston Street immediately comes to mind. New Yorkers, of course, say "House-ton," not "Yews-ton," as hinterlanders are prone to do. I had always thought that the reason for this was that the name of this thoroughfare was derived from the Dutch word huys-tuyn, *meaning "house-garden." However,* The Street Book *by Henry Moscow (a splendid book) says this is not so and Houston Street is named for William Houstoun, a Georgia delegate to the Continental Congress, and so the origin of the New York-ese pronunciation remains a mystery (unless Mr. Houstoun of Georgia was, unlike Mr. Yews-ton of Texas, actually called Mr. House-ton).*

Respectfully,
William T. Johnsen
Brooklyn, New York

Dear Mr. Safire:

The name of New Hampshire's capital city, of which I have the honor to be mayor, fits precisely into your "shibboleth" category.

It is my understanding that there are approximately seventeen municipalities in the United States which bear the name Concord. In New Hampshire and Massachusetts, the locals pronounce the name approximately as if it were spelled "conquered." However, in all the other Concords in the United States, the locals pronounce it with approximately equal emphasis on both syllables, i.e., "Con-cord," the same pronunciation given to the variety of grape and the Catskill resort.

The "password" value of Concord's pronunciation was dramatically demonstrated to me in 1977, when American Motors brought the mayors of most of the Concords in the United States to Detroit, to attend the unveiling of AMC's new automobile the Concord (pronounced like the grape). I was immediately able to recognize the representative of Concord, Massachusetts, and to distinguish all the others. AMC's public relations people were dismayed to learn about the difference in pronunciation but recovered gallantly and immediately began pronouncing the word both ways.

Locally we can always detect the inadequately tutored presidential primary candidate or the "foreign-made" television commercial through the way our city's name is pronounced.

Yours very truly,
Martin L. Gross, Mayor
Concord, New Hampshire

Dear Mr. Safire:

My colleagues have asked me to present our concerns about "shibboleths." The Concise Oxford Dictionary *(thumb index, mind you) states that "shibboleth" derives from the Hebrew word for "an ear of corn," not "stream," as you report. Perhaps you base your information on rabbinical authority that would eclipse Oxford.*

Yours sincerely,
Ian A. N. Sainsbury
Toronto (TRAW-na), Ontario

Dear Mr. Safire:

You state that "shibboleth" is the Hebrew word for "stream." That is not quite correct. It means the current *of a stream, not the stream itself. It is used with this meaning in verse 2 of Psalm 69.*

The word, which is pronounced "shibolet" in modern Hebrew, also means "an ear of corn or a spike." It is also the Hebrew name for the star Spica.

Very truly yours,
Michael L. Ticktin
Roosevelt, New Jersey

Note from W.S.: The current etymology is in the following letter from an eminent lexicographer.

Dear Bill:

The Hebrew word שבלת, *from a Ugaritic root, has several meanings: flowing stream (as in Isaiah 27:12 or Psalms 69:2), ear of corn (as in Ruth 2:2 or Isaiah 17:5), or twigs or branches (as in Zechariah 4:12). The first meaning makes most sense in the Judges narrative precisely because the incident took place at a stream. Seems like a logical password.*

And add to your list: In Cheyenne you're a furriner unless you say "shī an'," in Terre Haute it's "ter'ə hut'," and in Vienna (Ohio) it's "vī en'ə."

Yours,
David B. Guralnik
Dictionary Division
Simon & Schuster
Cleveland, Ohio

P.S.: "Help" in Hebrew is ezer *or* ezrah, *but if you're in real trouble, yell* gvalt! *or* rahtevet!

Dear Mr. Safire:

The piece on shibboleths reminded me of a World War II story I had heard from a Dutch friend. It is interesting because it almost exactly parallels the story of the Gileadites and the Ephraimites. The Dutch underground during the war had to be very careful about Germans infiltrating their ranks. This was difficult because many Germans speak very passable Dutch. But one word nobody except a native Dutchman can pronounce correctly is Scheveningen, the name of the Dutch seaside resort. Accordingly, Dutch underground members, in conversation with recruits, would bring the conversation around to seaside resorts in general and Scheveningen in particular. According to my friend, the recruit's pronunciation of the word was an infallible test of nationality.

Russell Fessenden
Ashfield, Massachusetts

Dear Mr. Safire:

It might be good to investigate what happened to Los Angeles. I'm a native Californian (a rarity in my time), and we were properly smug when a visitor would say "Losanjulus" or even "Losanj'leez." The natives in my day pronounced the g *on the hard side, as in "anglophile" or "angostura." We insisted it was closer to the original Spanish which makes the* g *a soft guttural—"Losanghelez." Today, via television tutelage, broadcast mainly from "Losanj'leez,"* that's *become worldwide. Or has it? Am I the last of the breed who insists on coming close to the original Spanish? There must be others.*

Also try San Francisco. We still hear it done in three words: "San Fran Sisko." Pure tourist. The natives, of course, swallow it all in one gulp: "Sanfrnsisko." The a *following the* r *simply does not exist. (And to say "Frisco" within a native's hearing is instant death.)*

The biggest shock I got last week was from a New Yorker on his way to a California vacation. He was planning a side trip to "Yoz'em-Ite!" I did not correct him. Mean.

M. Seklemian
New York, New York

Dear Mr. Safire,

You asked for city pronunciations for a piece on shibboleths. One comes to mind relating to Wilmington, Delaware, where I spent most of my earlier life. To the native "Du Pont" means E. I. du Pont de Nemours & Company, which has its headquarters there, and "Du Pont" refers to a member of the family whose ancestors founded the company and who are still prominent in the community. They pronounce the word with the accent on the second syllable consonant with its French origin. Visitors and outlanders tend to put the emphasis on the first. I recall asking a salesgirl in a small store in the area for "Du PONT ceMENT," and she replied, "You mean DU pont SEEment."

Sincerely,
Thomas Spackman II
Peach Bottom, Pennsylvania

Dear Mr. Safire,

Two Wall Street Journal *Dallas bureau reporters, Neil Maxwell and Steve Frazier, playful about your request, listed in a bar in Dallas late Good Friday afternoon a raft of shibboleths from the Midwest and the South, which I promised to record and send or deliver to you.*

The Arkansas River runs through Frazier's home state, Kansas, as the "Ar-KAN-zass" River, but it's the "AR-kan-saw," Maxwell says, by the time it reaches Tulsa, Oklahoma, where he's lived. Kansans embarrassed to call it the "Ar-KAN-zass" call it the "Ark," and Arkansas City (that's "Ar-KAN-zass," again) is known, similarly, as "Ark City." Salina, Kansas, is "Sal-EYE-na" to Kansans, but "Sal-EE-na," often, to other folks. Olathe, Kansas, is known within the state as "O-LAY-tha"; outsiders sometimes figure it's akin to the carpenters' tool. Nevada, as a town in both Iowa and Missouri, is "Ne-VAY-da." Prairie du Chien, Wisconsin, is, to its residents, I'm told, "Prairie-doo-SHEEN," but its name often is "mispronounced" "Prairie-doo-SHAYNE."

Palestine, in Texas, is "PAL-us-TEEN," not "PAL-es-TYNE." Mexia, Texas, carries the Spanish pronounciation "Me-HAY-a," but its residents have heard transients call it "MECK-si-a." Similarly, San Antonio's Bexar County is "Bay-HAR," but that isn't, you can be certain, what one always hears.

An apparently once-French name, Metairie, Louisiana, is, to residents, "MET-ar-ie"; it's sometimes pronounced "Met-AIR." Kissimmee, Florida, is pronounced locally "Kiss-IM-ee," but tourists sometimes stress the first or third syllable, I'm told.

In Georgia, Hahira is "Hay-HI-ruh," Alapaha is "Uh-LAP-uh-hah," and Albany is "All-BEN-ny."

The only two shibboleths I thought of are "Pa-GOH-da," New Jersey, which is spelled Bogota, like Colombia's capital, and Oxford University's "MAWD-lin" College, known in print as Magdalen.

Sincerely,
Holly Neumann
New York, New York

Dear Mr. Safire,

Speaking of shibboleths, any self-respecting Canadian would take issue with the statement that "the cities in Canada that Americans call 'To-RON-to' and 'Kwa-BECK,' [but] Canadians call 'TRON-na' and 'Kuh-BECK.'" In Canadian nomenclature, Quebec is termed a province. The capital located therein is Quebec City, *not to be confused with Montreal (pronounced "Mon-ray-AL"), believed by many Americans to be Quebec's capital city.*

Sincerely yours,
Debbie Jacobovits
New York, New York

Dear Mr. Safire:

I may be the 392nd person to write in in amazement to your saying that people born in Chicago say "ChiCAWgo" rather than "ChiCAHgo," but here goes.

I *always thought that you could tell a foreigner from a native American by the way he pronounced the name of the Windy City. An Englishman might err and say "ChiCAWgo" or even "ChiCAHgo," but* all *native Americans know that it is pronounced "ShiCAWgo" or "ShiCAHgo" and always has been. Come to think of it, native Chicagoans say "ShiCAAgo."*

You English or something?

Sincerely,
John P. C. Matthews
Princeton, New Jersey

Dear Mr. Safire:

Were you, sir, to be running a scam, and I to be your mark, and you were to try to ingratiate yourself by saying, "What a coincidence! I, too, was born and bred in Rocky River, Ahia," I would have the law on you before you could say "Metropolitan Northern Ohio." (That last word begins and ends with a clear, round O.*) "Down-Ohio" and Appalachian accents are considered decidedly substandard in this area.*

Sincerely,
Jean Guyot
Vermilion, Ohio

Dear Mr. Safire:

You state, according to Judges 12:6, "42,000 Ephraimites were slain." My Bible puts this as "forty and two thousand" which can be interpreted as 2040 or 42,000. Which is it? At the Battle of Gettysburg, which I remember reading about somewhere, the casualties were abnormally high—some 23,000 plus of which about 7,000 plus were listed as killed. So 42,000 seems to be in error. Particularly since the biblical battle occurred sometime about 1000 B.C., when the warriors weren't up on the high state of technology we now have for killing people.

Sincerely,
Edward J. Grabowski
Germantown, Maryland

Dear Mr. Safire:

My consternation this week comes from what is now supposed to be the accepted pronunciation of the Afgani city of Kabul. I knew I was in trouble when I first heard Walter Cronkite pronounce it "Cobble." "Arthur," I said to myself, "Arthur, if Cronkite calls it 'Cobble,' the whole world will now be calling Kabool 'Cobble.'"

I object! Really, Mr. Safire, do you think that an English army could have been annihilated on its way out of "Cobble"? Do you think that Richards would have avenged this murder at a place called "Cobble"? I submit, with no humility whatsoever, that these atrocities could not, I repeat they could not, have been committed at a place called "Cobble." However, these things could easily happen, as a matter of fact they had to happen, at a place called "Kaboool."

Cordially,
Arthur L. Finn
Los Angeles, California

Dear Mr. Finn,

Many thanks for your excellent letter to Mr. William Safire. You're absolutely right, of course—and so is he, and Mr. Cronkite.

Let's face it, the correct pronunciation *is "Cobble"**—if *you feel it incumbent on yourself to go around pronouncing it with an Afghan accent. In which case, why don't Mr. Safire and Mr. Cronkite, when speaking English, pronounce Paris as "Paree" and Moscow as "Moskva"? Because they know that the* received pronunciation *of these places in English is, simply, "Paris" and "Moscow." Just as the received pronunciation of Kabul is "Kabool."*

Kipling, incidentally, appears to favour "Cobble," to judge from his poem "Kabul River," where only "Cobble" scans. But if only "Kabool" had suited, I'm sure he would have used that.

I first heard of the place as a child, when I discovered in a magazine called The Wizard*—unknown, I imagine, in the U.S.—some heartening stories about* *a character called "The Wolf of Kabul." Obviously it had to be pronounced "Kabool." The Wolf of Cobble—I ask you!*

How would my old friends the Gilzais pronounce Beverly Hills, come to that?

Yours sincerely,
George Fraser
Isle of Man, Britain

**Or "CAWBLE," or "KAHBLE."*

should, *see* craven conditional

signs of the times

The most threatened man in the English-speaking world must be named William Stickers. Throughout Great Britain, blank walls and freshly painted fences bear the admonition BILL STICKERS WILL BE PROSECUTED. His accomplice, Bill Posters, has also been widely warned, although in the United States the sign painter usually prefers the antimail POST NO BILLS.

Time now for the first annual "Signs of the Times" awards, for the most engaging, cryptic, or confusing notices posted on purpose by serious people. (From the injunction in the New Testament: "O ye hypocrites, ye can discern the face of the sky; but can ye not discern the signs of the times?")

The sign requiring the most patience: At the Howard Johnson restaurant near Cornell University, patrons are greeted with a notice reading PLEASE WAIT FOR HOSTESS TO BE SEATED. Reports student Leslie Sara Goldsmith: "I waited patiently for about ten minutes, but the young lady failed to sit down, and feeling rather neglected, I felt compelled to sit first."

The most glaring example of unparalleled construction: NO BALL PLAYING, BIKE RIDING, LITTERING, SPITTING, OR DOGS. Runner-up in this category is seen on Indiana highways: WATCH YOUR SPEED/WE ARE.

The most imaginatively phrased, hand-lettered notice at City College of New York was submitted by Ed Early of Stamford, Connecticut: MAILMAN, PLEASE LEAVE BOOK WHICH WAS DROPPED IN HERE YESTERDAY WITH THE ELEVATOR MAN.

The most schizophrenic directive—actually, two signs that beat as one—was sent in by Thomas Clinton of the University of Pittsburgh: NO

SMOKING ON ELEVATORS/USE STAIRS IN AN EMERGENCY. (Mr. Clinton, a chemistry teacher, also reports he saw a sign in an eyeglass shop that advertised: EYES EXAMINED WHILE YOU WAIT, which he finds "by far the most comfortable procedure.")

The sign that most evokes sympathy for inanimate objects can be found, says realtor Robert McKee of New York, on Connecticut's Merritt Parkway: DEPRESSED STORM DRAINS. The sense of helplessness this sign summons is akin to WATCH FOR FALLING ROCKS. Perhaps the sign writer means "fallen." Illinois motorists are still trying to figure out the South Lake Shore Drive advice DISABLED CARS REQUIRED TO PULL OFF ROADWAY.

Most ubiquitous mistake in a sign is TEN ITEMS OR LESS at speedy checkout counters in supermarkets. Perhaps we could do with fewer, or less, supermarkets. A more creative semantic foul-up is reported by Selma Fischer to be in Woolworth's on Seventh Avenue and West Fiftieth Street in New York: NO ERROR MADE WITHOUT CUSTOMER BEING PRESENT.

Graphic design takes an award at Harold's Chicken Shack in Hyde Park, Chicago. David Harmin describes a sign that has a large NO on the left, and smaller lettering on the right saying: DOGS/EATING/BICYCLES. Though this may have been intended as an admonition against three sins, taken together it warns of an event that has not often been witnessed. (My pet, Peeve, munching a tire, acknowledges the regards sent from Paula Diamond's bête, Noire.)

Competition was keen for the sexiest sign. SOFT SHOULDERS was a frequently submitted entry; a subtler message was sent in by Fritz Golden of Philadelphia, who read a *Kama Sutra* meaning into the countertop signs at ticket windows: NEXT POSITION, PLEASE. But the best can be found in Manhattan, at many intersections. "I picture people prostrating themselves in the crosswalk," writes Barbara Nicoll of Hartsdale, New York, "to be seduced or even just tickled by passersby. . . ." The romantic grabber: YIELD TO PEDESTRIANS IN CROSSWALK.

Dear Mr. Safire—

I've tried and tried to persuade my local exterminating company to reform. Its bill invariably describes the services as EXTERMINATED ABOVE PREMISES. It's a wonder that I have a roof over my head!

Arminé Dikijian
Brooklyn, New York

W.S.,

The Holiday Inn folks have evidently succumbed to hedonism. Why else would they add the advice BUSSES WELCOME to many of their billboards across the country?

Makes one wonder what Sheraton will be doing for us lately, kissing booths?

Fred Prichard
New York, New York

Dear Mr. Safire:

Guarding the entrance to the parking lot adjacent to Kate Gould Park in Chatham, Massachusetts, where band concerts are given on Friday evenings in the summer, is a sign bearing the legend:

NO PARKING
AFTER 6:00 P.M.
FRIDAYS ONLY
EXCEPT FOR
BAND CONCERT

You figure it out.

Very truly yours,
William B. Lee, Jr.
Rochester, New York

Dear Mr. Safire:

You mentioned Connecticut's concern for its DEPRESSED DRAINS. *Massachusetts is also considerate of the mental health of the vehicles that drive down its roads. The whole length of Route 6 on Cape Cod is marked with signs saying* BREAKDOWN LANE.

Sincerely,
Joan Adler
Brooklyn, New York

Dear Mr. Safire:

*My favorite sign, after years of observation, is one I saw in a Peck & Peck storefront in Newport, Rhode Island—*BATHING SUITS—HALF OFF.

Very truly,
Philip Ahrens III
Yarmouth, Maine

signs of the times II

"Our hospital recently posted a sign," writes Dr. Harris Clearfield of Bala-Cynwyd, Pennsylvania, "stating: THIS DOOR IS ALARMED AFTER 6 P.M. I also get a bit nervous in this neighborhood after dark."

Unnoticed humor can be found in notices. When a nuclear warhead was taken from the scene of an accident to a Titan 2 missile, reporters noted a stenciled warning on the side of the roped-down canisters containing the weapon: DO NOT DROP.

To cram a message into a few words, new linguistic forms have been invented. Richard Gould of Washington points to an imperative phrase that has been turned into a noun: METROBUS FARE ADJUSTMENTS, SEE TAKE ONE FOR DETAILS. "There are containers for leaflets elsewhere in the buses," Mr. Gould explains, "and they bear the injunction TAKE ONE. Thus, the sentence 'See take one for details.' "

Some signs are insulting. If I were a workman, and a supervisor put up a sign that read, SLOW MEN AT WORK, I would walk off the job. Another locution, SLOW BUMP, has become a fixture on New York's Fifty-ninth Street bridge, which also causes motorists to look twice for artwork upon seeing BRIDGE PAINTING AHEAD.

Other signs boast of furious activity. WE CLOSE ALL DAY MONDAY suggests that the entire day is spent in the business of closing. A simple CLOSED MONDAY would suffice.

Lawrence Grossman of the Public Broadcasting Service sends along a curious little sign taken from an American Airlines aircraft:

CIGARETTE SMOKING
ONLY PERMITTED
ON THIS SIDE OF SIGN

Mr. Grossman wonders if riders on "this side" are prohibited from doing anything else—sleeping, talking, eating, reading the instructions on barf bags, and the like. The sign should read SMOKING PERMITTED/ON THIS SIDE OF SIGN/CIGARETTES ONLY.

Other readers are encouraged to send in signs that advertise ignorance. My own favorite—for many years on the Triborough Bridge—seemed to many drivers to be an invitation to panic. Others considered it a suicidal form of resignation or a fruitless protest:

IN EVENT OF
AIR ATTACK
DRIVE OFF BRIDGE

Dear Mr. Safire:

My hands-down favorite is a sign over the subway turnstiles under the Citicorp building: TOKEN ENTRY TO ALL TRAINS. It seems to me that now the ridership is compelled to pay seventy-five cents a pop, we should gain more than token entry.

Molderingly yours,
Sara B. Stewart
Allston, Massachusetts

Dear Bill:

Fie, fie and shame!!! "First annual!!" If you had had the same tough city editor to break you into this business as rasped the rough edges off me, you would never make that mistake. As he preached, there is no such animal as "a first annual." A second annual, yes; and a third annual, etc. etc., ad nauseam, *but the first, originating event cannot be an annual. That requires the passage of a year. We had to write it thus: "The Lady Elks Lodge 1,076 will hold what is planned as the first of an annual series of . . ." Awkward, possibly, but correct.*

Sincerely,
Paul
[Paul J. C. Friedlander]
Former Travel Editor
The New York Times
East Hills, New York

Dear Mr. Safire:

For your collection of "signs that stop you cold"—here's what you see as you go from your plane into the airlines' building at Columbus, Ohio:

TERMINAL
BAGGAGE

Some baggage does come off in terminal condition, but do the airlines really want to call attention to it?

Sincerely,
David Weingast
Ridgefield, Connecticut

Dear Mr. Safire:

As a member of your Lexicographic Irregulars I am compelled (impelled?) to add to the "Signs of the Times."

It seems Freud has influenced even the highway department. On country roads in Connecticut, New York, and New Jersey you will see signs that warn: HIDDEN DRIVES.

Maybe they're meant to prevent hidden run drivers.

Marian H. Mundy
Alias Bessie Mae Mucho
Mendham, New Jersey

Your next "Signs of the Times" roundup might well include the soft-porn come-on displayed beside the security X ray on the way to the TWA gates at La Guardia:

PASSENGERS
MAY SUBMIT TO
PHYSICAL INSPECTION
IF DESIRED

Something for everyone!

Harry Carruth
Pompano Beach, Florida

Dear Mr. Safire:

Falling Rocks was an Indian in love with the chief's daughter and sought her hand in marriage. The chief said if he could go out in the woods for two weeks with just the clothes he had on and manage to survive for two weeks and return safely, he could marry his daughter. Falling Rocks never returned, and that's why the Indians put up all those roadside signs: WATCH FOR FALLING ROCKS.

Sincerely,
Will Harrison, Jr.
Arcadia, California

sleep in, *see* New York-ese

slowdown speedup

An apology is due to the *Journal of Commerce*, a newspaper that was shut down during the Civil War by a repressive Republican administration, for a hoot of derision registered here recently at a headline that read: "Slowdown Is Accelerating."

That metaphor was neither skewed nor mixed. Although a contradiction is apparent, the contradiction is not real, as many physics students and other velocity freaks have pointed out.

"Acceleration is commonly thought of as the rate of change of velocity," writes Ted Senator of Ithaca, New York. "Hence, positive acceleration refers to a speedup and negative acceleration (or deceleration) to a slowdown." But such common thought is mistaken: "Velocity is the rate of change (with respect to time) of position, and acceleration the rate of change of velocity."

In case that whizzed past you in slow motion, consider this example by Jeffrey Saldinger of New York City: "A car going 60 miles per hour slows uniformly to 57 miles per hour in three seconds, then from 57 to 50 in the next three seconds, and finally from 50 to 30 in the next three. The car has been slowing down more and more with every three seconds—hence, an accelerating slowdown."

In common use, "accelerate" means "to go faster"; in technical use, it means the rate at which you go either faster or slower. The language is biased, then, in the direction of increased speed; for example, there is "speedup" but no "speeddown." Such are the brakes.

I don't want to be an alarmist, but a look at the last three months' industrial-production figures suggests that the slowdown of the American economy is accelerating to a screeching halt.

---

smarmy

Some adjectives are used only by reviewers. "Pert" is a reviewers' description of an ingenue; "luminous" can be found only in raves about soulful actresses; and "trenchant" is book-review blurbery. Now the vogue word in reviewerese is "smarmy."

On the same day, two *New York Times* movie critics used the term. "This approach might be purely smarmy," wrote Janet Maslin, "were the film's nature photography not so lovely." And critic Vincent Canby described a character in a Robert Redford film as "a smarmy building contractor." Reader John Fishkind of Maplewood, New Jersey, has demanded an explanation.

"Smarmy" is a British usage that has oiled its way across the Atlantic. The English dialect verb "to smarm" means "to smear with grease." "Some English *smarm down* their hair," explains lexicographer Stuart Berg Flexner. "They also *smarm up* to someone, try to ingratiate themselves." This development of meaning—from "smear with grease" to "flatter," or seek to curry favor by acting in a servile manner—has produced the popular adjective "smarmy." Citations now exist for "smarmily" and "smarming." You cannot get the word off your hands.

It seems to be replacing "unctuous," rooted in the Latin word for "ointment," as a word to describe today's Uriah Heeps. Perhaps because it sounds like "swarm"—as in "to swarm all over someone," or to pay excessive attention to him—the British term has been taken to the American bosom. I'm a convert to smarmism—we do not have enough words that fairly drip with the oil of ridicule.

Dear Bill:

Read your piece on the word "smarm" etc. . . . the other day in the Paris Herald. *It occurred to me that no one, you included, seems to react to the word in the way that I do—viz., the charm of the word to me is that it suggests both "smear" and "marmalade" in one oleaginous monosyllable. The first time I heard it, it was almost onomatopoetic (soundlessly so), and instantly I fell in love with it.*

Regards,
José Ferrer
New York, New York

---

soda jerk, *see* hashslinger slang

---

spazz out, *see* out is in

---

spokesmanspeak

"Positive" is a word that used to mean "sure." Am I sure? I'm positive.

In spokesmanspeak, however, "positive" now means "affirmative, constructive, encouraging." The old meaning of "definite"—its root meaning "a specific place or position"—lingers on, but in vogue usage the word no longer denotes a person's certainty. It is now the encouragement or forwardness of a development or a step.

The most meager concession is hailed as a "positive step," perhaps taken from mathematics, where the word means "greater than zero." But the opposite is not what might be expected: There are no "negative steps" yet. Rather, the trendy opposite of "positive" is "not helpful."

Do not be irked by this year's spokesmanspeak cliché. "Positive"—in its sense of "That's good, but nothing to get delirious with joy about"—is better than last year's hot word, "forthcoming," which confused "forthright" with "soon to come" with an added twist of "helpful."

What will next year's favorite expression of cautious optimism be? Though this may be considered unhelpful, it won't be "positive"—of that you can be sure (but he didn't say, "Positively").

Dear Mr. Safire:

To take a positive step forward (to use an atrocious, or at least redundant, phrase) in helping your understanding of mathematical jargon, please be advised that "positive" means "greater than or equal to zero." The correct words for "greater than zero" are "positive definite."

Otherwise, I positively enjoyed your column of today.

Sincerely,
Richard M. Spector
Huntington Woods, Michigan

Dear Mr. Safire:

When the bacteriologist Dr. Wassermann devised his diagnostic test for syphilis, also known as Wassermann reaction, he examined the blood serum of a physician friend and wired him one word: "POSITIVE." The friend immediately wired back: "ARE YOU POSITIVE?" To which Wassermann, according to the story, answered: "NOT ME, YOU."

Sincerely yours,
Zellig Bach
Caldwell, New Jersey

spokesperson, *see* missing persons

stiffed, sandbagged, and set up

Republican presidential candidates have been indulging in what broadcaster Dan Schorr calls "the language of political victimization."

Using the alliteration of Shakespeare's "cabin'd, cribb'd, confined," the various put-upon politicos complain of being "stiffed, sandbagged, set up."

"Stiffed" was first used by Ronald Reagan, who complained of having been, "frankly, stiffed" by a reporter who asked about an ethnic joke. A few days later, Senator Bob Dole picked up the usage in complaining of his exclusion from a debate: "They stiffed us."

The noun "stiff" is best known as slang for "corpse," derived from the stiffness of rigor mortis; from that comes the use of "stiff" as a synonym for "dimwit" or "deadbeat." However, another meaning of the noun "stiff," deeply rooted in British slang, is "banknote" or "promissory note"—from the stiffness of the paper used.

Perhaps from that banknote background, as a verb, "to stiff" has occasionally been used to mean "to swindle": A waiter denied a tip has been "stiffed," or cheated. More likely, the verb form has a priapic origin, and would ordinarily be considered as taboo as the obscene word it euphemizes. But, like "shaft" twenty years ago, the verb was used in a public forum by a famous person, which lessened the taboo. The user of "stiffed" can always say he thought it came from "stiff-armed," a football term.

"Sandbagged" was used by George Bush in response to the charges of stiffing. "We feel we were sandbagged," he said, repeating the slang verb used first by his New Hampshire campaign manager. Concurrently, Joe Scott wrote in his newsletter, "The Political Animal," that Governor Jerry Brown was "sandbagging Kennedy's surge."

In Farmer and Henley's turn-of-the-century dictionary of slang, a sandbag was described as thieves' argot and defined as "a long sausagelike bag of sand dealing a heavy blow that leaves no mark." In American use, its meaning was narrowed to "hit from behind."

"To set up": "His candidate had been set up by his rivals" was the position taken by a Bush campaign chief, as paraphrased by reporter Adam Clymer of *The New York Times.*

As a noun, a "setup" is the fixings or accouterments for a highball; or an organization; or furnishings and layout ("What a lovely setup"). As a verb, the term had been used in the United States for more than a century to mean "to weaken" or "to lead someone to the point of being duped."

The origin is pickpocket's slang: the "stiff" sets up the "mark" by putting him in a position that best enables the "wire" to dip into his pocket.

In current usage, then, "to stiff" means "to harm by deceiving," "to sandbag" means "to clobber stealthily," and "to set up" means "to ensnare or entrap." Please observe the distinctions, or you may be ganged up on.

Dear Mr. Safire:

Even Homer nodded, and on "stiffs" you missed out. Presumably you were never one yourself. Hoboes, who had their own argot between 1880 and World War I, when they practically passed into oblivion, knew each other as "stiffs." There were fast-traveling "passenger stiffs" who disdained slower and grubbier freights. "Bindle stiffs" were not recognized by the upper-caste "blowed-in-the-glass stiffs" as socially acceptable because they were really itinerant workers "beating" the railroads.

Sincerely,
Karl Baarslag
Tequesta, Florida

Dear Mr. Safire:

That was a grand bit you had on "sandbagging." But I learned the word in a quite different sense.

In the late 1930's, as a child actor, big canvas bags of sand were used backstage to "fly" scenery: counterweights. Stagehands would pull a rope, and up would go the backdrop, or a section of wall. Down would come the sandbag. So don't get in the way of stagehands at work, or "you'll get sandbagged."

And stagehands were often hostile to actors who'd tell them, "Can't you do anything right? Your timing was off." Stagehands could get even by sandbagging the snobs. Since there were dozens of nonworking sandbags up in the fly gallery, they could target one to hit a guy as he came offstage, but lightly, by holding back on the rope.

I don't argue your version, but mine is different. And from what I know, it was a theater tradition dating back to Edwin Booth. The hoods may have picked up the word—and idea—from the boardinghouse thespians.

Regards,
Edward Langley
Flushing, New York

Dear William Safire:

It is true that the excellent Dictionary of American Slang *(Wentworth and Flexner) does concur with the view that "sandbagging" means a stealthy clobbering, especially from behind.*

There is, however, a much more specific meaning: the operation a poker player carries out when he first checks (does not raise a prior bet), then raises on the next turn around. Sandbagging is sometimes explicitly forbidden; if not, a player cannot usually get away with it more than a time or two without losing his plausibility.

Yours for precision,
Matthew B. Miles
Tappan, New York

Dear Mr. Safire:

Regarding "sandbagging," this word has a different meaning for players of tournament chess. "To sandbag" is intentionally to lose some games in a tournament in order that one's "rating" will drop sufficiently to enable one to play in a lower section in a subsequent tournament. The idea is to encounter weaker players, win more games, and take a money prize. This escalates the player's rating to a higher class, where he would have difficulty winning sufficient games for a money prize. So . . . the sandbagger sandbags again in the next tournament, etc. etc.

Sincerely,
David Stoughton
Venice, California

Dear Mr. Safire,

In automobile racing (other than drag racing), time trials are held to rank the cars according to speed. In some races, such as the Indianapolis 500, the slower cars are placed at the back of the starting pack, but in others the fastest cars are placed at the rear. This supposedly makes the race more challenging, as the faster drivers have to work their way through the pack. In such a race it's better if you drive at less than maximum speed in the qualifying rounds; the slowest qualifying car gets the "pole" position in the first row. A driver who holds back a little in the qualifying trials, either to get a better starting position or to make other teams think he's slower than he really is, is said to be "sandbagging." The term probably derives from the negative effect sandbags in the trunk have on performance.

Sincerely,
James E. Kearman
Collinsville, Connecticut

Dear Mr. Safire:

Sandbagging is a betting technique which, while acceptable in some circles (including mine), is illegal under the house rules of many friendly neighborhood games. "To sandbag" in poker is to check and raise—to check (pass) at the beginning of a betting round and then, after another player has opened the round by betting, to raise that bet rather than just seeing (meeting or equalling) it. To be sandbagged at the poker table is, as in the rest of life, to be hit from behind.

You're welcome at our game any Friday night you're in town.

Cordially, (Truly? Sincerely?)
Elizabeth A. Zitrin
San Francisco, California

Dear Mr. Safire,

*I think you're all wrong about "*stiffed.*" The image is not priapic and is only partly physical. A stiff is straight, rigid, unbending, too highly starched . . . and a bunch of stiffs make for an uptight situation. The verb usage is related: "to behave in an unbending or ungiving manner." Usually it means "to hold out on." Thus, in cards, when your opponent fails to respond to a finesse, he stiffs you; thus, the untipped waiter got stiffed; and thus, Bob Dole, excluded from a debate, says, "They stiffed us." Ronald Reagan is a stiff and seems to think that "to stiff" means "to shaft."*

On sandbagging, I think your definition—"to clobber stealthily"—is right on the mark. But surely "sandbagging Kennedy's surge" has more to do with building levees when the river's rising than conking someone on the head.

Finally, I think "ensnare" is too restrictive a definition for "set up." After all, you can set up a person to win an election (when the dying actress gets an Oscar, it's a setup) or you can set yourself up for a witty riposte. Perhaps the image is theatrical; certainly, the definition I prefer is to "stage-manage."

Sincerely,
Lucy A. Breyer
Waterford, New York

---

stoop, *see* New York-ese

---

stringer, *see* molar mashers and sob sisters

---

subjective pronoun, *see* me Jane

---

substantive, *see* ives have it

---

suffixes, *see* ives have it *and* taking a whack at wacko

---

superlatives, *see* the usefulest adjective

---

swingy, *see* neatness counts

---

synonymy, *see* living in synonymy

---

take a card

Is John Anderson becoming Ronald Reagan's ace in the hole? Will Jimmy Carter call the bluff, or has he something else up his sleeve? All three of those expressions—along with "fast shuffle" and "dealing from the bottom of the deck"—are from the world of card playing, which the bridge expert Ely Culbertson called "a world of pure power politics where rewards and punishments were meted out immediately."

The card metaphor, as New Dealers know, is part of America's political language. Warren G. Harding described his selection in a smoke-filled room in these terms: "We drew to a pair of deuces and filled."

Of late, however, the metaphor's game has almost been solitaire: Diplomacy dominates. In the late 1970's diplomats began speaking of the need to "play the Chinese card"—to rattle the Russians with our relations with the People's Republic of China. The phrase was given international linguistic status by Leonid Brezhnev in 1978: "Attempts are being made... to play the 'Chinese card' against the U.S.S.R." Recently, turnabout was considered fair cardplay, as Peking's moves toward expanding trade and military relations with the United States were described as "playing the American card."

Who played the first card? Whence this useful expression? According to Conor Cruise O'Brien, editor in chief of the *Observer* in London, the coiner was Winston Churchill's father, Lord Randolph Churchill, in 1886.

"Home rule" for Ireland was a great issue of the day. It was opposed by the people of Ulster, the northern counties of the Emerald Isle, who were largely Protestant, and who called themselves "Orangemen," after William of Orange. When William Gladstone—Great Britain's "Grand Old Man," or "GOM"—declared in favor of Irish home rule, Lord Churchill saw a way of using this issue to oust the Liberals in favor of the Tories.

"I decided some time ago," Randolph Churchill wrote a political ally, "that if the GOM went for Home Rule, the Orange card would be the one to play. Please God, it may turn out the Ace of Trumps and not the Two."

Editor O'Brien informs me that "as far as I know, the phrase 'the Orange card' was first used by Lord Randolph Churchill, and certainly it did not become a current phrase in politics until after he had used it."

A good find; the metaphor has become fixed in the language now, and its provenance is in as controversial a context as it is used today. If ever I am faced with trumped-up charges, I will play my linguistic card.

Dear Mr. Safire,

You refer to Lord Randolph Churchill as Lord Churchill. He should be referred to as Lord Randolph.

As the younger son of a duke he was entitled to use the courtesy title of Lord as a prefix to his name. He was not a peer, which is what the style Lord Churchill would indicate. His wife would be Lady Randolph Churchill or, when addressed, Lady Randolph, but not Lady Churchill. She would be entitled to use her own name after Lady only if she were the daughter of a duke, marquess, or earl.

Yours truly,
Paul H. Silverstone
New York, New York

---

taking a whack at wacko

"Billy Carter is not a buffoon, a boob or a wacko, as some public figures have so described him," said President Carter's brother before a Senate subcommittee.

In that statement, prepared by his attorneys, Mr. Carter made a significant contribution to the clarification of the spelling of a newly popular word.

The public figure who first used "wacko" to describe the President's brother was Mayor Koch of New York. When the mayor said he thought Billy Carter "happens to be a wacko," reporter Clyde Haberman of *The New York Times* spelled the word with an *h*, and it appeared on the front page as "whacko." This was because the word did not appear in the dictionaries. I was on vacation.

On sober second thought, Mr. Haberman dropped the *h* when next he used the term, because most dictionaries spell "wacky" or "wackiness" without an *h*, and "wacko" is the noun form of the adjective "wacky."

Although most authorities readily agree on the adjective's range of meanings—eccentric, crazy, irrational, crackbrained—a great deal of harrumphing goes on when you get to the etymology. The word probably comes from the verb "to whack," or hit over the head, which resolutely and consistently carries an *h*: In early English, "whack" was "thwack," imitative of the sound made by a stick whooshing through the air and crashing on a head.

The *h* is important in the verb "whack"; in British English, the sound can be heard—reversing the *w* and the *h* as "hwack." (This is a customary

English quirk—from time immemorial, Britishers have been saying "hwen" and "hwere" and spelling them "when" and "where.") In America, the term "whacked out" is current, as an intensified form of "spaced out" or "zonked out," meaning "soft-headed after prolonged and excessive use of drugs."

Why, then—if "wacko" is derived from "one who has been whacked silly," as most etymologists agree—have "wacky" and "wacko" dropped the *h*? Big mystery.

For a moment, after "whacko" with an *h* appeared on *The Times*'s front page, some word watchers hoped the *h* had returned and all would be consistent; but Mr. Carter's formal statement dropped the *h*, and in a subsequent editorial on an unrelated subject—the Trilateral Commission—*The Times* wrote that "not all the conspiracy theories come from what Mayor Koch would call 'wackos.' " The word is firmly de-*h*'d.

A second subject has been raised by the rise of "wacko": the decline of the suffix *nik*, and its replacement by *o*. After "sputnik," the way to transform adjectives into nouns was to add *nik*, a Slavic device influenced in the United States by Yiddish: hence, "beatnik," "spacenik," "no-goodnik," and "sicknik." That has declined in favor of the British and Australian method of forming nouns with *o*. One who is weird is a "weirdo." (Nobody fascinated by words has yet been labeled a "wordo.") Americans who long ago adopted "kiddo" are slinging around "sicko," "sleazo," and "wrongo." (When the *o* is added, the final consonant is sometimes doubled, as in "kiddo," but erroneously, I think, in "wronggo"—doubling the *g* makes the word look as if it intended to sound like a Bert Lahr high note.)

The *o* suffix, Anne Soukhanov of the *American Heritage Dictionary* points out, can also replace a missing element in a base word—for example, "psycho" for one who is psychoneurotic or "combo" for combination. When used as a form of address, the suffix is often hyphenated. (Got it, daddy-o? Intense, boy-o.)

Finally, about the meaning: "Wacko" connotes zaniness, a mind askew; "boob" connotes simplemindedness, a brain benumbed. "Boob" comes from "booby," a stupid seabird that allowed itself to get caught and placed in a "booby hatch" aboard ship. That became the cruelly jocular term for "insane asylum," which is now properly called a "mental hospital" by those who look askance at "funny farm." Mr. Carter made his Senate appearance denying wackohood on the "boob tube," which derogates the watcher rather than the one who is watched.

Dear Mr. Safire,

Your article refers to "a customary English quirk" of reversing the w *and* h *in words beginning with* wh. *This is simply not true! To an Englishman—and certainly to this expatriate—the aspirated sound signifies that the speaker is (i)*

Irish, (ii) Scottish, (iii) an American intent on "refined" pronunciation. In Irish speech, of course, the h *sound intrudes in words where there is no written* h, *but it is particularly marked in the* wh *words. A well-known American speaker who adopts the practice is William Buckley. The surname suggests an Irish background, and in any case, his convoluted vocabulary readily attests to an interest in "refined" speech. Another American who aspirates these words is Johnny Carson; since he hails, I believe, from Nebraska, the reason for his adherence to aspiration is less clear.*

Fowler's Modern English Usage *has some comments of interest (I quote from my 1965 edition): "The aspirated sound is natural to the Scots, Irish, and the Americans; in England (except in the extreme north) 'w' was long the normal pronunciation, but 'hw' is gaining ground under the influence of the speak-as-you-spell movement." Leaving aside the fact that to say "hwen" is not to speak "when" as one spells it, I doubt that the last statement is really accurate. Certainly, none of my English acquaintances aspirates the* wh *words.*

Yours sincerely,
Wilfred J. Westlake
Philadelphia, Pennsylvania

Dear Bill:

Can't believe you're so innocent!

"Wacko" comes from "wacking it" or "wacking off" (sometimes with an h*). Like "jerk" or "jerkoff," it refers to the kid who is a bit weak in the brain from "beating his meat" or "beating off" too much. All from the time-honored legend that excessive masturbation (or any at all) causes or results from mental disability* (cf. *the "village idiot").*

Other words now in wide use that have lost their X rating: "jazz" from "jizz" or "gism" (seminal fluid); "swell," from erection; "aw, nuts!" or "nuts to you!" from testicles (not to be confused with "you're nuts" or "he's nutty"—they derive from "nutty as a fruit cake," much as "he's bats" comes from "bats in his belfry").

Best,
Mark Lawrence
Boston, Massachusetts

Dear Mr. Safire,

You made a statement that might have been misleading: "(This is a customary English quirk—from time immemorial, Britishers have been saying 'hwen' and 'hwere' and spelling them 'when' and 'where.')" For well over 500 years the Old English initial spelling hw *generally* was *used in such words until the early Middle English period late in the thirteenth century.*

If one were to look into any Old English dictionary, he would find the orthography for many of our common words listed that way. Thus, a person would come upon: hwaeþer *("whether"),* hwǣer *("where"),* hwanne *("when"),* hwȳ *("why"), and so on. A few people may even remember the initial word in the first line of* Beowulf:

"Hwaet, we Gar-Dena in geardagum. . . .

Yours truly,
(Br.) Francis J. Markert, CFC
English Department
Iona College
New Rochelle, New York

Dear William Safire,

It is not a "customary English quirk" to spell the hw *sound (as in "when" and "where") as* wh. *It is a French scribal error that became official in the Middle Ages, when the Anglo-Norman aristocracy imposed French practices on English. As every graduate student in English knows (or ought to know), Old English texts would quite properly spell these words as "hwen" or "hwere." You will recall that God once told the unmusical monk Caedmon to sing a song: "Cedmon, sing me hwae thwugu [a little something]," to which Caedmon eventually replied, "Hwaet sceal ic singen?" While the French scribes gave the British the strange reverse spellings, they have by no means existed "from time immemorial."*

Best wishes,
Susanne Woods
Associate Professor
Department of English
Brown University
Providence, Rhode Island

Dear Bill,

A small point, perhaps, but I thought I'd mention it. "Hwen," "hwer," "hwak," etc. are not really characteristic of British English, at least not of the standard dialect, Received Pronunciation (RP), the cultivated speech of southern England, including London, and of the professional theater. As we all know, the British generally knock the h- *out of the language.*

Such a pattern, however, has *prevailed in the major U.S. dialects, especially in nonurban areas. I remember teachers who, apparently under the mistaken notion that it was British, hence more elegant, tried to impose it on us, along with "nyooz" and "tyoozday." Not too successfully in my case.*

Regards,

Yours,
David B. Guralnik
New World Dictionaries
Cleveland, Ohio

Mr. Safire:

You're hwacko.

It's the English who, more often than not, drop the "haitch" at the front of what, where, and when.

Standard American still has it. Keep your ears open. You and I don't, I guess, because we're easterners. Are we?

Frank Scalpone
New York, New York

Dear Mr. Safire:

The use of the hyphen with the o *suffix would seem to be less connected with forms of address than with attempts to transcribe what were originally verbal, slang forms into print. There could be no mistaking the pronunciation of "weirdo." The word "daddy-o" or "boy-o," if left unhyphenated, could be easily misspoken. "Boyo" could be interpreted either as "boy-o" or as "bo-yo"—that is to say, the* y *could be read either in vowel or in consonant form. It would thus seem that the ultimate letter of the word governs the use of the hyphen.*

Yours,
Edward Levin
Assistant Professor of Architecture
Syracuse University
Syracuse, New York

taking over

Last summer this department reported with all suitable horror that the 800-pound gorillas who rattled their executive cages in Movieland liked the locution "taking a meeting." Lithe orangutan amanuenses would never say, "He's in a meeting"; always, "taking a meeting."

As stealthily as "tax-bracket creep," this grabby usage has moved into its next stage. Reports from the Lexicographic Irregulars across the country show that the old "making a decision" is changing to "taking a decision." When you have a meeting, you make a decision; when you take a meeting, you take a decision.

You make your own choice about vogue verbs from Tinselville. As for me, "having" meetings and "making" decisions is the decision I've just taken.

Dear Mr. Safire:

If memory serves, the expression used in the UN Summary Records *in the 1940's when I worked there was "*take *a decision." I believe that is the British expression, and official UN English usage was always British.*

Yours very truly,
Mrs. Helen Geberer
The Bronx, New York

Dear Mr. Safire:

I discovered a twenty-nine-year-old usage of one of your "vogue verbs." In The History of the Joint Chiefs of Staff: The Joint Chiefs of Staff and National Policy, *Vol. 4,* 1950–1952 *(Wilmington, Del.: Michael Glazier, forthcoming), p. 276, Walter S. Poole quotes from a message of 18 December 1951 from Colonel George A. Lincoln, a member of the U.S. NATO delegation in Paris, to his superiors in Washington. Colonel Lincoln notes that NATO's Temporary Council Committee has proposed the preparation of a report which will give the council "a manageable paper on which to take decision." (I enclose a copy of the original message, which I obtained from the Records of the Joint Chiefs of Staff in the National Archives.) That Hollywood is reviving a usage apparently current during the Korean War is perhaps a comment on the state of creativity in "Tinselville."*

> *. . . TCC proposes that countries submit comments by 15 January and that TCC meet in late January to consolidate comments as basis for supplementary report, thereby giving council a manageable paper on which to take decision.*

Sincerely,
Terrence J. Gough
Historian
General History Branch
Department of the Army
Washington, D.C.

---

taxi dancer, *see* c'mon, big boy

---

tenterhooking

Reporting on the mixture of wonderment, skepticism, and excitement in the nation's capital as its denizens await the descent of the Reaganites, Bob Schieffer of CBS said: "Washington is on tender hooks."

Many tough-minded people pronounce it that way, but the word is "tenterhooks." "Tent" comes from the Latin *tendere*, "to stretch"—a tent is made of stretched cloth. The frame upon which cloth is stretched is a "tenter," and the hooks that hold the cloth in place are "tenterhooks." In 1748 the novelist Tobias Smollett used it metaphorically—"I left him upon the tenterhooks of impatient uncertainty"—and that has been the word's primary meaning ever since.

Though Washington is tense (same root: stretched nerves), the President-elect is relaxed about using arcane or archaic words. Mr. Reagan called a Republican governors' conference to assure them that he hoped to "reinstitute this nation as a federation of sovereign states."

"Reinstitute"? The word is not in *Webster's Third* unabridged. "Reconstitute" has been getting a good run lately, what with adding water to dehydrated food, and "reorganize" is a Washington byword. But you have to dig in the *Oxford English Dictionary* for "reinstitute," with a nice citation of "There will never again be any reinstitution of slavery."

Now the old word will go back in most big dictionaries, part of the Reagan "new beginnings" theme. That's a power a President has—to bring back old words, as Harry Truman did with "snollygoster"—a linguistic power that Mr. Reagan will soon discover. He will also discover that Washington has no tender hooks.

Dear Mr. Safire:

The first paragraph of "tenterhooking" is fraught with ambiguous words. Let us take "descent" as in "the descent of Reaganites." According to Funk & Wagnalls Standard Collegiate Dictionary, *"descent" has seven definitions. One is "A sudden onslaught or attack" (Reagan on a horse leading a posse of whooping Republicans); another definition, "A decline or deterioration" (not an unreasonable assumption). The rest of the definitions are genealogical or legal and would not seem to have any bearing in this case. Perhaps "influx" instead of "descent" would have been a better choice.*

The other words in question are "capital" and "denizen." "Capital" is correct if "denizen" is defined as "one who lives in a place." However, if "denizen" is defined as "one who frequents a place," then "Capitol" could be used.

Sincerely,
Albert P. Carmichael
Port Washington, New York

Dear Mr. Safire:

It seems to me that he meant "reinstate," not "reinstitute," in the sense of bringing back to a former state or condition. However, "reinstate" usually refers to a person. Thus, the second error would be that he probably meant "reestablish." The entire phrase, then, ought to be reformulated as "revive the premise that this nation is a federation of sovereign states."

S. Robert Lehr
New York, New York

---

their, *see* down with "one"

---

they say, *see* down with "one"

---

throat, *see* words for nerds

---

thumbsucker, *see* molar mashers and sob sisters

---

thunderstorm activity, *see* nature boy

---

ticky, *see* getting down

---

to a tee

"Whence 'to a tee'?" I wondered in passing, and Harrison C. Coffin of Schenectady, New York, snappishly advises, "The correct expression is 'to a T,' not 'to a tee.' It means 'precisely' . . . as though measured by a T square. Try to get access to a good dictionary." Man sounds teed off. He's right about derivation, halfway right about spelling—"to a tee" is preferred.

Another reader, Marie Borroff of the English Department at Yale, thinks the expression might have been influenced by "to cross your *t*'s," and, while she's at it, adds: "Have they also told you that the phrase 'the last jot and tittle' is of similar provenance? A 'jot' (from *iota*) is the small letter *i*, and the 'tittle' is the dot over it. I used to think the jot was the dot and the tittle was the cross stroke of the *t*."

Dear Mr. Safire:

Your correspondent's suggestion that the expression "jot and tittle" has its origin in the "small letter i *. . . and the dot over it" goes to show how careful we have to be in this business to avoid assuming that what is plausible is also true.*

The i *is certainly the skinniest letter, but does that make it the smallest? In any case, when the Founder of Christianity said that "not one jot or tittle of the Law shall pass away," he wasn't likely to have had in mind the Latin* I *(not really so small) or even the Greek* iota. *Galilean Jews in those days spoke Aramaic and, depending on background, were also familiar with Hebrew. The two cognate languages shared what we now call the Hebrew alphabet, the smallest letter of which is the* yodh *(whence the Greek* iota *and the English* jot*).*

The Torah scrolls from which the Law was then read in the synagogues—and still is—use the conventional Hebrew alphabet modified by certain traditional strokes shown in the attached figure. These strokes are, much more convincingly, the "tittles" of the Gospels.

This theory has been around a long time and isn't original with me. I think it hangs together pretty well. Copacetic, you might say.

Sincerely
Myron Robinson
Flushing, New York

Dear Sir:

The explanation of "jot and tittle" is about half right. In the sixteenth-century translations of the Bible, Matthew 5:18 is rendered "jot, tittle"; recent translations have abandoned these words generally. The Latin was iota, apex, *and the Greek was* iota, keraia. Iota *is indeed the smallest Greek letter, although Jesus, speaking Aramaic, would certainly have said* yodh *(the smallest Hebrew letter).* Keraia *means "horn" and refers to the tiny flourishes that distinguish one Hebrew letter from another—*beth *and* kaph, daleth *and* resh.

Hence Jesus was saying that not even the smallest letter of the Law, even the smallest part of one letter of the Law, would be done away with but would be perfected in the New Law.

To describe the dot over the i *or the stroke through the* t *is to put the English language in the mouth of Christ before it existed.*

Very truly,
Rev. Jerome F. Weber
Holy Trinity Church
Syracuse, New York

---

tool, *see* words for nerds

---

to to or not to to

Showing off the length of my research arm, I recently wrote that "I wrote the British Library." (Most Americans call it the British Museum, but that leaves them cold in London.)

The absence of the preposition "to" was noted by Gerry Loughran of Brooklyn: "I walked my corner store this morning, chatted the storekeeper, picked my copy of *The Times*, and found you had given your respected imprimatur this new form of drastically edited English. I thought I would write you and protest it."

Although I have written a few books, when I wrote, "I wrote the British Library," I did not intend to claim having written the entire contents of that institution. Rather, I meant: I (subject) wrote (predicate) a letter (direct object) to the British Library (indirect object). The question is this: When the direct object ("a letter") is understood, is the preposition "to" needed before the indirect object ("the British Library")? Put less pedantically, do you have to write that you are writing to somebody, or can you just write somebody?

In England, accepted usage calls for the "to"; in America, after more than two centuries of independence, you can forget the "to" after the verb "to write." Don't fuss about logic; that's the way it is. Idioms is idioms, and respect no imprimaturs. The English laugh at our "bums"; we laugh at their "I'll knock you up in the morning."

Peggy Miller, the researcher who handles much of my international linguistic correspondence, summed up her findings with the most scrupulously correct sentence that can be put together on the different usages: "You may write the Library of Congress, but you must write *to* the British Library."

Dear Mr. Safire,

In your admirable weeding of our verbiage garden I urge you to spare words that have a functional role in assisting clarity—namely, "to." While this word may not be helpful to native Americans, pity the poor foreigner. How many innocents abroad are under the impression after last Sunday that you are, in fact, the author of the British Library? After all, you said you were.

Why not take your trowel to the truly superfluous, such as "that." I am no semantic scholar, but I suspect "that" is a descendant of the French que. Que, *in French, introduces an entire line of useful compressions:* Je pense que oui, *for example. In English it is frequently extra baggage.*

"That" alone can be the subject or object of a sentence, in cases where its reference has been previously established: "That's right," for example.

"I dreamt I dwelt in marble halls" stands nicely on its own. Common usage, however, would probably give it a "that"—unnecessarily lengthening the sentence and, worse, approaching tautology. As a current phrase would have it, bag that.

Yours sincerely,
Felicia R. Clark
Boston, Massachusetts

Dear Mr. Safire:

Your discussion of the missing "to" prompts me to send you an example which has been annoying me all summer. A commercial for Polyglycoat Weatherizing Sealer has been aired each morning for the last six weeks and jars me into painful consciousness each time. Its claim is that "You may never need wax your car again."

Now the mere mention of Polyglycoat elicits, Pavlov-style, an uncontrollable cringe and usually sends me back under the covers for a few more minutes of sleep. Too *much!*

Susan Forte
Canton, Connecticut

Dear Mr. Safire:

Your recent discussion of the dropping of the "to" in "I wrote the British Museum" leads me to comment on the dropping of a different "to," the infinitival form in that phrase beloved of newspapers— "He or she or it declined comment."

One must decline to do something, as comment, or one must decline to accept something, like an invitation. But in the phrase as used by the print media (ugh), the newspaper is simply stating that in accord with its lofty high standards of fair play, it offered someone an opportunity to reply to one charge or another and he (or she or it) said, "Thanks, but no thanks."

The late Mr. Bernstein, commenting on this complaint of mine and ignoring the fact that newspapers do it both ways with the "to" and without the "to," sometimes in the same issue, said it was just usage. My conversational opportunities may be limited, but I have yet to hear anyone remark, "You know, he [or she or it] declined comment." Or "declined to *comment," for that matter.*

Whenever I read the "declined comment" phrase, I envision someone being offered a platterful of tastefully worded comments and regretfully saying, "No, thank you, I'm on a low-comment diet."

Sincerely yours,
James E. Hague
San Diego, California

---

tude, *see* getting down

---

unacceptable

"The corvine postures of some leaders during the Carter years," wrote William Toombs of Kent, England, to *The New York Times* recently, "notably Senators Henry Jackson and Edward Kennedy, standing by to see how popular the President's initiatives might be before offering public support, is unacceptable."

Good word, "corvine"; it means "like a crow or raven." Occasionally, the obscure adjective is used to mean "black," but the word also can be used to call up an image of crows on a fence, just looking and waiting.

"Unacceptable," however, won't do. It is a 1960's word, in great vogue during the Great Society, nearly as favored by liberals as "compassion." Conversely, "won't do" is unacceptable—it has a British establishment ring and carries a connotation even more elitist than "unacceptable."

Roget's II, American Heritage's new thesaurus, has a good suggestion to denote the arousal of disapproval which is not such a cliché as "unacceptable": "objectionable." Try it, during a corvine mood; and if you are really worked up, go all the way to Arthur Schlesinger Jr.'s favorite term: "odious."

Dear Mr. Safire,

Regarding "unacceptable," "won't do," etc.

Won't you consider using "reprehensible"?

Yours,
R. Bharath
Marquette, Michigan

Dear Mr. Safire:

I agrees with you and Mr. Toombs. "Corvine postures" is *always unacceptable.*

Better luck in the New Year.

Cordially,
Steven Delibert
New York, New York

Look here, Safire, it just won't do. You lose all the marks you've earned in turning down "unacceptable" by saying that "won't do" has a British establishment ring and is even more elitist (what kind of word is that, Safire?) than the word you've turned down. Twaddle, Safire. The two simple words, made of about the least number of letters possible, have authority, and they carry just the meaning intended. Your sneer at us British, who gave you freely the most noble language of them all, just won't do, you know. We WASPs may have lost our sting, but we still know the difference between fair and foul.

Edwin Tetlow
High Falls, New York

uncommon prayer

"As an Episcopalian layperson," writes David Murphy of Barneveld, New York, "I am having a little trouble with the emphasis in the Lord's Prayer having to do with 'trespasses.' We usually hear: 'Forgive us our *trespasses* / As we forgive those who trespass *against* us.' Since I cannot conceive of anyone trespassing *for* us, I suggest that the proper reading should be: 'Forgive us *our* trespasses / As we forgive those who trespass against *us*.' "

Good thinking (though that "layperson" made me wince). However, Mr. Murphy's concern may be overtaken by events: In the Alternative Service Book, which the Anglican Church has prepared to update the Book of Common Prayer, the plural noun "trespasses" has become "sins." Beyond that, the hallowed "Our Father, which art in Heaven, hallowed be thy name" has been edited to "Our Father in Heaven, hallowed be your name."

Every time a translator fiddles with the familiar prayers—especially with the King James translation of the Bible—fuddy-duddies the world over loudly complain that their birthright has been stolen. Prayer is supposed to be communication with God, assert the modernists—why not use the current, most widely understood form of communication? We don't say "thy" in conversation—why say it in church?

On this, count me with the fuddy-duddies. (I am thy fuddy-duddy traditionalist.) "Dearly beloved," begins the pastor and we all get ready to cry. "We are gathered here in the sight of God, and in the face of this congregation, to join together this man and this woman in holy matrimony." Somehow, that memory-laden old form—despite the redundancy "join together"—is more of an emotional grabber than the newly recommended "We have come together in the presence of God to witness the marriage of ..."

Or try this from a dramatic moment later in the old marriage ceremony: "Therefore, if any man can show any just cause, why they may not lawfully be joined together, let him now speak, or else hereafter forever hold his peace." I much prefer that hold-your-peace drama to the new version: "But first I am required to ask anyone present who knows a reason why these persons may not lawfully marry, to declare it now." (I envision a wedding guest—all prepared to yell, "But that cad is a bigamist!"—missing his cue at the new ceremony.)

"Liturgy is not something that can be allowed to become fossilized," says the Bishop of Durham, the Right Reverend John Habgood. "People say we've spoiled the prayer book," adds the Very Reverend Ronald Jasper, Dean of York. "That is a downright lie." (Presumably, these fossil-free clerics would not mind being hailed with a trendy "Hi, Reverend!" To most others, that would be an error: "Reverend" is an adjective, not a noun. "Right" is a higher grade of Reverend than "Very" in Episcopal terminology.)

But there is something to be said for fossilization—it preserves and reminds; it transmits a sense of awe. When scholarship reveals new meaning to old manuscripts, or when the old translations are misleading, modernization is called for. In the Bible's Book of Job, for example, the King James line "My desire is . . . that mine adversary had written a book" is better translated as "If only my adversary had written an indictment," or "had shown me a bill of particulars." Job did not want to criticize a book; he wanted to see what charges God was making against him. That's when modernization helps.

Otherwise, the prosaic approach to poetry leaves me cold. The church, of all institutions, should revere tradition—making the obscure understandable when necessary, holding fast to the memories that resonate when possible. That debate will never end, but I thought I should speak now, rather than forever hold my peace.

Dear Sir:

In the matter of the wording of the Lord's Prayer and the Book of Common Prayer, I have always suspected that the Episcopalians speak for the landed gentry when they use the word "trespasses" and those denominations that prefer "debts" speak for the shopkeepers of the nation. Both limit the scope of the prayer unnecessarily and give it a class bias it shouldn't have. For this reason, "forgive us our sins" makes better sense. (As a retired church organist, I have listened to various preachers trying to explain the continued use of "trespasses" or "debts" by vapid generalizations, without any notable success that I could detect.)

On the other hand, the language of the Book of Common Prayer is a precious heritage that should no more be changed than the language of Shakespeare or Milton. There are those who would alter the traditional English version of Martin Luther's Ein' feste Burg *also, on the ridiculous assumption that the world is no longer "with devils filled." More seriously, the sanctuaries offered by human temples, whatever the creed, are special places of renewal, of spiritual refreshment, apart from the everyday world, and need a special heightened language suitable to their ambiances. To introduce words or music or art from other and alien provenances is to obscure and very likely trivialize what is proper to the sanctuary. The fact that we use "you" in everyday speech is a reason for keeping "thou" in the liturgy, not for eliminating it. The language of the circus* no more belongs in the church than does the language of the church in the circus.

Best wishes,
R. A. Athearn
Stoddard, New Hampshire

~~No reply is necessary.~~
A reply is not necessary.

Sir,

Your comment about the "old" marriage ceremony and its phrase "why they may not lawfully be joined together" reminded me of the delicious spoonerism uttered by a nervous young cleric performing his first marriage ceremony. The words came out, it is said, thus: "If any man can show any just cause why they may not joyfully be loined together . . ."

Cheerfully yours,
(Rev.) Vern Hansen
Lutheran Church in America
Philadelphia, Pennsylvania

Dear Mr. Safire:

As you indicate, today's iconoclasts would have us greet God as Big Buddy or Pal Joey. We must strip ourselves of all awe-reverent fear. So you do not reserve special language for Him but simply address Him as you would the man next door.

Re this, you recalled an amusing incident in my young life. We had such an idol breaker teaching us religion and music. The class "fuddy-duddy" reported to his father—a Ph.D. fuddy-duddy from way back. The father emitted a proper roar and told his scion, "You keep the Doth, Thee, and Thou. And in her music class, when she teaches you the patriotic song 'My Country 'Tis of Thee,' you sing 'My country 'tis of you, Sweet land of libertoo.' "

Gratefully,
Rev. William D. Lyons, P.E.
Immaculate Conception Church
Long Island City, New York

Dear Mr. Safire:

I was particularly alerted by your remark that " 'Reverend' is an adjective, not a noun." What might be pointed out, further, is that it can be used only in conjunction with the man's *first* name, not with his surname. In other words, "The Reverend John Jones" is correct; "The Reverend Jones" is not. One might as well speak of "The Honorable Carter" or "The Honorable Reagan." Yet invariably one reads references in print to "The Reverend Jones" as a designation for Protestant ministers, and—increasingly—to "The Rev. O'Keefe" rather than "The Rev. Francis J. O'Keefe" (initial identification) or *(after that) "Fr. O'Keefe" for Catholic priests. "Reverend" goes with the first name, never with the surname alone. Rabbis are luckier in this respect as they can use "Rabbi" with the full name or with the last name alone. Evidently, "Ayatollah" can be used that way, too.*

Sincerely,
George Lane
Department of English
Lasell Junior College
Newton, Massachusetts

Dear Mr. Safire:

Your "the prosaic approach to poetry" leaves me hot, not cold, from the measures which would be required for such an impossible approach.

Sincerely,
J. Vuillequez
New York, New York

Dear Mr. Safire,

Your column contained a tiny, and possibly not very significant, error. However, so widely is your column read and so influential is it that like Caesar's wife, it ought to be above even the suspicion of error.

So then: The Anglican Church could not issue an Alternative Service Book because there is no such thing as the Anglican Church; rather, there is the Anglican Communion which encompasses ten autocephalic churches throughout the world. It is these churches which prescribe their forms of worship. The Alternative Service Book was issued by the Church of England, the oldest member of the Communion. Here in the United States we have the Protestant (ugh!) Episcopal Church in the U.S.A. (PECUSA), which has issued its own updated (1979) Prayer Book.

I've tried not to make a mountain out of a molehill, but your Episcopal readers will relax just a little if they know their language pundit is au courant *on Anglican jargon.*

Delightedly yours,
(The Rev.) Walter L. Lawrence
Non-stipendiary Curate
Holy Trinity Church
Collingswood, New Jersey

Dear Mr. Safire,

I stand with you as a fuddy-duddy on the Prayer Book. But why didn't you take to task the "Episcopalian layman"?

Correctly, he is an Episcopal layman. Ask any good Episcopalian.

Sincerely,
Liz Winkler
Bloomington, Indiana

upmanship

"I'm only going to say this once, so listen up."

A Washington sportswriter put that now-hear-this command in the mouth of an imaginary pro-football star, and on the same page, another writer covered the Redskins' practice with "Listen up, faithful followers." That means only one thing: The expression "listen up" is sweeping the pro-football coaching staffs and is certain to embed itself in mucho *macho* lingo this year.

I point this out so that the reader will not be "blindsided," a vivid locution explained on page 25, and to call attention to the rise of "up." In linguistic circles, "up" is a fighting word. Its use transforms a normal verb into a phrasal verb—into "hurry up," "wake up," "start up"—which burns up some people and cheers up others.

Joseph Alsop, the retired columnist, who taught me that thumbsucking was meaningless without shoeleathering, writes: "This is to suggest a crusade against the ghastly usage 'ended up.' ... I find the phrase more and more widely, by now even in otherwise excellent historical and art-historical studies by younger British scholars of the most exigent kind.

"My chief objection to the phrase," opines Mr. Alsop, "besides its clumsy sound, is that the 'up' is almost invariably superfluous. It is just as correct to say, 'She ended a whore,' as it is to insert the 'up' in the usual position. And it is certainly much more succinct; and therefore more desirable."

Who will stand up for "up"? To join the issue, I turned to the world's leading defender of "up," Sol Steinmetz of Barnhart Books.

"You can tell Joe to stop fretting," declares the upbeat Mr. Steinmetz, popping no downers. " 'End up' is a perfectly acceptable English idiom and there is nothing superfluous about the 'up,' which emphasizes the completeness or finality of the verb's action. (The same goes for 'finish up.') The phrase 'end up,' incidentally, is recorded in the *Oxford English Dictionary* since 1874. H. Rider Haggard used it in *King Solomon's Mines* (1886): 'We should only end up like my poor friend Silvestre.' "

Now just wait up, Sol—are you saying that the "up" in "hurry up" or "listen up" is not redundant?

"The sense of 'completely, entirely' is a discrete meaning of 'up,' " Steinmetz one-upped, "a natural extension of the basic meaning, 'to or toward a higher, greater, fuller state.' This sense is quite apparent in phrases like 'eat up,' 'to consume completely,' 1535, 'grow up,' also 1535 [evidently 1535 was the breakthrough year for "up"], and 'take up,' 1400, though it is perhaps less apparent in 'hurry up,' 'speak up,' 'start up,' 'fire up,' and 'work up,' where the 'up' signifies an intensification (of speed, activity, excitement, etc.) or increased output of energy."

Then I tried to trip up my lexicographic friend with a letter from Moe Kregstein of New Milford, New Jersey. "I must always hurry up, but I may slow down or up. If I write *down* my problem, will you write it *up*?" How about that, Sol—aren't "up" and "down" just cluttering up the language and mixing up all of us? Why must we drink up the milk that we drink down?

"The 'up' in 'slow up' has the function of emphasizing abruptness in the slowing process," explained Steinmetz, "while in 'slow down,' the 'down' emphasizes gradualness. Both 'drink up' and 'drink down' emphasize completeness of the action of drinking, but whereas the 'up' suggests the raising of the head to empty the cup or glass, the 'down' suggests the downward course of the liquid as it is drunk. One 'writes up' a report because a report is a complete statement, but one 'writes down' a name or address because the emphasis is on the downward action of the writing hand, not on the result of the action."

Warming to the defense of his roughed-up adverb, he added, "Ask me about 'burn up' and 'burn down.' When you 'burn up' a piece of paper, you consume it completely; when you 'burn down' a house you also consume it completely, but the emphasis is on the leveling of the house."

I settled him down before he could settle up other accounts. Surely, I argued, the rise of "up" has led to excesses. What about the insertion of "up" in the phrase "to beat on"? Writes Lincoln Rothschild of Dobbs Ferry, New York: "A ghettoism that has emerged recently is 'beat up on.' You can beat *on* a door, but you beat *up* an opponent, and never the twain shall beat the same person, place or thing." Right—I was shook up at the usage of a *New York Times* editorialist who denounced the mayor for "beating up on judges."

" 'Beat up on,' like 'get off on,' " counters the lexicographer, "is a slang phrase probably formed on the analogy of 'check up on.' 'Beat up on' differs in meaning from either 'beat' or 'beat up': to 'beat' a judge means to defeat him; to 'beat up' a judge means to strike him repeatedly; but to 'beat up on' a judge means to attack him with verbal or other abuse. The richness of English is beautifully exemplified by this threefold distinction achieved with a maximum economy of expression."

I'll sign off on that. But I am not persuaded that "up" should be allowed free rein, much less free reign. In cases where phrasal verbs are followed by nouns, the marriage does not always work: You do not muddy up the water, you muddy the water; you do not split up hairs, you split hairs. On the other hand, I wish my daughter would clean up her room.

But what of "listen up"? Isn't that a barbarism—fumbled footballese, flat gridironing? On this point, shouldn't those who respect tradition in English insist on choosing up sides?

Steinmetz hangs tough. " 'Choose up' is an extended use of the sports term for forming sides by choosing alternately from available players. The meaning of the 'up' in this phrase is 'completely,' the same as in 'split up,' 'match up,' and 'dress up.' 'Listen up' sounds like a dialectical use meaning 'listen well, listen with complete attention.' "

I give up. Rather, I give you "up"—the intensifier of the future, a usage that Joe Alsop and I will end up by loosening up on.

Dear Mr. Safire:

My question is this: Who typed up your column?

Sincerely yours,
Esther F. Russell
Hampton Bays, New York

Dear Mr. Safire,

I've just finished reading "Upmanship" and did not find the following:

"One cuts a tree down,
then cuts it up."

It certainly belongs in the list.

Tom Panzera
Brattleboro, Vermont

Dear Bill:

Your column on "Upmanship" was one of your most brilliant pieces, sparkling with wit and glitzy puns on the subject of that much overused particle "up." But who, pray, is that pugnaciously pedantic permissivist Sol Steinmetz, whom you quoted so generously and even dubbed "the world's leading defender of 'up' "? No doubt he's an invention of yours, though not a very amusing one, I'm afraid, with his ludicrously extremist notion that every word in the language, no matter how petty, has some meaning and usefulness.

Really, you have given much too much space to Steinmetz's libertarian views, and your avid readers, including myself, might get the wrong idea that you actually believe some of the nonsense he sputtered. What we need is more attacks on the abuse of language, not approval and vindication of its multifarious misuses. I am certain that the John Simon-pure segment of your readership is up in arms over your popularization—albeit cleverly disguised as satire—of the most flagrantly redundant uses of "up." With prices, wages, and everything going up, up, up, the last thing in the world we need is more "ups."

With thanks and best wishes,
Sol
[Sol Steinmetz]
Barnhart Books
Bronxville, New York

Dear Bill,

"Upmanship" now has a proud place in my scrapbook. Reading it, I must add, I found myself wondering whether my own prose had not grown finicky and old-fashioned. But Mr. Steinmetz is wrong all the same. Verbs like "end," "hurry," and "burn" need no intensification. Either you end or you do not end, hurry or fail to hurry, and burn or burn incompletely. It is a vulgarism to add "up" or, in the case of burn, "down" as an intensifier. One of the secrets of good prose, in my opinion, is to leave words alone when they convey finality of one sort or another.

Vulgarisms, by the way, are another subject you ought to investigate. I have just been reading Boswell's great Life *for the umpteenth time, and I find that Dr. Johnson had much to say about the constructions which were still considered vulgarisms in his day, but were already "gaining on us" like the sons of bitches in the old story. These are constructions which are perfectly acceptable today, whereas those favored by Johnson would now sound a bit old-fashioned, though rather vigorous and succinct.*

As ever,
Joseph Alsop
Washington, D. C.

Dear Mr. Safire:

I thought you might be interested in another use of "up" which I heard frequently in the recent two years that I lived on the Eastern Shore of Virginia (and had never heard before).

"It was the hottest day of the summer, and my air conditioner went up." "Could you drive? My car has gone up." "Wouldn't you know my washer would go up when I have all this laundry to do?"

Yours truly,
Janet H. Pfeiffer
Richmond, Virginia

Dear Bill:

"Upmanship" reminded me of the expressions we used while we were "growing up" in the early forties in the German-Slovak section of the city.

Threats were: "Look out or I'll beat you up"; commands were: "Hurry you up"; the police would "write you up"; and the Italian kids would toast a drink with "drinka you up."

In fact, quite a few of the expressions referred to in your discourse had the "you" before the "up." "Wake you up" and "start you up" are expressions I can recall.

I wonder whether there was Dutch, German, or Slovak influence in these expressions.

Henry J. Bartosik
Gilboa, New York

Dear Mr. Safire:

You did a piece on up-down that made me think of a headline in the Los Angeles Times *that, twenty years ago, had a Belgian friend scratching his head and very confused, up in the air and very down on himself.*

A linguist who had Chinese, he had been staring at the headline for at least a half hour trying to figure it out. Finally, he gave up and came to me for help. It was, of course, an idiom that had tripped him up, er, down.

The headline: "Things Looking Up Down Under."

A word in your ear,
A. V. Dela Rosa
Madison, Wisconsin

Dear Mr. Safire,

You omitted what to me is the weakest and fastest-growing "up" expression, "meet up" ("Let's meet up after work"). It can't be justified by your friend Steinmetz for adding the sense of completeness or for indicating a physical direction. Mercifully it is still rare in Canada; it will reach us soon enough.

The next stage is inevitable and already common, to add "with" ("Meet up with me after work" = "Meet me after work"). I'd like to hear Steinmetz defend that.

Yours sincerely,
R. E. Bell
Montreal, Quebec

Dear Mr. Safire,

As I was sitting here at my desk at the SoHo News *(where I'm an editor), I found myself invited to cover a particular event—to which I replied, "I can't get it up for that." This is odd, for two reasons:*

1. *I'm a woman.*
2. *I never use crude or sexual vernacular.*

It seems this certainly anatomical reference has worked its way into the language of the "negative superlative"—"That's loathsome," "I wouldn't touch it with a ten-foot pole," "I wouldn't buy it for all the tea in China."

And I realize it is in my vocabulary because it's an expression which seems to [be] moving around the town.

Why? I suppose because it's a bit vulgar, and we live in vulgar times, because we are all pretending there is no such thing as vulgarity (which is truly *vulgar), and also, it just may refer to the metaphysical distance "up"—up to God, to hope, to heaven, to aspiration. I can't get my enthusiasm up, my dander up, my temper up. Up from where? From the solar plexus? From dreams and the unconscious? Every anatomical joke has* some *element of seriousness in it.*

I hope you can get it up to discuss this in your column (I hope you don't presume I'm being too familiar . . .).

Up, up & away!
Merle Ginsberg
New York, New York

the usefulest adjective

Here comes the usefulest reading you will do all day.

The trained syntactician, upon reading that catchy topic sentence, would say: " 'Useful' is most commonly inflected to the superlative degree by combining the base word with 'most'—that is, 'most useful' rather than 'usefulest.' " Most other readers would say, " 'Usefulest' looks funny," a reaction linguists call "the sensitivity of the native speaker."

To make the most of a word, when do you use *est* and when do you use "most"?

"I was startled the other day," writes Seymour Amlen of ABC Entertainment, "when I came across the word 'loyalest' in *The New Yorker* magazine." The sentence, written by Andrew Porter, who comes from England, reads: "Amelia is the wife of his secretary, closest friend and loyalest supporter, and Warwick loves her."

Mr. Amlen dimly remembered a rule that "comparative adjectives may end in *est* if the adjective has only one syllable ('great') or ends in *le* ('gentle') or *y* ('pretty')." He cannot figure out why there is no commonality to the exceptions: "For example, I could hear myself saying 'stupidest' but not 'rapidest.' I would not feel appalled at hearing 'tenderest,' but would at hearing 'chipperest.' Is there any aid for the perplexed in this matter?"

Anne Soukhanov, an *American Heritage* editor, gives the very, very best advice on superlatives. Confirming Mr. Amlen's recollection of the rules, she points out that *est* is used with most monosyllables (being great is the "greatest," being hard is the "hardest") and with two-syllable words ending in *y* ("lazy-laziest"), *le* ("noble-noblest"), *ow* ("narrow-narrowest"), and *er* ("tender-tenderest").

That's simple and direct. So are the rules for "most": Use it with adverbs ending in *ly* ("eagerly" becomes "most eagerly"), with predicate adjectives ("to be afraid" becomes "to be most afraid," not "afraidest"), and with disyllables having foreign origins ("bizarre," "antique," "burlesque" all take "most," not *est*).

Generally, you should also use "most" for longer words, words ending in *ive* ("active" and "passive" would sound like something else if you added an *est*), *s*, *ish*, *est* ("honestest" wouldn't work), *ed* or *ing*, and "absolute" words—"real," "right," "just" would not go with *est*.

But what about all those words that fall between "great," which obviously needs an *est*, and "honest," the superlative of which sounds silly without a "most"?

When in doubt, go with "most." So "loyalest" is wrong, right? No. Miss Soukhanov writes of Andrew Porter's "loyalest": "He is using the *est* form with a word to which it ordinarily would not be affixed so as to afford more emphasis on the nature of the relationship he is describing, and to make the whole sentence tighter and more effective...."

That trick of breaking the rules for comparative-superlative dramatic effect has been used for years. Lewis Carroll put a catchy comparative in Alice's mouth: "Curiouser and curiouser!" Thomas Carlyle writes, "Surely of all the 'rights of man,' this right of the ignorant man to be guided by the wiser ... is the indisputablest." And Mark Twain found the most emphatic denunciation in "the confoundedest, brazenest, ingeniousest piece of fraud."

If you want to be brutal about "brutal," go beyond "most brutal" to the "brutalest"—not the most common use, but you may want to describe the uncommonly brutal. Same with "crooked" or "damnable."

"The upshot is that both 'loyalest' and 'most loyal' are correct," writes Miss Soukhanov, "but that the latter is by far the most usual formation. The honor of *The New Yorker* remains intact, and Mr. Amlen can remain a loyalist." That is a good trick: by using "loyalist" right after "loyalest," she shows how the uncommon usage can be confusing and makes the case in her conclusion: "Had this not been the case, it would indeed have been the most unkindest cut of all...."

Safire's Law: Only use superlatives like "usefulest" when the outlandish is most useful.

Dear Mr. Safire:

I may be dating myself, but I don't think the song would have been nearly so popular if it had been called "Saturday Night Is the Most Lonely Night in the Week."

Sincerely,
Ruth Toor
Berkeley Heights, New Jersey

Dear Mr. Safire:

Your piece on "The Usefulest Adjective" recalled my four-year struggle with the superlative. Daily I wondered how to write the biography of Johann Most and use the superlative without evoking a grating echo. "Most was the most important anarchist in Europe and America in his time" is one of many justifiable superlatives about him, but how to say them with accuracy and grace? Importantest? Eloquentest? Terrifyingest? Picturesquest?

When I told a colleague I was writing a book in which "most" should not appear, he said: "That's impossible." Other writers on Most, apparently less concerned than I with grace, seem to have done the utmost to attribute to Most the most of almost everything. His obituaries bristle with the likes of "Most was the most notorious man of his day." Notoriousest?

Refusing to commit such stylistic atrocities, I struggled and struggled to write the superlative with accuracy and grace. The struggle prolonged the completion of the book. But I succeeded. Forthcoming from Greenwood Press is The Voice of Terror: A Biography of Johann Most, *in which, to the best of my knowledge, the superlative with "most" appears only twice, both times intentionally and (I hope) with accuracy and grace.*

Sincerely,
Frederic Trautmann
Glenside, Pennsylvania

Dear Mr. Safire,

Anyone who learns English grammar is told a fixed rule on the use of comparatives and superlatives: -er *and* -est *with Anglo-Saxon words, "more" and "most" with words deriving from Latin or French.*

Sincerely yours,
Joachim Themal
New York, New York

Dear Mr. Safire:

There is one word that to me is sufficient without being inflected to superlative *degrees without combining with "more" or "most." The word is "honest."*

A person is either honest or not. There are no degrees of honesty.

Yours very truly,
Frank A. Moran
Rocky River, Ohio

Dear Sir:

*Safire's flaw: Use superlatives like "useful*est*" only when the outlandish is most useful.*

Yours truly,
Marlow Sholander
Cleveland, Ohio

Note from W.S.: Only I misuse "only."

Mr. Safire:

I feel I should tell you about another legitimate use of est. *My friends tease me about my small bladder. They say I am the bathroom-goingest girl they know.*

Sincerely,
Randi S. Londer
Boulder, Colorado

P.S. My friends are mostly very literate people.

Dear Wm. Safire—

How could you offer "usefulest" as a prime example of the perfect way to express the ultimate in superlative superlatives when "onliest" is far and away in a class by itself. The first time I heard a southern black use the word, I realized immediately that he had transformed used-to-death "only" into its real meaning, so that everybody would sit up and take notice of what "only" really means. So celebrate with me the impact value of "onliest," for it's at the top of the list in this age of "only 99¢, only $9.99," day after day of only, only, only.

Wolf Larson
Loleta, California

verbiage

"The verbiage can be argued," said Senator Robert Byrd about whether the War Powers Act applied to the rescue raid launched into Iran, "but in spirit and intent I don't think there was any violation."

The second meaning of "verbiage" in several dictionaries is "style or manner of expression," and the senator can find support for use of the word in that. But such a definition has mainly to do with diction.

The meaning of "verbiage" to most of us is not "wording," as Senator Byrd wanted to say, but a running on at the mouth or typewriter. Excessiveness is built into the primary meaning, as if "verb," for "word," were being melded with "foliage" or "garbage."

"Wording" is one thing; "wordiness"—or "verbiage"—another. Let's leave it at that.

vetting

"Twice in two weeks," complains Arthur Harris of Arlington, Vermont, "*Newsweek* has used this verb 'vetting.'" Attached was a piece about a Ronald Reagan speech, including the comment "His edited version was routinely retyped without further vetting."

"I became enraged," fumes Holly Butler of Weston, Connecticut, "and scrawled all over the Op-Ed page of yesterday's *New York Times*." The page, attached, cited a submission to "the C.I.A. for official vetting." Expostulates Miss Butler: "*Time* and *Newsweek* happen to be the worst offenders so far.... Add this letter to a list you will keep of others who find the word offensive until identified and properly noted in dictionaries."

Some dictionaries have it: *Webster's New World* defines the word as "to examine, investigate or evaluate in a thorough or expert way," adding that it is a colloquialism.

The word comes from "veterinarian," which originated in the Latin from one who took care of old beasts of burden—the "vet" means "old," as any veteran wordsmith can tell you. In nineteenth-century England the verb was used in scholarly circles in this way: "Have you had this manuscript vetted?" The meaning was "Has this been examined thoroughly, as a veterinarian carefully goes over an animal?"

The Briticism is in vogue use in America today, along with "early on" and "trendy," and shows the first signs of becoming more active and less passive. I've heard "Vet this for me." Soon we will hear of manuscript vetters, antique vetters, social-acceptability vetters, bed vetters, etc.

If not overused or tossed off with a lifted pinky, the word is a good substitute for "peruse," whose meaning has been changing from "examine" to "glance at." A more specific word is "edit," and a narrower command is "Check this for factual errors." "Vetting" is a useful activity that deserves a special new name, and I welcome it; so does my pet, Peeve, and the copy editor who vets my prose.

Dear Mr. Safire:

A careful vetting of the Lewis and Short Latin Dictionary *will show you that the* vet- *of "veterinarian" does not mean "old," for "veterinarian" is not based on the adjective* vetus, -eris, *"old."*

"Veterinarian" is derived from veterinarius, *"cattle doctor," which in turn is derived from* veterinus, *"of or belonging to carrying or drawing burdens"; cf.* veterinae, *"beasts of burden." The* vet- *of* veterinus *is a contraction of* vehit-, *from* veho, vehere, *"to bear," "to carry."*

Accordingly a veterinarian takes care of beasts of burden of all ages, not just old ones.

Sincerely,
Robert J. Martin
Brooklyn, New York

Dear Mr. Safire,

I fear that your hospitality may have got the better of you when you welcome so heartily the Briticism "vetting." Had you had the word vetted more carefully, you would have uncovered its seamy connections with the world of espionage—connections close enough to make the word, and anybody introducing it as an innocent immigrant, highly suspect. A similar situation in Britain would lead to people asking: "Has this man Safire been vetted?" meaning "Has he been cleared to see security-classified documents after a check of his background, acquaintances, and so forth." They might even ask: "Has he been 'positively vetted'?" or cleared for access to the real burn-before-reading stuff, an in-depth investigation that is usually reckoned to take three months. Documents and other inanimate objects may also be vetted, but again the idea is to make sure they give nothing away, and I would say that in Britain now the concept of vetting carries almost exclusively the narrow meaning of security checking.

Yours faithfully,
Gavin Lyall
London, England

Dear Mr. Safire—

Your column concerning "to vet" sent my memory back to somewhere about twelve years ago, when there was certainly no American vogue for the verb, and when I, free-lancing in London, wrote for the San Francisco Chronicle *that the British security services were "vetting" posted (mailed?) messages, possibly illegally. An alert subeditor (which, as you may know, is British for the much preferable "copy editor") changed it to "vetoed." Make of that what you will, if only to demonstrate the truism that articles on language generate dotty letters.*

Yours sincerely,
Larry Klinger
London, England

Dear Mr. Safire:

You noted the chagrin of two wordniks at the use of the term "vetting."

One of the critics was "enraged" (I wonder if she was contentious or wrathful?) because of something submitted to "the C.I.A. for official vetting." She urged you to add her letter to "a list you will keep of others who find the word offensive. . . ." Please do not confuse this letter with those which properly belong on that list!

I don't find the term particularly offensive. I must admit it doesn't have a seemly feel to it—much like wearing one's pajama tops in lieu of a shirt.

Actually the term is part of the patois of the "intelligence community" and is used with greater frequency in England than it is in the United States. To "vet" a person means to screen him in order to determine his suitability for a position of trust. In this country we just run BIs (background investigations).

The arcane world of intelligence is actually a cornucopia of strange words, many of which (like the people who use them) are steeped in mystery. The skills of espionage and counterespionage are collectively known as "tradecraft" (itself an interesting word). People who seek out intelligence services for the purpose of volunteering information are "walk-ins" (where I come from, walk-ins are big refrigerators) whose "bona fides" must be ascertained in order to establish their credibility. Dare I go on?

Why do people in intelligence work have such a penchant for creating their own jargon? I suspect that the reason lies in the fact that since so much of what they do must be hidden from public scrutiny, they are more comfortable with words which likewise conceal more than they reveal.

Sincerely yours,
Nick McDowell
Greensboro, North Carolina

---

wacko, *see* taking a whack at wacko

---

watchpot, *see* Haigravations II

---

watch your baggage

Sometimes politicians carry "baggage," a word that has come to mean "unwanted burdens," the equivalent of an albatross perched on the shoulder. Sometimes historical phrases carry such baggage, and the user cannot always find a redcap to handle the unintended associations.

Our hod-carrying State Department spokesman, who trendily substituted "this" for "the," said after the United Nations commission had glumly left Teheran: "This Government believes that the situation requires, first, watchful waiting."

Putting "watchful" before "waiting" gives a kind of purpose to hanging around, and it has a Wilsonian ring to it. That's because Woodrow Wilson said it. On December 2, 1913, he reported to Congress about America's relations with Mexico, where a dictator had temporarily detained some United States seamen: "We shall not, I believe, be obliged to alter our policy of watchful waiting."

Four months later President Wilson sent 4,000 marines to take Veracruz; the bloodletting in association with this assertion of national prestige cannot be what the present State Department spokesman had in mind.

Better phrases, with less baggage, were coined by Sir James Mackintosh in the early nineteenth century: "Masterly inactivity" went over well, topped only by his "disciplined inaction." Until Mr. Carter's spokesmen can find a similar term for resolute irresolution, they are better advised to let the dust settle.

Dear Mr. Safire,

You refer to an "albatross perched on the shoulder" as an example of unwanted baggage. Perhaps you are referring to Coleridge's "The Rime of the Ancient Mariner." The mariner, having wantonly shot a friendly albatross, was forced by his colleagues to replace the cross on his neck by the dead albatross. This usage makes the similarity to unwanted baggage much clearer.

Sincerely,
D. Eric Greenhow, M.D.
Media, Pennsylvania

Dear Mr. Safire:

Please note that the albatross which you've chosen to perch on someone's shoulder belongs around the neck. To quote from Samuel Coleridge's famous "Rime of the Ancient Mariner" (lines 141-142):

Instead of a cross, the Albatross
About my neck was hung.

Sincerely,
Solomon Kunis
Bellerose, New York

Dear Mr. Safire,

". . . 'baggage,' a word that has come to mean 'unwanted burdens.'. . ." It came to mean that quite some time ago—the Latin word for "baggage" was impedimentum.

Art Morgan
New York, New York

---

weasel subjunctive, *see* **craven conditional**

---

well, *see* going to the well

whatever

"And so on and so forth" was replaced by "et cetera, et cetera"; that was followed by "yakety-yak" and "stuff-stuff-stuff," which in turn fell before "blah-blah-blah." Recently the vocabulary of the summarized remainder (*et cetera* is Latin for "and others") has centered on "and all that stuff," and like that.

Now comes "whatever." As a pronoun, "whatever" is a word that emphasizes variance: "whatever you say." As an adjective, "whatever" stretches the degree or quality of the noun: "whatever diamond you buy."

However, it is as a device to help the speaker dribble off authoritatively that "whatever" is now coming into its own. The word has overtaken "and like that" and is now used as a short form of "and whatever else comes to mind."

What post are you being considered for in the new administration? "Defense secretary, arms control chief, First Lady's press secretary, whatever . . ."

wienie, *see* words for nerds

wimp mush, indeed!

The *Boston Globe* was embarrassed recently when a prankster in its midst removed a headline above an editorial and substituted a poke at the White House. The editorial supported President Carter's anti-inflation announcement and was supposed to have been headed: "All Must Share the Burden." The changed line, which went through 140,000 copies before the hoax was caught, read: "Mush from the Wimp."

"Wimp" is a curious locution. It has replaced "drip" and is more pejorative than "nebbish," carrying an obsequious, overly solicitous, weepy, listless, out-of-touch connotation.

The word cannot be rooted in "wimple," the medieval veil that is still part of a nun's habit. Stuart Berg Flexner, the sultan of slang, thinks that the noun "wimp" might have come from the verb "whimper."

The question is: Was Wimpy—the character who loved hamburgers in the comic strip *Thimble Theater,* starring Popeye the Sailor—named after the slang noun, or was the term taken from his own shy, sleepy-eyed character? I'm inclined to believe that Popeye's friend may have had an influence on the word's adoption, but "wimp" was not an eponymous word: Wimpy was too ingenious to have been the model for the present meaning. Forbidden more hamburgers by Olive Oyl, he would ask for a bread sandwich, which turned out to be a slice of bread between two hamburgers. No wimp, he.

In commenting on the *Globe*'s intended headline—"All Must Share the Burden"—*The Washington Post* confessed, "Some awful, sinking feeling tells us that we ourselves ... must have used that headline a thousand times. In fact—or as we Big Thinks like to say, *'Indeed'*—just put us in the presence of that headline and we can't help ourselves, we start automatically and compulsively writing the editorial that goes with it."

"Indeed!" There's a sneaky word, its wings neatly pinioned for the first time by the *Post* editorialist, who is probably the watershedding Meg Greenfield. "Indeed" can be used to mean "certainly, assuredly, truly" and can also turn in an honest word's work meaning "undeniably," but it has a pompous side that has been puffing itself out lately.

I have no quarrel with those thousands—indeed, millions—who use the word as an intensifier or emphasizer; indeed, the word can succor a friend in need. What bugs me is the sense the word is often intended to carry when used at the beginning of a sentence. "Indeed, there are those who say..." "Indeed, despite the circumlocution of my opponent..."

That "indeed" says, "I am telling the truth, and what you have heard or are about to hear from anybody else is a bunch of nonsense." An arrogant word, which I've used too often myself. (All Must Share the Burden.)

None of these observations about "wimp" and "indeed" should be taken as a derogation of the President's anti-inflation effort. I am making a determined attempt to be antipartisan in this space; indeed, the mush that was ladled out of the White House that day would have made any self-respecting wimp blush.

---

words for nerds

"Collegians now register for 'guts,'" writes Faith Heisler of the University of Pennsylvania, "...to lessen the necessity to become 'throats.'"

This prime example of campusese, instantly understandable to any college student, was submitted in response to a query in this space for a current review of the slang that has replaced the hip expressions of yesteryear.

Remember "snap course," the subject you took for a breather? That is called a "gut course" today, presumably because you know the answers in your intestines, and has been growing in use since the early fifties. Variations include the middle western "cake course" (from "a piece of cake," or "easy") and the Californian "mick course" (not an ethnic slur, but a derivation of "Mickey Mouse," or "inconsequential.")

Examples of gut courses—where "gut gunners" get an "easy Ace" (A) as opposed to a "Hook" (C) or "Flag" (F)—are on the analogy of "Rocks for Jocks," a generation-old put-down of a geology course attended by athletes. More recent examples are astronomy's "Stars for Studs," art's "Nudes for Dudes," psychology's "Nuts and Sluts," European civilization's "Plato to NATO," anthropology's "Monkeys to Junkies," and comparative religion's "Gods for Clods." Students of linguistics engage in "Blabs in Labs." Courses on the art of film are referred to as "Monday Night at the Movies," music appreciation is "Clapping for Credit," and any science course aimed at liberal arts students includes a technocrat's derogation of the generalist as "Physics for Poets."

Students take these courses to avoid becoming "throats," which is the term for what used to be called "grinds," which in turn replaced "bookworms." "The term 'throat,'" explains Mitchel A. Baum of the University of Pennsylvania, "is short for 'cutthroat' and refers to a person who wants an A at any cost and who would dilute your standardized solution of hydrochloric acid if given half a chance. At Penn, these students are often called 'premeds,' regardless of their postcollege plans."

Other replacements of "grind" are "squid" (an ink squirter), "pencil geek," "spider," "cereb," and "grub." "'Grub' is often used as a verb as well," writes Philip Frayne of Columbia University, "as in 'He's in the library grubbing for a history exam.'" At Yale, the grind is a "weenie"—not "wienie," as spelled here not long ago—and at Harvard, the excessively studious student is derided as a "wonk," which Amy Berman, Harvard '79, fancifully suggests may be "know" spelled backward. (In British slang, "wonky" means "unsteady.") At some southern colleges, such people are "gomes," which Sean Finnell describes as "those who carry a calculator hooked onto their pants belt or, off campus, wear black socks with loafers and shorts (sorry, Dad). The derivation of this word undoubtedly comes from 'Gomer,' as in 'Gomer Pyle.'"

"Here at MIT," observes Robert van der Heide, "we refer to someone who studies too much as a 'tool.' At MIT, 'nerd' is spelled 'gnurd.' There is a distinction between gnurds and tools. Tools study all the time, perhaps to get into med school. Gnurds study all the time because they like to. Gnurds are a subset of tools." (Not so at Colgate, reports Mathi Fuchs, where a tool is one who exploits others.)

"Nerd," no matter how spelled, is a big word with the youthful set.

Its origin is probably in a forties variation of "nuts"—as in "nerts to you"—and a "nert" became a "nerd," probably influenced by a rhyming scatological word. Like so many campusisms, the noun is turned into a verb with the addition of "out." "At Brown," writes Alison Kane, "the sons and daughters of the previous generation of 'bookworms' are called 'nerds' instead of 'grinds.' Rather than 'grind away' at their books, they prefer to 'nerd out.' "

What about "cramming"? That word is still used a lot ("alot," on campus, is one word), though a variation exists. "Staying awake the whole night through to 'cram' is called 'pulling an all-nighter,' " writes Susan Chumsky of Penn, noting: "An 'all-nighter' is never 'spent,' never 'had,' but only 'pulled.' "

New terms for "cramming" are "shedding" (from "woodshed"), "speeding," and "heavy booking" or "mega-booking." At schools of architecture, "charretting" is used. " 'Charretting' (to describe pulling an all-nighter)," write Carey Reilly and Peter Fein of Yale, "comes from the French word for cart. A cart was used to collect the architectural drawings of a student in any atelier of the Ecole des Beaux-Arts in Paris, mostly between 1860 and 1930. The word has come to mean the harried period in which a student's drawings are completed, or simply working all night to complete the next day's assignment." (Professor Susan Fiske of Carnegie-Mellon spells it "charette," which is the spelling *Webster's Third New International Dictionary* prefers, but ascribes it to a drawing tool.)

In the event that the all-night pullers do not succeed in passing the exam, their reaction is vividly described in an "out" verb used at Cornell, situated high above Cayuga's waters. "One threatens to 'gorge out,' " testifies Michele Cusack, "which does not refer to eating three banana splits (that's 'pigging out'), but to jumping off one of the many scenic bridges on campus." Other schools prefer "veg out," soft *g*, or to turn into a vegetable, after one "blows off," or fails.

A traditional, generation-spanning campus activity is vomiting. Accordingly, students have their own terms for the habit. In my college days, "upchuck" was the preferred euphemism, and since then the alliterative "losing your lunch" and the debonair "tossing your cookies" have been in use. Today the activity—usually from an introduction to overindulgence in alcohol by a "pin," or an innocent with a weak stomach—has upchucked the verb "to boot." The origin of "booting" may be to use your shoe as a receptacle, but that is speculative. Mathew Shapiro of Columbia submits the most descriptive: "Praying to the Great White Porcelain God (kneeling required)."

" 'Power' is a common prefix at Dartmouth," reports Rick Jones, "e.g., 'power book' or 'power boot.'" A "tool" or "grind" is sometimes called a "power tool" or an "auger"—a boring tool. The "Power Tower" at many schools is the administration building.

Whatever happened to "Big Man on Campus"? He's gone—sometimes remembered only in acronym form, as "bee-moc"—though Anne Griffin says he is called a "politico" at the University of Virginia, and J. Barrett Hickman recalls a Hamilton College usage of "Young God." Nobody remembers what a "co-ed" is, though the term is sometimes used now to refer to men who attend colleges that formerly catered to women. A "stud"—the horse-breeding term used recently to admire sexual prowess—is now a derogation of a BMOC.

Remember the pleasures of cutting classes? "'Cutting' is practically never used anymore," says Audrey Ziss at Skidmore. "The new terminology is 'bucking.'" This newly favored verb is not to be confused with the sixties favorite, "to bust"—to arrest. Today, with sit-ins and other demonstrations only dimly remembered, a "bust" is no longer a police raid and "busting" is not a dreaded activity. "One is busted on the basketball court when one's shot is blocked," explains Bob Torres of New Brunswick, illustrating "busted's" new meaning of being bested. "One is busted in conversation by snappy rejoinder. 'Busting GQ' means to dress in high fashion.... GQ refers to *Gentlemen's Quarterly,* the men's fashion magazine. Hence one has outdressed the exemplar when one 'busts GQ.'"

The term for "farewell," which was the inane "bye now" a generation ago, is "later," from "see you later," but pronounced "lay-tah." Parents are "rents," reflecting a tendency to clip a syllable rather than any gratitude for payments of upkeep. Pizza has been shortened to "tza," pronounced "za." Nancy Pines of Mount Holyoke reports: "You guys want to go in on a za?" Reply: "Intense!" For years, the most common intensifying adjective was "teriffic" or "cosmic"; it is somehow fitting that the leading intensifier has become "intense." Its only competition at the moment is "flaming," as in "flaming youth."

A word that kept cropping up in this rewarding response by the Lexicographic Irregulars was "random." My happiest days at Syracuse U. were spent just strolling about, determined to be aimless, and that wandering wonderment now has a verb: to random. The word, normally an adjective meaning "haphazard," is also a college noun that Edward Fitzgerald of MIT interprets as "a person who does not belong on our dormitory floor," or, by extension, a welcome foreigner.

We'd better conclude this megabooking before some Young God gorges out. Lay-tah.

Dear Mr. Safire:

I think that I can offer a better explanation for the origin of "booting," though still speculative.

Two years ago, at the University of Florida—Gainesville, I was at a party, along with about ten other students and one life-size glass boot. *The owner of the boot had been in Germany for a year as a foreign exchange student and had brought it—and a drinking game—back with him.*

As my friend explained the game, fellows in Germany play the boot game in Ratskellers *where brew costs marks and pfennigs. Initially the boot, which holds about two pitchers, is filled at common cost. Then the game begins. The first player taps the table once with his elbow, then gently slaps the boot with both the front and back of his hand. The tapping and slapping ceremony is very important to the solemnity of the game and is known as "addressing the boot." The player then drinks his fill, sets the boot down, and says "good-bye" with some more tapping and slapping. The boot goes around the table from player to player, each in turn addressing the boot, drinking, and saying "good-bye." The object of the game is to drink as much as you want without paying for refills, which object is accomplished either by emptying the boot (causing the player who last had the boot to refill it at his expense) or by leaving enough beer in the boot when you say "good-bye" so that the subsequent player cannot empty it.*

The game is great fun and involves consumption of much beer all around the table. Not surprisingly, some zealous players drink more than they can humanly stomach, and they vomit, though not into the boot or even into their own shoes. One might say that they "boot out," but the practice is to keep playing the game, even if some are booting, and to laugh.

Sincerely,
Patrick J. O'Hara
Salt Lake City, Utah

Dear Mr. Safire,

The most descriptive phrase I ever heard at Cornell for upchucking was "driving the porcelain bus." Note how the position of the hands is identical for both activities.

Sincerely yours,
Lynne Federman
New York, New York

Dear Mr. Safire—

Yes, Mathew Shapiro's "Praying to the Great White Porcelain God" is quite *descriptive, but may I offer my own personal favorite? "Blowing your chunks" is, of course, one colorful term, but indisputably the ultimate in regurgitation is "to feed the fish," a common occurrence during Bates's infamous Portland Booze Cruises!*

Sincerely,
Ann E. Colten
Lewiston, Maine

Mr. Safire:

"Drinking" is "pounding," "kissing" is "making it" (the assumption is that everyone goes all the way all the time), "sleeping" is "crashing" (a sleeping swine is a . . .), and "eating" is "munching." "Dinner" is a "major munch." Unless it's squat.

So much for slang.

Catch you on the rebound,
Hal Goodtree
Montclair, New Jersey

Dear Mr. Safire:

Slang, as I see it, essentially derives from an attempt by a group of people to set themselves apart from the masses and to move themselves closer together. Imbibers at different institutions are no different from followers of a certain sport or a member of a specific age-group.

Your "tossing your cookies" is my "blowing his/her lunch." "Blow" seems to more accurately describe the movement of material during this bodily function. The newly indoctrinated, your "pin" is my "eunuch." The "eunuch" drinks a few and "chirps" like a mother bird regurgitating while it feeds its young. In serious activities such as chugging contests or Wales Tales games there is the potential for greater fireworks as the intake exceeds stomach capacity. This alleviation of excessive pressure is called a "power blow." (Here Dartmouth is close.) The "power blow" can either be a scattered affair, like the discharge of a blunderbuss, or a long-range projection similar in trajectory to a load of grapeshot.

Yours truly,
Hedden V. Miller, Jr.
Chicago, Illinois

Dear Mr. Safire,

I've got to go book for my Govy final as I got hosed on the midterm and if I get really used in this course, it could shoot my cum (noun, clipped form of cumulative GPA). I might rally later when my roomies fish me for a "za ra" down at a local pub where we can pound a few brews and scope the local units (who are all too often grimbos). If I do too much brew, I'll get wicked-faced, boot, and maybe even pass. Wait till the rents find out.

Later,
Matthew R. Joyner '81
Editor-in-Chief
The Dartmouth
Hanover, New Hampshire

Dear Mr. Safire,

I submit a line which my son came up with several years ago when he was in college: "God didn't really make heaven and earth in six days. He fooled around for five days and then pulled an all-nighter."

I don't know what your study habits were in college, but that struck a nostalgic chord for me. Being the king of procrastinators, I must have pulled more of them than the entire engineering school. (Engineering students at Michigan were notoriously well organized and dull.)

As for "nerts," I know it dates back at least to 1933, when I was thirteen, because I had a friend (whom I haven't seen since) who used to say it all the time. I think it was actually coined as a sniggering euphemism by some radio comic because, incredibly, "nuts" was a bit risqué for the airwaves in those days.

In the upchuck department, I recall a couple of variations on terms you mentioned: "blowing your lunch" and "flashing your cookies."

At Ann Arbor in 1940, we called a gut course a "pipe" (I'm not sure why), and the pipe science course for lit students was called "Gentlemen's Physics."

Sincerely,
Art Hill
Stoughton, Wisconsin

Dear Bill—

You betray your (youthful) age by suggesting that "gut" and "grind" were born in the fifties. Both my wife and I at our respective colleges (Princeton '34 and Bryn Mawr '38) were very *familiar with those terms in the* thirties. *They were in current use then and perhaps earlier.*

Yours,
John B. Oakes
The New York Times
New York, New York

Dear Mr. Safire:

"To boot" may come from the computer people. Bringing a computer up is booting. A cold boot is starting a computer that has been turned off, and a warm boot is resetting a computer that has "bombed out." (In order for a computer to operate, instructions have to be loaded into the memory.)

Donald C. Wiss
New York, New York

---

worriation, *see* getting down

---

would, *see* craven conditional

---

writering

"Parenting" is a good new word. "Mothering" carries a connotation of protection or nurture; "fathering," or "siring," means causing an offspring to be born, metaphorically extended to a country, cause, or invention (Edward Teller is known as the "father of the H-bomb"; nobody can be called "mother of the H-bomb").

Because mothering and fathering have gained specific connotations beyond parenthood, "parenting" is a useful way of being specific about being a parent without getting bollixed up with the role of each parent or bogged down in sex arguments.

However, the new word is in danger of being vogued to death. (What could be vogueier than to use "vogue" as a verb?) Not every stern refusal to part with car keys or indulgent willingness to install a separate telephone line is an example of "parenting"; to me, the word means "conscious attention to a child's upbringing." A good parody of the word's excess usage comes from Mary Ellen Donovan of Plainfield, New Hampshire.

"I'm writering to request a bit of advisering about a problem I've been having with parenting," she corresponds. Eschewing sour-graping, Miss Donovan worries "that there's been all this talkering and seminaring about parenting of late and none about aunting, uncling, or siblinging. Do you think my resentment toward parenting could stem from something that happened while I was childing?"

Having conceived this word, let us give it a good home, and not keep nagging at it, lest the act of marriage become "espousing."

yank his chain, *see* ding!

zonk out, *see* out is in

Acknowledgments

As I have become more cocksure on the subject of language, certain editors—usually new people, filling in for Old Copy Pros—have become intimidated. When they see some egregious error, they refrain from striking it out, and call instead: "Did you mean to spell cohort with an 's'? Is the language changing and have I missed something?"

Fortunately, most editors know I am as prone to error as they are, and do not hesitate to make a fix and save me embarrassment. At *The New York Times Magazine,* first Phyllis Shapiro, and then Sherwin Smith, pull me out of the quicksands of solecism, as do my daily column watchmen, Steve Pickering and William Meyers. I cheerfully blame them for all my mistakes. (Now, that's not what you're supposed to do in an acknowledgment; the line should read: "Although of course all mistakes are my own responsibility.")

At Times Books, Ned Chase is in charge of the bookification of my columns, which then goes to Pam Lyons who supervises the intellectual gruntwork of copy editor Pearl Hanig and proofreader Sharon Kapnick (it must kill them to leave in the mistakes for the readers' letters to correct.)

In my office, Peggy Miller used to help me with research and has now gone on to a higher plateau; Angela Hoover now handles that job in the mornings with a strong assist from my full-time aide, Ann Elise Rubin. My daughter Annabel keeps me up to date on teenage lingo. Typist Ramona Doss comes in to send out a blizzard of postcards acknowledging receipt of about 300 letters a week. (I get a few letters on my political columns, but no passion drives readers to write like an unused "whom.")

My sources are legion. The lexibiggies are all cooperative: Robert Burchfield at Oxford, David Guralnik at Simon and Schuster, Sol Steinmetz at Barnhart Books, Frederick Mish at G. & C. Merriam, Frederic Cassidy at the Dictionary of American Regional English, Stuart Flexner at Random House, and Anne Soukhanov at Houghton Mifflin never fail to respond to a "Where did the dollar sign come from?" or "How many words have five consecutive vowels?" (You'll have to start queueing up for that one.)

In matters of usage, Jacques Barzun at Scribner's is my favorite guide; for new words, I. Willis Russell in Alabama is the nabob of neologia. At *American Speech* magazine, John Algeo and Ronald Butters have been illuminating on matters linguistic, and if you liked this book and have twelve bucks to spare, subscribe to that quarterly by writing Box 2877, University, Alabama 35486. (You don't write the box, you write *to* the box, but the American idiom permits the dropping of the "to," so long as you know you're doing it. If you think that should read "as long as" and want to write to me about it at 1000 Connecticut Avenue, Washington, D.C. 20036, you're a Lexicographic Irregular.)

And those good-humored, argumentative, frustrated, helpful readers have stuck to me through thick and thin (as S. J. Perelman used to say, "like leeches"). They are the inspiration for most of my columns and the indispensable co-authors of all my language books. I thank them most of all.

Index